WOMEN AND THE IDEAL SOCIETY

WOMEN AND THE IDEAL SOCIETY

Plato's *Republic* and Modern Myths of Gender

NATALIE HARRIS BLUESTONE

THE UNIVERSITY OF MASSACHUSETTS PRESS
AMHERST, 1987

LC 87–6002
ISBN 0–87023–580–x cloth; 581–8 paper
Set in Linotron Goudy Old Style
Printed and bound by Thomson-Shore

Library of Congress Cataloging-in-Publication Data

Bluestone, Natalie Harris, 1931–
    Women and the ideal society.

    Bibliography: p.
    Includes index.
    1. Women.   2. Plato.   Republic.   3. Feminism.
4. Political science—Philosophy.   I. Title
HQ1206.B48   1988   305.4′2   87–6002
ISBN 0–87023–580–x (alk. paper)
ISBN 0–87023–581–8 (pbk. : alk. paper)

British Library Cataloging in Publication data are available.

For Max Bluestone
In Memoriam

Do you accept the community of the women with the men in education, children, and guarding the rest of the citizens; and that both when they are staying in the city and going out to war, they must guard and hunt together like dogs, and in so far as possible have everything in every way in common; and that in doing this they'll do what's best and nothing contrary to the nature of the female in her relationship with the male, nothing contrary to the natural community of the two with each other?

> Plato,
> *Republic*, Book V, 466d.

Christian morality . . . introduced into the world the purest idea of marriage, and the most perfect form of domesticity. . . . Plato's view on the contrary misled him . . . to an utter destruction of both; and this is what every individual of sound mind . . . would gladly erase out of his work, even to the very last trace. . . . [H]ere is concentrated all that was mistaken in the development of the Hellenic mind.

> Friedrich Schleiermacher,
> *Introductions to the*
> *Dialogues of Plato*

Contents

Preface

I owe an enormous debt to Aron Gurwitsch, George Boas, and Ludwig Edelstein, teachers and mentors, who, in the 1950s when such views were heretical, fostered in me the belief that woman's intellect was in every way equal to man's. These three scholars, although not social radicals, truly believed that the life of the mind, which they valued highly, was in no way gender-connected. It was a time when female undergraduates were being discouraged from continuing their studies, when as a young teaching assistant—then called a "section man"—I could eat at the Faculty Club only on specified Ladies' Days, and membership in the campus literary society was closed to women. It is all the more remarkable, then, that these rare scholars rejected the prevalent wisdom and taught me to ignore Aristotle's dictum, "*Gunai, gunaixi kosmon hē sigē pherei.*" Indeed the present volume is an attempted refutation of this idea that "Silence is a woman's glory." And I can only hope to repay my debt to Gurwitsch, Boas, and Edelstein, now—alas—all dead, by passing on the flame of scholarship and egalitarianism to my own students, and hopefully to my readers.

My aim in this study has been to present a consistent, coherent, logical argument to show that a systematic bias against women philosophers has pervaded scholarly thought. I do not wish to rant bitterly or denounce in anger, for it is my belief that a careful demonstration of my case can encourage men and women of good will, interested in Plato and in the truth, to examine what has been done and what is to be done. My second goal has been to reveal and assess the contribution of recent feminist writers who have brought to center stage for the first time the idea that Plato's *Republic*, and indeed any ideal commonwealth, requires not only Philosopher-Kings, but also Philosopher-Queens.

In my efforts I have benefited greatly from the help of colleagues and friends. Parts of the manuscript have been presented to the Research Colloquium of the Alliance of Independent Scholars, the Radcliffe College Alumnae Board of Managers, and the Graduate Philosophy Colloquium, York University, Canada. I particularly want to thank Judith Amory, Hugh Amory, Michael Bennett and my other friends at HCHP, Nancy Downey, Renate Hanauer, Abigail Housen, Judith Kantrowitz, Eugenia Kaledin, Annette Pringle, Chris Paci, Mary Paci, James Shen, and Nancy Zumwalt. I am especially grateful for the incisive criticism of Mona Harrington, who read the entire manuscript and whose encouragement was indispensable. My greatest debt is to my children, Hanya and Sasha, and most of all to my husband, George Bluestone, whose patience, devotion, concrete help and emotional support sustained me throughout the work.

N.H.B.
Cambridge, Massachusetts

WOMEN AND THE IDEAL SOCIETY

Introduction

COMMENTARY ON PLATO'S *REPUBLIC*, BOOK V AND THE EXCLUSION OF WOMEN FROM THE PHILOSOPHIC LIFE

In Plato's *Republic*, the most influential philosophical work ever written, Socrates proposed an ideal society in which superior men and women would rule together equally. The Athenian philosopher thus became, more than twenty-three hundred years ago, the first advocate in human history of a measure of sexual equality. The guardians of his society were to be true philosophers, passionately committed to reason and trained in its rigorous application. Believing that some women possessed the necessary capacity for reason and philosophy, he introduced the then startling proposal that identical leadership roles required identical education for the most capable members of both sexes.

From Aristotle onward, writers and scholars have explored all aspects of Plato's great dialogue on the nature of justice and the just society. Some commentators had even expressed vague enthusiasm for greater civic participation by women. But until recently only a very few bothered to discuss the advisability or feasibility of identical education from earliest infancy for gifted boys and girls. And not until the 1970s has there been a single commentator who wholeheartedly agreed with the Platonic suggestion of identical leadership roles for both genders. In fact, throughout the centuries, Plato's passage on sexual equality has suffered a singular fate; it has been largely dismissed, deplored, or ignored.

In earlier eras, the excision of Plato's discussion of women rulers was deliberate. Modern awareness of the *Republic* begins in the fifteenth century when Marsilio Ficino reintroduced Plato into the mainstream of Western thought by translating all the known dialogues into Latin. Before Ficino, Leonardo Bruni had translated several of the *Dialogues* and the *Letters*, but declined to translate the *Republic*. He feared that its radical ideas, particularly those on women, would upset his readers. This dedicated classicist at least did not underestimate the importance and subversive character of the Platonic suggestions. He found Plato too searching, unconventional, and disturbing. And at a time when very few in the West knew Greek, he made the decision in effect to suppress the *Republic* because he knew its suggestion of the "community of wives" as he put it, would be offensive to his Florentine audience.[1]

Later scholarship, starting with the renewal of serious interest in Plato in nineteenth-century Germany, dismissed the subject of women rulers in a different way. Scholars in the German tradition did not censor Plato where they found his ideas threatening. On the contrary, beginning with Friedrich Schleiermacher's careful early nineteenth-century translations, scholars made a conscious commitment to strict objectivity. Philosophers and historians of philosophy returned to the actual Greek texts, seeking to distinguish the authentic views of Plato from those of earlier translators and interpreters. Widespread attempts were made to establish the definitive Greek text, to offer the best translations in many languages, to explicate difficult passages. The ostensible purpose of all these efforts was solely to make clear what Plato really meant.

But in the numerous translations, explications, and "companions" that have continued to appear down to our own day, hostility toward the Platonic suggestion of equality persisted. Unsubstantiated views of women's differences and unexamined assumptions about women's limitations occurred repeatedly. Further, despite their stated aim of complete objectivity in rendering Plato's thought, commentators frequently offered their own beliefs that men and women cannot or should not play the same leadership role in society. In short, on this highly charged issue, objectivity faltered and scholars dealt with Plato's radical proposal for equality with a bias they themselves did not recognize.

This bias, although sometimes glaring, was far more often subterranean and subtle. Most of the commentators whose work I examine in this book would vociferously deny any outright contempt for women or their abilities. Such disdain is well documented among the Greeks; traces of it appear in Plato himself.[2] But scholars of the last hundred years are far less likely to avow such feelings openly.

Nevertheless, a pervasive, unexamined resistance to the idea of female rule has characterized most nineteenth- and twentieth-century scholarship. Since virtually all scholars had been male, their attitudes no doubt reflected the age-old fact of male dominance in Western society. However, the assumption that it is right for males to rule, carried into philosophic thought, also helped to sustain and even shape the anti-female biases of scholars, educators, and politicians across the generations. The very students who were most likely to speculate freely on fundamental questions and criticize prevalent social practices received no encouragement from the Plato scholars to examine freshly what came to be known as The Woman Question. By downplaying or disregarding Plato's provocative proposals for women rulers, philosophers, whose task it is to question the dominant assumptions, instead reinforced the tendency of the "educated gentleman" to ignore the matter of sexual equality as an important element of justice.

With the advent after 1960 of a new feminist movement and the entry of more women into the field of philosophy, Plato's argument for women rulers has been revived. The commentators of the 1970s and 1980s have made a significant contribution by successfully focusing attention on the long-neglected passage calling for Philosopher-Queens. They show that Plato's admirers failed to see the inconsistencies in his beliefs about women, and some even expressly desire to dethrone and discredit Plato. Many also recognize the hostility of previous commentators to the suggested reforms. For generations of commentators have perpetuated attitudes, often despite protests to the contrary, which have kept women excluded from the realms of reason, philosophy, and civic authority.

But there are problems also in this revisionist effort. In many cases, feminist commentators use the Platonic text as a mere pretext for making sectarian points. Instead of explicating the relevant passages, they devote themselves only to praising Plato for a total egalitarianism he did not in fact profess, or to condemning him for not having gone far enough. Some feminists—primarily women, but also male enthusiasts—plunge into analyses which betray a painful lack of preparation for scholarship, a disregard of the original Greek text, and little or no acquaintance with Plato's other works.

On occasion they even outdo male misogynists in suggesting that women need not rule since they have other intuitive gifts to contribute. Some feminist scholars condemn reason itself. They do not, like Luther, denounce it as a whore. But they do not value it as a true mistress, nor, like C. S. Peirce, urge that we cling to logical method like "the bride we have chosen from all the world."[3] Instead, reason becomes a false master foisted on us by a male establishment, by a tradition which begins with the ignoble paedophilic Plato. In the eagerness of feminist commentators to re-evaluate female contributions to history and validate women's role as homemakers and emotional foci of family life, they downplay the worth of intellectual activity and call for separate but somehow equal standards for evaluating human achievement.

The new Plato scholarship, therefore, while providing a corrective for the male biases of the past, has added biases of its own. In some cases it has also produced an odd alliance between scholars still writing in the misogynist tradition which denies that women are equal to men in their capacities to reason and to rule, and a feminist school which denies the importance of reason and political leadership, and thus minimizes the need for women's participation in public life.

In my view, denigrating intellectual activity as a game not worth playing is ultimately self-defeating. There is little to be gained from undervaluing the rich, varied humanistic tradition of great books, great scientists, great artists, theologians, and civic rulers. And, we must face the truth that women have contributed far less than men to this heritage. Rather than denying the importance of public effort and achievement, the message should be the one Socrates forced on his reluctant audience. Women must now participate in these activities fully.

It is of crucial importance now to assess rationally the proper role of women. In this study, I seek to show the continuing relevance of the questions and arguments first formulated by Plato. Starting with the original text, I trace the interpretation over the past hundred years of the passage on women guardians, seeking to separate objective comments on its meaning from those reflecting the prejudices of particular scholars.

In setting out on this enterprise, I acknowledge fully the extraordinary complications surrounding the problem of bias in philosophy. Throughout this book my assumption is that no interpretations can be independent of their social context. Like many post-Renaissance, post-Kantian thinkers, I see all truth as "the daughter of time." We can only base our beliefs on the evidence available at a given time, and the pursuit of certainty is a hopeless quest. Scholars must endlessly seek objectivity or, as Huntington Cairns has said, their enterprise is not philosophy. "When ideas are manipulated for class or group interests, the name for this in Plato's day was sophistry."[4] Similarly, one of the most distinguished of the British Plato scholars, A. E. Taylor, declares, "The last thing I should wish is that the reader should see Plato through my spectacles."[5] Still, the objectivity Taylor calls for is only relatively possible to achieve, no matter how scrupulous and vigilant the interpreter. In the end, one can only see ancient writers through one's own experiences, convictions, and assumptions.[6]

Nevertheless, even if distortion of vision is ultimately inevitable, it is still possible to avoid some of the blind spots which distort and obscure the meaning of a text. That is, while no one can be wholly free from the biases of a particular culture and time, other forms of bias *are* avoidable. These are sometimes personal and idiosyncratic, sometimes the result of group partisanship of which scholars can and should be aware. And they can and should minimize such departures from objectivity by realizing and declaring where their allegiances lie in such controversial areas as that of sexual equality.

The undeclared, underground anti-female prejudice that has marked much of Plato scholarship until recent years has been as damaging to a clear discussion of sexual equality as overt discrimination. As American blacks discovered, it was in some ways easier to fight the Southerners' outright exclusions and declarations of racial inferiority than the more subtle prejudices of

Northerners. If there are philosophers today who genuinely believe that women's training and role should not be identical to men's, that women can never be true philosophers, they must not be prevented from arguing their case freely and openly. Few of the commentators that I consider in the pages that follow have been willing to state forthrightly that half of the human race was automatically disqualified from the pursuits of reason. Even the professor who aggrandized Hitler's *Mein Kampf* did not see himself as anti-female. Instead, he declared that the Nazi program was actually implementing Plato's egalitarian aims for women in the *Republic!*[7]

The persistence of subtle bias against women arises partly from the very ambience of classical scholarship. The atmosphere of Plato's *Symposium,* with its gathering of men who through their erotic attraction for each other will reach a higher love of truth and beauty, has for centuries had its appeal. Whatever their sexual preferences, many young men have found that male-bonding genuinely fosters intellectual growth. The picture of beloved teacher and brilliant youth that we find in the Socratic dialogues has had a powerful influence. Victorian Englishmen openly admired this ambience of ancient Greece, and even repressed and homophobic Germans valued discipleship and quasi-father/son relationships in university circles. The presence of a large number of females might well have disturbed this growth-enhancing atmosphere.

Scholars have made varied use of the *Symposium* in their interpretations of the egalitarianism of the *Republic.* These uses will be discussed later at length. But it is important to note at the outset that no necessary connection exists between homosexuality and misogyny or any prescribed attitude toward women's ability or societal role. Homosexual males have on occasion displayed particular sympathy for, and understanding of, women as victims of discrimination. But in some intellectual circles, the existence of an all-male homoerotic atmosphere has tended rather to inhibit and discourage female students.

The intellectual excitement of such circles as that around Ludwig Wittgenstein at Oxford undoubtedly was conducive to the mutual exploration of philosophical issues. But despite a few exceptions membership in the circle was predominantly and pronouncedly all-male. Even at mid-century the linguistic usage of British scholars reflected this exclusion of females. In his influential book, *The Concept of Mind*, Gilbert Ryle talks repeatedly of the "lad who thinks" with no consciousness that some of his readers might be female. Thus, even at mid-century the linguistic formulations of British philosophers reflected this exclusion of women. From the fourth century B.C., when one of the few women said to have attended Plato's Academy was reputed to have worn men's clothes, to anecdotes about the economist Keynes' and other famous professors' willingness to accept female assistants only so long as they appeared indistinguishable from men, women have found, and still today continue to find, scholarly doors closed to them.[8] Well into the last quarter of this century, the full participation of women in the life that philosophers have always told us is most worth living, the life of rational decision-making, is far from accomplished.

Women have made advances, however, and the historical moment may finally have arrived when for the first time there is a genuine possibility of joint leadership in the society as a whole and of genuine exploration of the question of equality between the sexes. At such a juncture, it becomes all the more important to explore the ways in which avoidable bias on the subject still persists, particularly in the institutions of learning. One classicist has suggested that unfortunately democracies discourage research into unpalatable or unpopular truths like the essential inequality which he himself believes to exist between the abilities of men and women.[9] In my view, such suppression is indeed unfortunate. Those who maintain unpopular opinions must be encouraged to bring them out into the open where they can be scrutinized, supported, or refuted.

As part of this scrutiny, I aim, in the intellectual history of Plato scholarship that follows, to reveal the preconceptions and inconsistencies that have through the years distorted commentaries on Plato's proposal. I do not embark on this enterprise in the spirit of those post-revolutionary Chinese women taught to "speak bitterness." Nor do I wish solely to add to the litany of anti-female references in Western thought, an exercise which one theorist has aptly described as "tedious and depressing."[10] My aim is rather to correct the record so that future readers of the *Repub-*

lic and its commentaries will be particularly wary of unconscious bias and special purpose and will return to the text itself, engaging with it in the spirit of inquiry championed, if not always followed, by Socrates himself.

In the dialogues Socrates describes himself as a midwife who assists others in the delivery of ideas. If he had been female, able to function literally, not only figuratively, as a midwife, he might well have noticed further unexamined assumptions in his audience. But the enterprise of discovering the nature of the just and virtuous life through rational analysis would ultimately have been the same.

Much of the feminist commentary I deal with in the second part of this book extends this inquiry. Although the writers I cover would not all claim to be Plato scholars, many of them make significant contributions to the on-going discussion. I shall try to show, however, that in the process some have undervalued "the greatest philosopher that ever lived" and overemphasized the emotional excellences of women.[11] If I am sometimes harsh in my criticism of female colleagues it is perhaps because one is often hardest on one's own. My object throughout has been not rancor, but rather the restatement of the value of careful scholarship and the importance of continuing the tradition with a passionate, and ultimately gender-free, commitment to ferreting out the truth.

DETAILS OF THE PLATONIC PROPOSALS FOR SEXUAL EQUALITY AND SOME EARLY INTERPRETATIONS

Plato's proposal to include women among the true philosophers appears in Book V, from 449c to 473e.[12] There, Plato's teacher, Socrates, protagonist of the dialogue, presents his listeners with three paradoxical features of his proposed "city of speech." These he describes as the Three Waves of his argument in defense of the arrangements for an ideal *polis.* The First Wave which threatens to drown his listeners is his suggestion that just as male and female sheep dogs are equally responsible for guarding the flock, so female and male rulers will guard the city, protect it in war and rule it in peace. The fact that there are differences between males and females, that as Plato puts it, the "female bears and the male mounts," is not a difference relevant to the governing of the state.[13] Just as the bald and the long-haired are opposite in one respect, but that respect does not affect their ability as shoe-makers, so the differences between men and women are not differences with respect to any art or practice connected to the organization of the city. For Plato, it is true that the class of men excels that of women in all practices; however, many individual women are better than many men in many things. Plato puts it, "There is no practice of a city's governors which belongs to woman because she's woman, or to man because he's man; but the natures are scattered alike among both animals; and woman participates according to nature in all practices, and man in all, but in all of them woman is weaker than man."[14] Since women and men have the same natures in regard to ruling, they must follow the same practices in preparation for ruling. They must be equally trained in gymnastic and music; this would be what Plato calls "according to nature," whereas the Athenian practice of highly dissimilar education he considers "against nature." For Plato, to reach truly just practices we must understand what is natural as opposed to what is merely conventional, legal, or cus-tomary. Women's participation in the gymnastic training that will ensure the necessary physical strength and discipline requires that female guardians must exercise naked in the gymnasium as men do. Although initially this will seem laughable, the practice can be seen to be beneficial if it is properly considered. In fact, Plato assures his listeners that in the last analysis his entire proposal of equal opportunity for both sexes is both possible and advanta-geous for the society.

The Second Wave of the Platonic scheme is that male and female guardians are to live communally, eliminating private mar-riage arrangements and also abolishing what we would call the nuclear family. Children will be raised communally with parents and offspring unaware of the biological connections between them. Marriages are arranged by the state with periodic festivals where temporary unions are consummated. Subtle lots must be fabricated, one of Plato's "noble lies," to assure that citizens will blame chance rather than the rulers for each union. As the off-spring are born the task of caring for them will be taken over by the male and female officers designated for this job. With the help of wetnurses and governesses the women will be spared the "wakeful watching" and other labors connected with infancy, making for what Glaucon, Socrates' interrogator, calls an "easygoing kind of childbearing" for the women guardians.

The offspring must be born of those in their prime, which is between twenty and forty for women, twenty-five and fifty-five for men. When the women and men are beyond the age of procreation they are free to have intercourse with whomever they wish with certain exceptions. However, the partners in these unofficial pairings must be especially careful to avoid conceptions. And they must understand that should a fetus force its way into the light of day, "there's to be no rearing for such a child."

Plato believes that the abolition of private property and of the family will keep the usual causes of dissension, the fighting over money, children, and relatives, from disturbing the tranquillity of his ideal state. His arrangements will promote very strong ties among the rulers. And although they will live simply, they will be rewarded by seeing the preservation of the whole city as well as by the support, prizes, and honors given them by the public.

The Third Wave, the final paradox of Socrates' argument, is that these guardians, men and women alike, must be true philosophers, reaching knowledge of the good through reason and dialectic. Only the rule of such philosopher-guardians can guarantee the welfare of the State. Plato thus calls for Philosopher-Kings, and—if the terminology be properly extended, as it rarely is—Philosopher-Queens to rule. For, as he puts it: "Until the philosophers rule as kings or those now called kings . . . genuinely and adequately philosophize, and political power and philosophy coincide in the same place . . . there is no rest from ills for the cities . . . nor I think for human kind."[15]

These are the bare outlines of the Platonic plan. My aim in this book is to trace the history, from roughly 1870 to the present, of the treatment of these passages on women guardians. Before the time at which this study begins, there was a period of a thousand years, from Proclus in the fifth century until the flourishing Platonism of the Italian Renaissance, in which we hear almost nothing of the *Republic*. Although the text may have been available to the medieval churchmen, there is no extant commentary in the West on the dialogue. Surprisingly, some later commentators have suggested that the medieval Church itself was an embodiment of Plato's ideal republic. The noted classical historian Ernest Barker, although making no claim for a direct influence, thinks the Church's own principles make it *naturaliter Platonica.* He compares the papal monarchy to the Philosopher-Kings. And he suggests that the hierarchy of priests, monks, and laity correspond to the three classes of Plato. For Barker's analogy to hold, he must overlook among other aspects Plato's insistence on female guardians. The medieval Church—and for that matter the Catholic Church today—had no women equal in ruling power to the male leadership.

The argument for an "unconscious debt" of the Church to the *Republic* is convincing only if one judges the call for female rulers to be peripheral. In discussing views of Plato's scheme, Ryle makes a related point about the connection between the interpreter's interests and his judgments. Plato's view of the body politic as an organism, Ryle drily remarks, is apt to appeal less to those who are told that they are constituted by nature only to be the body's feet. The appeal, he points out, is bound to be greater to those who are assured that their role is that of the body's eyes or brain.[16] Likewise, the omission of women from the dominant group can be expected to be of more concern to female commentators, most of whom do not appear on the scene until late in the 20th century.

Any direct influence of Plato's utopia on medieval thought would probably have had to come from the *Timaeus,* which is the one book of the Platonic corpus that we know was extant. That work, which contains a brief summary of the ideal city of the *Republic,* is notorious for its misogyny. In it, Plato warns that a man who lives an ignoble life will be demoted after death, condemned to live as a woman.[17] Misogyny of this sort is more characteristic of the attitudes of the early Church than is any program for identical roles.[18] Of course, all that can be said of the contempt for women that appears in the *Timaeus* as well as in most other Greek writers is that it coincided with the prejudices of the educated man of the Middle Ages. And, despite that much-noted Christian emphasis on equality of souls in men and women, it is hard to see how the structure of the Church exemplifies a belief that women's and men's natures are qualitatively identical.

There was, however, a direct Platonic influence on the philosophy, if not the practice, of Islam. From about 800, Islamic thinkers were translating Greek philosophical works into Arabic and attempting to harmonize them with Islamic theology. In the tenth century, al-Fārābī proposed a theory of a philosopher-caliph based on his reading of the *Republic*. But he, too, in keeping with the Islamic assumption of the inferior status of women, takes no note of the egalitarianism of Plato.[19]

On the other hand, Averroës, the last and perhaps greatest of the Islamic philosophers, wrote an extensive three-part commentary on the *Republic* in which he discusses the proposal for sexual equality with sympathy. We have only a Hebrew translation of his work, but if it is a faithful rendering of the original, then Averroës' support for sexual equality is astounding. There are no biographical or sociological details available that would account for the fact that this Arab thinker, although a committed Muslim, seems to have been far more open in the twelfth century to the idea of female guardians than some American university professors are in the late twentieth.[20] As in William James' definition of the true philosopher, Averroës on this issue is able to "fancy everything different from what it is . . . to see the familiar as if it were strange, and the strange as if it were familiar."[21] And even if, as I believe, he was somewhat less consistent and less completely egalitarian in his acceptance of Plato's program than some assert, he was nevertheless remarkably openminded.[22]

Averroës finds it deplorable that in his own states women who are not being fitted for any of the human virtues often resemble plants. He writes: "In these States the *ability of women is not known* because they are only taken for procreation" (*my emphasis*).[23] This stands out particularly when compared with the views of scholars I present in this book who are quite certain they do know what women's abilities are. As we shall see, some are even sure that Plato actually placed women among the guardians solely for their role in procreation. Averroës' belief that for Plato "women are essentially on the same level with men in respect of civic activities in the same classes" makes his agreement with the

Greek philosopher even more striking.[24] Since he seems mistakenly to have believed that Plato clearly intended that men of
every class would have intercourse only with women like themselves who had training identical to their own, what the
egalitarian Averroës approved was even more far-reaching than
what Plato actually proposed. Such enthusiasm for the Platonic
proposals is unmatched so far as I can discover in the Western
tradition.

Although we hear of the *Republic* from the Italian humanists,
extended commentary does not appear again until the eighteen-
hundreds. There are a few translations and paraphrases earlier in
the century, but the period I shall explore in this book begins
with the important publication in England in 1871 of the first
English translation of Plato's complete dialogues by the distinguished scholar Benjamin Jowett. The *Republic* was the subject of
Jowett's first course of lectures at Oxford. His notes to the Greek
text and the portions of his projected but uncompleted analytic
essay have been of interest to scholars. But it is his translation
which has had the most significant influence on generations of
students and general readers.

Concurrent with Jowett's work, notable Plato scholarship also
flourished in Germany and a rich cross-fertilization took place
between writers in both countries. And from that time on, new
translations and interpretations have appeared in numerous countries and continue to be published in books and journals
throughout the West. One of my main aims in the chapters that
follow is to analyze the presuppositions of the voluminous commentary from 1870 to 1970 on the egalitarian proposals in
Book V.

My second aim is to focus attention on the feminist writers of
the last decades who have at last entered the dialogue. When a
new class or group is finally empowered to participate in scholarly
endeavors, previously overlooked meanings are bound to emerge.
Just as labor historians viewing the documents of the industrial
revolution from the vantage point of the factory workers have
come up with new interpretations and evaluations, so too women
writers have seen new implications in Plato's ancient text. They
have turned to the *Republic* in the process of rethinking the per-
ennial questions about the nature of the complete life. In asking

how women, as well as men, can best participate in a society geared to the well-being and fulfillment of all, they have reexamined the plan for male and female guardians of the state.

The outstanding classicist-philosopher Martha Nussbaum clearly articulates the questions involved. Understanding Plato, she believes, will aid us in deciding what kind of education women should have and what they will become as a result. Will the idea of a separate women's sphere disappear? Will women still love and care for their children as before, or is some radical change in the structure of the family like that proposed by Plato for his guardians necessary? Plato valued both gentleness and assertiveness. Nussbaum reminds us that in thinking about the ideal society, we still need to ask what kind of emotional attachments are compatible with public and private gentleness. She sees that the most important question about women's upbringing and education is still whether they will and should "become free and autonomous citizens just like men."[25]

Plato's text has frequently served as the jumping-off point for disagreement among feminists in their answers to these questions. In the second half of this book I shall survey and evaluate these recent examinations of Book V. In order to show exactly why the text has supported varying interpretations, it will sometimes be necessary to dwell on small details. The general reader may want to scan these quickly, although I believe that only by examining many trees can we legitimately make generalizations about the forest.

One of the purposes of my analysis of details and nuances in the new feminist explication is to show certain dangers implicit in contemporary rethinking of the *Republic*. My aim is to steer a course between the Scylla of sexism and the Charybdis of separatism. Just as I reject the anti-female bias of the great Plato scholars I also regret some recent writers' underestimation of the human accomplishments of the past, simply because they are the work of the dominant male culture. I consider it a mistake to elevate the supposed female virtues over the worth of logical analysis and rational principles.

An alarming trend among feminists in general appears clearly in some of the scholars' condemnation of Plato. Many consider current educational methods and ways of thinking about morality

to be defective because societal practices are wrought in a "masculine mold." They consider competition a masculine trait and
the disregard of loving affiliations a masculine failing, and consider both the source of much of the world's ills. But there is no
convincing evidence that cooperativeness or the valuing of emotional life is sex-linked. Plato advocated unifying affiliations, and
his true philosophers were meant to be *lovers* of truth. Religious
moralists, almost all of them male, have always stressed the affec-
tive side of human existence. In the Platonic ideal of the
examined life, the kind of reason advocated requires both
logical operations and the intuitive thinking he called "direct
vision."

In the pages that follow I shall try to show that some feminist
writers in their zeal to validate the emotional strengths and family
contribution of women through the centuries have unwisely mini-
mized the importance of rationality. They have unduly praised
women's separate virtues practiced in a private sphere. Fearing
that women will become "just like men" they lead us away
from the truth that indeed *identical* traits should be valued in
both.

This is not to side with those writers who wholeheartedly
embrace the Platonic proposals and seek to sweep under the car-
pet the inconsistencies in Plato. The Athenian philosopher,
although a great thinker and a great artist, was also a purveyor of
the biases of the ordinary Greek male. And in the fifth century
BC the ordinary Athenian was guilty of an extraordinary degree of
misogyny. Even in Book V Plato speaks disparagingly of the
beliefs of a "small, womanish mind" (469d). "Imitating a woman"
in sexual encounters, that is assuming the submissive position, he
considers humiliating (395c, 397c). In the *Apology* he reproaches
those who plead when they are condemned to death as "no better
than women" (35). Within the framework of the *Timaeus* myth,
as I have mentioned, to exist as a woman is to be in an inferior
state (42b–c). In the *Laws* he describes women as secretive and
crafty, less capable of virtue than men (780e–781b).

Besides such evidence of misogyny, he also exhibits the bias of
most ancient Greek philosophers against democracy. As often
noted there are elitist and authoritarian elements in his social
planning, elements which it is doubtful would produce the eudae-

monia he envisaged. Plato was concerned with gender equality only for the best and the brightest. If he intended similar changes for the class of manual workers as his own theory of justice would require, he said nothing of plans for such changes.

Nevertheless, his work deserves repeated attention.
For even though the contradictions in his thought cannot be reconciled, the fact that he was the first to raise the crucial issues puts us in his debt. Without worshipping him uncritically we still should admire his wisdom in concluding so long ago that the physiological differences between the sexes must not affect their participation in civic life.

In my conclusion I shall argue that sociobiologists are still addressing the same questions about the relevance of biological differences that Plato formulated. Scientists seek evidence for inevitable female disadvantages as well as special excellences. But their recent attempts to prove that there is a male human nature and a separate female human nature are no more convincing than the arguments Socrates expected from his listeners. Nor can the ethical questions be turned over to the biologists as the founder of sociobiology has suggested. Scientific research, the very questions we ask, involve assumptions about value. Male and female philosophers are needed to examine these assumptions. Genetic investigations cannot themselves tell us how we ought to live. Those who proclaim that the diversity desirable in human communities is, and therefore ought to be, determined by gender are mistaken. They are promulgating myths, not in the neo-Platonic sense of illuminating stories which provide otherwise unreachable insights, but myths in the vernacular sense of unwelcome distortions of the truth.

Besides my examination of these distortions I have one further aim which underlies this entire study.

I want to underscore the value of the scholarly enterprise and pay tribute to that activity of explicating the texts of others which is so often disparaged or underrated. Through the traditions of interpretation, new generations of students are helped to learn about the past and acquire the resources to shape the future. As intermediaries between the readers and the ancients, commentators perform a great service. By reinterpreting in the light of their own world views the meaning and relevance of the thought of the past, they help to determine which works will be influential in the future. These scholars surely deserve much gratitude for the crucial role they play in keeping valuable texts alive.

The Prevalence of Anti-Female Bias in Plato Scholarship, 1870–1970: Seven Types of Hostility

EQUALITY AS A NON-ISSUE:
NEGLECT OF THE PROPOSALS

In an extensive survey of commentaries written from 1870 on in many languages, including French, Spanish, Italian, Russian, Hebrew, German—and English, and composed in Hong Kong, Canada, England, and the United States—I find an overwhelming antipathy to the proposal for women guardians in the *Republic*.[1] One of the most striking features is the complete neglect of what others in the same period have termed Plato's "radical, even revolutionary" proposals.[2] Very few give any serious attention to the central role Plato himself claims for the First Wave of his argument for a just society. Commentators often completely ignore the proposal for sexual equality while discussing the other two elements—abolition of property and the family—at length. Many of the writers, almost all of whom are male, are particularly concerned about the elimination of the family. Since even those who have no wives nor any interest in women's roles are or were part of a family, one can see how this idea of Plato's might be of more direct interest to them. But whatever the reason, there are a large number of writers who, while occupying themselves with minutiae of Greek religious practice and obscure literary allusions, do not even mention the complexities and contradictions in the Platonic text on female equality.

The prominent logician who has translated and annotated the chief Russian edition of the *Republic* is not averse to commenting on the contemporary relevance of the Platonic scheme and points out that the holding of property in common is not to be compared with the Marxist view. Plato's schemes are utopian rather than scientific. He takes the trouble to explain this Soviet sense of "scientific" but he does not have a single word to say on

the subject of equality of male and female guardians.[3] Since the
Russian Revolution paid lip service to egalitarian reforms for
women similar to those Plato proposed, one might expect comment not only on property relations but also on equality of
leadership roles. But none is forthcoming.

Likewise, the author of an annotated Hebrew translation
ignores the proposal of sexual equality both in his introduction
and in his notes on Book V. It is, of course, unfair to expect a
commentator to be objective and then condemn him for not
interjecting his own opinions as to what is important. But as with
the Russian, so, too, the Hebrew translator is not in fact averse
to connecting Plato's views to contemporary realities. Writing in
the early 1930s, this Israeli socialist refers in his introduction to
the current importance of Plato in the face of the "sinking of
human culture" reported in the European newspapers.[4] But he
makes no comment on the suggestion for equality of the sexes
despite the fact that the kibbutz system was founded on just such
joint leadership. Nor does he bother to note any similarity
between the original settlers' provision of communal child care
and the Platonic proposal for communal child-rearing.

Immediately after the war, Karl Popper published an opposing
view which sees Plato not as an antidote to European irrationality
but rather as himself a dangerous authoritarian. In *The Open Society and Its Enemies*, Popper seeks to combat the idealization of
Plato and condemn his anti-liberal, anti-humanitarian attitudes.
He calls Plato one of the founding fathers of racism and
denounces the deceit the philosopher recommended to keep the
masses subservient. According to Popper, there would be no room
in Plato's ideal state for an independent thinker like Socrates. In
Popper's attack on Platonic "totalitarianism," he accuses the Athenian of wanting to return "to the tribal *patriarchy* of the time
before the Fall" (*my emphasis*).[5]

Popper supports his conviction that in ancient Greece there
was a humanitarian "equalitarian movement" by citing Democri-
tus, Pericles, Antisthenes, even the historical Socrates, as
proponents of an open society. He discusses their anti-slavery,
anti-nationalist beliefs, their creed of "the universal empire of
men." In order to contrast Plato with this tradition and show
what a thoroughgoing, unmitigated "reactionary" the philosopher

was, Popper might be expected to attempt to reinterpret or explain away the seemingly egalitarian statements in Book V about women's capacity to rule.

In fact, Popper makes absolutely no mention whatsoever of Plato's views on women. In his praise for the more democratic Socrates, Popper might well have tried to minimize the importance of the *Republic*'s suggestion of sexual equality, perhaps attributing the views to Plato's teacher, as others have. But Popper makes no such attempt. In hundreds of pages of texts and references, Popper buries only a single example from the *Theatetus* of Platonic humanitarianism which he admits is difficult to reconcile with the thesis of Plato as totalitarian enemy. He assumes that the passage in which Plato equates masters and slaves, Greeks and barbarians, must have been written before (rather than, as is commonly held, after) the *Republic*. The *Republic* itself he finds wholly without any redeeming humanitarian features.

Popper's own definition of the essential features which would allow any doctrine to be considered humanitarian do not include a single mention of the female half of the human race, which has been persistently oppressed throughout history. As a spokesman for the downtrodden, Popper completely ignores Plato's advocacy of women rulers in a time when women were widely viewed as property. What in Popper's day and before was repeatedly called Plato's "feminism," has no role whatsoever to play in Popper's analysis. Even if there is justice in his denunciation of the aristocratic, anti-individualist bent of Plato, it is clearly not correct to accuse the philosopher of advocating a patriarchy. And it shows at the very least an insensitivity to a major egalitarian issue to write a lengthy accusatory volume without granting his ancient opponent some slight credit for the proposal on women guardians. Popper might well have been able to show that joint male and female aristocrats still involved a closed society; but he did not even consider the issue important enough to discuss.

It is equally surprising that there is no mention of the issue of female equality in a companion to Plato's *Republic*, published as late as the 1980s.[6] There was some reason to wonder how works appearing in England in the years immediately following Mill's historic *On the Subjection of Women* could ignore Plato's discussion. But then Mill's voice was a relatively isolated one in scholarly circles. It is far harder to understand how this current guide for students appearing in a world where a strong women's movement exists in many countries, and where serious readers will undoubtedly include women, can ignore the issue entirely.

WOMEN *ARE* DIFFERENT:
THE PROPOSALS AS UNNATURAL

The most common reaction among those who do consider Plato's proposals is to contend that in fact the equality, which Plato claims is "according to nature," is on the contrary "unnatural." Critics offer a variety of reasons to support their position. The argument takes many forms, from the well-meaning paternalism of Jowett to the blatant sexism of the American translator Allan Bloom. A few, like Ernest Barker, are aware of the pitfalls of trying to determine what is "natural." Barker admits that though his aim is to interpret Plato *sub specie aeternitatis*, despite the political crisis of the time in which he is writing, his efforts may be only *sub specie temporum suum*.[7] That is, he is aware of the difficulties of eliminating cultural bias. Nevertheless, the learned Oxford scholar explains that although many may sympathize with the emancipation of women, the fundamental argument which underlies Plato's scheme raises doubts. If the basic difference between men and women is that one begets while the other bears children, it produces a number of other differences "which cut deep."

> The fact of her sex is not one isolated thing in a woman's nature . . . : it colors her whole being. She is by nature the centre of the life of the family. . . . She has by nature a specific function of her own, which she will always refuse to delegate to a crèche, and the long period of growth and the need of nurture of her children (which finds no parallel in the children of "the other animals") will always make the discharge of this function the work of a lifetime. The unmarried woman may enter into the open field of the

world's activities; the married woman has her life's work
ready to her hand.[8]

Thus, what is really natural to women is a lifetime of motherhood. He concludes that the state ought not to abolish maternity
but rather to recognize it as a function and a contribution to the
community. Through child-rearing the woman will take "her station in the common life," and by doing the thing which pertains
to her station she will attain to Justice.

In another work, Barker tells us that it is not possible for men
and women to come together merely for sexual intercourse as
Plato proposes.[9] Given the current divorce rate and the statistics
on multiple partners for both sexes in today's America, we can
only conclude that his view of what is possible needs alteration.
Barker finds Aristotle's more sympathetic treatment of marriage
preferable to that of Plato, who he says failed to appreciate "the
real nature" of the marriage tie. Aristotle's view of marriage, it
will be recalled, is based on the natural domination of the male,
as in the master-slave relation. Aristotle considers the female by
nature inferior, born to obey and without the ability to be virtuous in the same way as a man.[10] Barker does not, however,
allude to this aspect of Aristotle's admittedly more enthusiastic
support of private marriages.

Benjamin Jowett also finds Plato's view of what is natural mistaken and offers his own idea of the natural differences between
men and women in character and capacity. Jowett's views are not
always easy to ascertain, since they are only hinted at in the periodic summaries and paraphrases in the margin of his translation of
the *Republic*. They can also be inferred from the vagaries of his
linguistic usage, as I shall discuss later. But in an interpretive
note in his edition of the Greek text, he spells out his ideas about
equal education for women and offers a theory about women's
true nature.[11]

First, he details four aspects of Plato's proposal which are
worthy of attention, that presumably should be considered sympathetically. He phrases them carefully so as to avoid offending his
readers and to persuade them that although Plato's views differ
from modern, that is, Victorian English ideas of education, they
nevertheless have merit. The meritorious aspects he finds are: 1)

the consideration of the subject independently of existing practice and with reference solely to sexual differences; 2) the implication that bodily health and strength and the training by which they are achieved are equally necessary for males and females; 3) the belief that both sexes have the same interests and duties and are capable of the same occupations in a degree greater than that allowed by social practice; and 4) the contention that false delicacy is a poor foundation for manners and morals.[12]

But despite the value of these considerations, Jowett decides that Plato has actually made a major error. The error "seems to arise" from the Athenian's failure to consider the other differences "to which the differences in sex give rise"; these are differences "in mind and feeling."[13] The problem is that Plato has forgotten a crucial fact. Jowett quotes with approval from an unidentified source that "women's best education is the training of their children."

Furthermore, Jowett finds that Plato has lost sight of the fact that education is relative to character, and the character of women is necessarily formed by the universal opinion of mankind. Evidently, Jowett loses sight of the fact that Plato considered character only in connection with capacity regardless of the opinion of the multitude. That is, one human being learns quickly, the other less so; one female has the capacity for medicine, another does not. This is the only sense of character relevant in Book V. And it is on the basis of such judgments of individual character that Plato believes the opinions of mankind *ought* to be formed. Exactly what Jowett himself means by the "universal opinion" which forms the character of women is not clear. Throughout history there have been a few who held the opinion that women have the capacity for an education identical to men's, and such opinions have increased markedly in recent years. Presumably, then, Jowett would have to admit that as views of women's nature changed, so too would the resultant character itself change.

But Jowett does not seem to allow for this possibility. Difficult as it is to be sure of his precise position, one aspect is entirely clear. Jowett assumes that his view and that of "modern philosophy" is preferable to that of Plato. Women in fact have "equal powers of different qualities" rather than the unequal powers of the same quality that Plato ascribes to them. Woman is not "undeveloped man" as he interprets Plato to have said. Her nature is diverse from man's, and it is therefore natural that she be educated differently.[14]

Unlike Barker, Jowett does not specifically comment on the unnaturalness of the prescribed mating arrangements for the guardians; but he does point out that the prohibited unions would no longer rest on any natural or rational principle.[15] In the interpretations of both thinkers two distinguishable but related issues regarding what is natural arise. There is 1) the question of "woman's nature" and its necessary consequences, and 2) the question of whether the monogamous (or perhaps more accurately, moderately polygymous, or "double standard") family is "natural." On both issues, the view of the eminent classicist K. J. Dover, who in his work has taken the issue of Greek homosexuality out of its Victorian closet, has much appeal. Dover declares himself unwilling to engage with any enthusiasm in debates about the naturalness or unnaturalness of human behavior. He observes that any community encourages behavior which it regards as possibly conducive to an eventual situation of a kind desired by that community. It discourages behavior which seems likely to hinder the development of such a situation.[16]

I agree with Dover that the absence of any clear correlation between "natural" and "desirable" is self-evident. Rape and homicide are species-typical in men and orangutangs; in the sense that they occur regularly, they might then be described as natural to these species, but not to other "lower" animals where such behavior never occurs. Few, however, would argue that rape and homicide are therefore desirable. Nor could Plato's commentators defend their use of "natural" as meaning "descriptive of a statistical majority of known cases in man's history." The majority of male humans that have lived thus far have died before their seventieth year; this too cannot be seen as *ipso facto* desirable.

Despite obvious ambiguities of the term, commentators throughout the period under discussion have automatically assumed that their readers would understand what they meant by "natural." They have repeatedly attempted to equate the natural with the desirable, or at the very least, by labelling a situation "unnatural," to convince us automatically of its impossibility or undesirability.

A typical example of this procedure occurs in the work of the well-known Victorian Platonist, Walter Pater, who opposes Plato's views on both issues, that of women's nature and of marriage. He forthrightly opposes the Platonic view of women's leadership role and informs us that such modifications of married life would "deprive mothers of that privacy of affection regarding which the wisdom of Solomon beamed forth." On the one hand, he complains that Plato would be dealing with humans in the same manner as a breeder of birds or dogs. The plan is a "strange and forbidding experiment," or so it should seem to us from the vantage point of "laws now irrevocably fixed on these subjects by the judgment of the Christian church."[17] Pater does not even attempt to answer Plato's contention that, despite the conventions of the day, the sharing of rule by men and women actually preserves the natural relations of the sexes. Instead, he merely states without argument that female equality and identity of role are "altogether out of harmony with the facts of man's nature."[18] (By "man's nature" he of course means "woman's nature," i.e., man in the generic sense.)

A later English philosopher, Bernard Bosanquet, is more sympathetic in principle than Pater to the need for similar education for males and females. He writes that the fact that the Greek household was almost Oriental in its seclusion of women makes Plato's revolutionary demands for women understandable.[19] Bosanquet doesn't find it surprising that Plato wanted to put an end to the Greek family because it was, he says, "a wretched institution." But his final word on the subject is the familiar refrain. On the matter of the lack of difference between the sexes except for the fact that one is weaker, he writes with careful phrasing that "we may be disposed to think that in this he was blind to essential facts of human nature."[20]

A. E. Taylor agrees that Plato is unaware of the true nature and purpose of human sex differences. He explains Plato's blindness by suggesting that Socrates' treatment of sex in the *Republic*, like that of all non-Christian moralists, involves an underestimation of the significance of sex for the whole of the spiritual life.

Taylor assumes that the impulses of sex and family affections are for humans intrinsically, that is, naturally, connected. Natural sexual impulses, Taylor concludes, are subjected to much severer restraints in Plato's state than in any which has ever been adopted by a Christian society.[21] The intolerable severity and self-denial are the chief reasons that Plato's scheme is unfeasible. (As a male Christian moralist, Taylor's interests, unlike those of the present writer, cause him to overlook entirely that Plato grants almost complete sexual freedom to women over forty.)

Taylor makes no attempt whatsoever to compare Plato's proposals with the actual sexual satisfactions of the upper-class Greek wife. Demosthenes' often noted view of fourth-century Greek women, even if it is only one possible account of their status, is relevant here: "We have *heterai* for pleasure, concubines for our day-to-day physical well-being, and wives in order to beget legitimate children and have trustworthy guardians of our households."[22] This clearly does not present a picture of extensive physical and consequent spiritual satisfaction for wives to be contrasted with the self-denial of Plato's ideal society. Unfortunately our knowledge of women's thoughts and experiences at this time comes almost entirely from literature written by men. Therefore, it is difficult to make reliable comparisons between the sexual satisfactions open to women in classical Athens as compared to those offered by nineteenth-century Christianity. Nevertheless, we have little reason to believe that throughout the centuries the ideal of Christian marriage has guaranteed more sexual satisfaction, for women at any rate, than actual Greek practices or Plato's reforms.

Taylor is also sure that the view of differences between the sexes which cause Plato to extend the duties of warfare and statesmanship to women is erroneous. He says Plato is wrong about sexual distinctions affecting the individual only in respect to procreating and—what Taylor includes as Platonic—to rearing a new generation. Here, this careful scholar actually and uncharacteristically misreads Plato. In the *Republic*, only the bearing is admitted as a relevant sexual distinction. The *trophe*, rearing, or upbringing of the children is alterable; and as Taylor surely knows, the raising of new generations will be communal in the ideal state. It seems to have been hard for him to accept that

Plato did not automatically assume, as he himself does, that children's upbringing is by nature a female task. For Taylor reproduction and child care are both natural to women, and these distinctions profoundly affect the rest of their functioning. Women cannot be soldiers or political leaders because sexual distinction "goes deeper and modifies the whole spiritual life profoundly."[23]

It is striking that scholars whose interpretations make the Platonic text vital and comprehensible in many respects are so much less careful when dealing with matters of female equality. It has been suggested that there is no topic in classical studies except that of homosexuality on which a scholar's normal ability to perceive differences and draw inferences is so easily impaired. Only on the subject of homosexuality is a writer "so likely to be thought to have said what he has not said or to be charged with omitting to say something which he has said several times."[24] But I contend that the subject of women's nature and role provides as great a tendency to misread, misquote, and suspend the usual standards of evidence.

Taylor, like most other commentators, feels no obligation to offer evidence for the way in which sexual differences necessarily alter women's consciousnesses or consciences. In general, none of the commentators find it necessary to offer biological, historical, or anthropological data to support their view that, in the modern vernacular, "anatomy is destiny." Even men writing in the 1960s and 1970s do not attempt to provide evidence. Nor do commentators entertain the possibility of suspending judgment on women's true nature until more information is available.[25] A scholar as intent on objectivity as Taylor proclaims himself to be in his Preface might in 1926 have called for more investigations on the actual connections between sexuality and psychic characteristics. He suggests that the historical Socrates was influenced in his views on female emancipation by the existence of women like Pericles' mistress Aspasia, who was famous for her intellectual attainments. However, he does not seem to have been influenced by the attainments of Queen Elizabeth I. Nor do most of the other writers who disparage women's abilities for leadership find it necessary to account for modern female parliamentarians and even heads of state who somehow, contrary to female nature, manage to display equal aptitude for statesmanship.

One of the most blatant distortions of Plato's view of what is natural occurs in the comments of a Canadian rabbi, Solomon Frank, in his study of Plato's theory of education. Like Pater, he makes the unself-conscious assumption that what he approves will be generally accepted as both desirable and natural. Frank uses as his chief source for Plato's theories the *Laws*, which contain the modified views of Plato's later years. These views constitute advantageous regulations for an actual Greek state rather than a description of what would be best in an ideal state. Although even in this latter book Plato advances reforms which would provide for more equitable treatment and use of the resources of half of the human race, his radical plan for complete equality is not sustained.[26] But even in discussing the arrangements in the *Laws*, Frank superimposes his own opinions without even a minimal attempt to guard against seeing Plato through the presuppositions of a twentieth-century conservative Canadian religious educator. In his paraphrase, he speaks of the stages of a girl's life as "maid, wife, mother, and matron" with no prototype for this division in Plato's texts at all.[27] The main emphasis of his discussion, which largely ignores the topic of education in the *Republic*, is on the contrast between expert and amateur in male and female training. Plato, he tells us, believes that women should learn some of the same things boys do, but always in an "amateurish spirit" in distinction from the boys' expertise in such matters, e.g., military drill. I am not suggesting that there is absolutely no basis for this distinction in Plato's *Laws*. However, to write as if this were all Plato had to contribute to the subject of women's education is to downplay the ideals of the *Republic* to such an extent as to distort Plato's total views.

It is worth quoting in its entirety the footnote in which Frank attempts to deal with what he admits might be considered contrary to his interpretation of Plato's sole view of the connection between women and warfare. This footnote is a striking illustration of the way in which prejudice can interfere with our reading of important philosophical texts, as well as with the disinterested consideration of what is best for society. Frank writes: "It is thus only women with a natural turn for warlike pursuits who are to be selected and educated for this function; and *at that*, they are allotted the less heavy duties of military life (457) and are 'never to violate, but always to preserve, the natural relation of the sexes' " (466).[28]

Frank intends this final quote from Plato to convince us that the "natural relation" for the Athenian philosopher, as for Rabbi Frank, is that even if girls did participate in war, they must be protected, as nature dictates, by their superior, expert menfolk. The reference given is to line 466d in the *Republic*. In fact, in that line Plato says exactly the opposite of what Frank intends. Having based his entire argument on *physis*, what is genuinely natural, rather than *nomos*, the merely conventional, Plato in this passage (only part of which is quoted by Frank) clearly restates that men and women should pursue the same tasks. Both when they are staying in the city and going out to war, they must guard and hunt together like dogs. He then puts it unequivocally that *by* doing this (Bloom translates "in doing this," but the meaning is the same), they are doing nothing contrary to the nature of the female in her relationship to the male, "nothing contrary to the natural community of the two with each other."[29]

The generous interpretation of Frank's misreading is that in his zeal to preserve the conventional relation of the sexes, as formulated in Jewish law and custom, he finds it hard to face that Plato genuinely stated the contrary. The fact, however, is that in this passage Plato is asserting precisely that since other animals share in aggression and ruling, such joint participation is in fact natural.

Later English and German commentators have not missed this point. Instead, they reinforce the oft-stated objection that Plato is mistaken in his view of female nature. There is no need to discuss at length the position of R. C. Crossman. He certainly cannot be accused of any concealed attempt to use the original text for a hidden agenda of his own. For the aim of his *Plato Today* is stated explicitly; his specific intention is to update Plato's views for the twentieth-century reader. This British scholar and politician considers himself to be in agreement with what he calls Plato's "feminism." But it is not complete identity of role that he finds desirable, for he fears that much will be lost if egalitarianism "goes too far."[30] As we shall see, there are many others who echo this cry.

One highly influential commentator who does not even profess sympathy with egalitarianism is Leo Strauss, who is a frequent target of feminist attacks in the 1970s. Like the feminists, Strauss attributes crucial importance to the proposal for gender equality. However, he views it in a diametrically opposed way. It is not a forerunner of modern equalitarian programs, but instead Plato's way of showing us that the just city could never come into being. Regardless of what Socrates actually says, Plato's real intention was for us to recognize that his utopia was ultimately unrealizable.

At least Strauss sees that a revolutionary change would be required to fulfill Plato's scheme. And he finds that, no matter how desirable, in the final analysis such reforms are unnatural; therefore, a just society in Plato's sense is impossible. Strauss himself accepts Plato's framework for discussing the good of societies and concludes with a realization that is intended to move us with its tragic overtones. The just city cannot come into being because absolute communism and the equality of the sexes—and that is the precise phrase he uses—"are *against* nature."[31]

Allan Bloom, whose translation contains an extended interpretive essay, follows Strauss in his reasoning on the unnaturalness of the proposals. Since Bloom, too, is the target of much criticism and controversy, and since many of his objections to female equality recur in his defense and rejoinders to these attacks, I shall postpone the bulk of discussion of his views until later. It is important to point out here, however, that he joins the voices of those like Taylor and Strauss who condemn Socrates for "forgetting the importance of the body."[32] Only on the precondition of such "forgetting" could Plato have made such a proposal. For if he had considered the body and its needs correctly, he could have seen that the differences between men and women are far more crucial than Socrates allows.

Bloom also finds Plato's abolition of the family unsatisfactory. For the family, by which he evidently means our current Western notion of a nuclear family, is "surely somehow natural."[33] The father, if he is anything, is the one who engenders the child. The strength of what Anna Freud has called "psychological parenting," so that in her view the parent is not necessarily the one

who contributes the sperm but the one who nurtures the child
emotionally, is not even considered. Nor does he consider animal
evidence. We know there are biological species where there is no
parental investment in the offspring, as well as animals where the
young are cared for by what we would call foster parents. I am
not suggesting that animal data is ultimately decisive.[34] However,
any commentator in the 1960s who wishes to pronounce on the
naturalness of parental feeling, and therefore on the impossibility
of communal rearing for males at least—he mentions only fathers—might be expected to adduce anthropological or biological
information to support his view. Instead, his assumptions are
baldly stated; he appeals evidently to "common sense."

An interesting contrast to Bloom written at approximately the
same time is a little-known commentary written in Hong Kong. I
include this study because the fact that it is addressed to students
culturally different from the audience of the other commentators
requires a less dogmatic approach to the naturalness of any given
kind of family. N. E. Fehl's *Guide to the Study of Plato's Republic* is
addressed to Chinese students at Chung Chi College to whom he
declares, "Plato is our contemporary here within these green hills
so close to the boarder [sic] of China."[35] His analysis revolves
much less around what is natural and relies much more on the
varying arrangements that have actually existed. He discusses how
the family types in ancient China differed from those of fourth-
century Athens and points to the similarity between the Greek
schema and the Hindu caste system. He also describes the varying
foundations of marriage in what he calls tribal and religious societies and the differences between the Catholic and Protestant
views of the purposes of sexual union.

Fehl's own view is hard to determine because of the question
and answer format he uses to stimulate students. The importance
of his discussion, however, is that unlike Taylor, Strauss, Bloom,
and others, he cannot call upon an assumed unanimity or self-
evidence for his own views about mating, incest, and the importance of the body. He can still, however, assume certain shared
assumptions about the preeminence of the male sex. So he tells
his Chinese theological students at a Christian college that just as
Eve was an after-thought of Yahweh, so women and the family
are dealt with in a parenthesis in Plato's dream of the ideal soci-

ety.[36] This disparaging of the issue no doubt has as much to do with Fehl's own bias as it does with a correct interpretation of the text.

On the other hand, his anthropological perspective, with its emphasis on the typology of family structures, leads him to consider seriously Plato's alternatives. Fehl distinguishes three types of family: the consanguine, the conjugal, and the communal. The first, which Plato took for granted, consists of a large family which includes not only parents and children, but grandparents and the male descendants of the grandparents and their wives and children. This was also the structure of ancient China and was in fact an obstacle to the development of a strong central government. Fehl sees Plato as suggesting another kind of family which he calls the communal. The third alternative, what he terms the conjugal family, where the structure is centered in the ego-spouse relation, he seems to agree with contemporary radical feminists is undesirable.

This conjugal family is the modern urban family in which frequently both mother and father are employed away from home. This type may be a necessity of urban industrial society, he states (using Hong Kong, I assume, as his model). Fehl asks whether this urban nuclear family is not worse than Plato's suggestion.[37] He thus implies that no one kind of family is more "natural" than another. As we have seen, this is not the view of the majority of the commentators from 1870–1970. The pervasive attitude is rather the one expressed by Desmond Lee in the introduction to his frequently reissued translation. He tells us that both the desirability and the very possibility of exact similarity of role are questionable. "To sweep aside the physiological differences as unimportant and ignore the psychological differences they *entail* is to be in danger of ignoring women's special excellences" (*my emphasis*).[38] He warns that if you merely expect women to do the same things as men, they are likely, as Plato in effect said, to end up as inferior men. Is it not better to recognize the difference rather than pretend it does not exist? he asks.

This solicitous concern that women might "end up" as lesser men, a concern shared by Jowett and others into the 1980s, will be discussed later. The important issue here is the dogmatism of Lee's final formulation. For the chain beginning with the suggestions that differences "cut deep," are profound, alter women's entire being, and several other metaphorical expressions alluding to women's diverse abilities, ends with a conviction of logically entailed consequences of biology. Lee gives us no hint of what those special excellences are which Plato denies women to possess. Nor does he expand on how female physiology inevitably produces psychological differences, nor why these differences exclude women from a leadership role.

The commentators we have been dealing with all share the assumption that women's nature is ascertainable and that it is other than Plato describes it. They all find the proposals of Book V in some sense unnatural and use this either as an automatic justification for the undesirability of gender equality or at the very least as strong evidence against its advisability.

WOMEN HAVE BETTER THINGS TO DO:
THE PROPOSALS AS UNDESIRABLE

Several commentators who deem Plato wise in many other respects find that his proposed changes in the relation between the sexes are clearly undesirable. These writers do not discuss the plan primarily in terms of its naturalness. When they do, they may even grant that some features of the arrangements in Book V are more natural, generally meaning more analogous to animal practice. Nevertheless, such changes would be bad for women and for society.

Chief among the influential scholars arguing for the undesirability of equality of role is the noted British scholar Richard Nettleship. Nettleship's Oxford lectures of the 1880s were reproduced from notes and published just before the turn of the century. His *Lectures on the Republic of Plato* have been continuously reprinted and have thus influenced students for over a hundred years. In many areas, his commentary is incisive and helpful, but on the matter of equality for women his arguments are suspect. He does make a contribution by pointing out, more than seventy-five years before the identical "discovery" is made by the twentieth-century feminists, that Plato is not concerned at all with the *rights* of women. For Plato, equality is solely a question of women's duties to the community. Socrates does not make his proposal in the interest of women as a class whom he supposes to be wronged, but in the interest of the state.

According to Nettleship, it is doubtful whether Socrates' plan would have struck an Athenian as favorable to women. "It might," he writes, "very likely have seemed to be dragging them out of a position in which they would rather be left."[39] Nettleship's phrase how it would strike "an Athenian" is unclear—does he wonder about the reaction of males or females or both? He does not address this question, but he does seem to imply that the austerity of the guardians' lives would have kept Athenian women from choosing it freely. But Nettleship surely knows that Plato was himself well aware that it would not be easy to convince his guardians, either male or female, to accept the austere life he outlined. Both males and females might rather be left in their ordinary positions, and this is why Socrates introduces his complicated measures of deception and rewards to motivate them.

Probably Nettleship believed that Athenian women would have found the life of leadership and equality even more distasteful than the men, would have resented being dragged out of the positions they occupied even more than the Athenian heads of households. He is expressing the view stated much more openly by an historian who contrasts the life of modern "emancipated women" with the advantages of Athenian wives. Although the former have more personal freedom, the Athenian women had all the advantages of being well-protected.[40]

The crux of the matter lies in how one evaluates the position of fourth-century Greek women. Some have stressed that they led a life of idleness and subjection. No male would willingly trade the absolute lack of control over marriage partner and choice of pursuits for such legal protection. Although other historians and commentators have in fact bemoaned the subject condition of women, Nettleship, here at least, does not seem to share their concern. In my opinion, Greek women might well have preferred to become rulers rather than remain the property of their husbands. At the very least, there seems no reason to believe that it would be any more difficult to persuade a woman than a man to enter the guardian class.

Nettleship thinks that hardly anyone would dispute Plato's

assertion that it is the real good of the community that ought to prevail. He agrees, too, that this good involves as much coopera- tion as possible between the sexes so that they can make the greatest contribution to the common life. But Plato's view of cooperation between the sexes Nettleship calls "narrow." Plato was mistaken in thinking that cooperation involves participation in deliberative, administrative, and military functions. He writes: "[A]s it might be put now, there are thousands of ways of contrib- uting to the service of society besides being a member of Parliament or a soldier. One has, then, to distinguish between Plato's principle and the particular application he makes of it, which is to a certain extent determined by the circumstances of his time."[41]

Nettleship interprets Plato as having said that the more coop- eration there is between men and women the better. But Plato does not speak of cooperation between the sexes in general, but only of identity of function among the superior. Nettleship clearly prefers the Victorian British idea of women as helpmates. He says he agrees with Aristotle that the difference between men and women is one which fundamentally affects their social functions. They ought not to do the same things, but to supplement each other. He seems to agree, too, that the analogy of the lower ani- mals proves nothing. For even if some male and female animals are not so widely differentiated in character, this is due to the fact that animals are not so highly developed as man. In man, the most highly developed animal, the differentiation of the sexes is greatest.[42]

Nettleship does not offer any reasons why this differentiation is the most beneficial arrangement for society as a whole. He cer- tainly makes no attempt to view the question of access to leadership from the point of view of the women then beginning to agitate for change. He simply assumes paternalistically that the many ways women could do service in his society were satisfactory for them and best for the common good. There are many other examples of commentators who believe the Platonic proposals would be highly detrimental. Their arguments are forcefully put by the great German scholar who proclaims that the arrangements suggested in Book V are "altogether intolerable and most corrupt- ing."[43] All of these writers prefer the *status quo*, the relations between the genders in their own societies, to Plato's innovations.

PLATO DIDN'T REALLY MEAN IT:
THE PROPOSALS AS UNINTENTIONAL,
UNWELCOME, OR COMIC

One minority view is that Plato himself never really meant—or at the very least was less than wholehearted about—his suggestion of female and male guardians ruling equally. Although other writers have asserted adamantly that there is no point on which Plato speaks with more decided conviction, these commentators insist that the entire proposal was never intended to be taken seriously. While some attempt to justify the arrangements by showing that they would not have seemed as paradoxical to the Greeks because of the presence of the Spartan example, the commentators that I shall now discuss find the plans not only paradoxical but basically amusing, absurd, ironic, and intended as a joke.[44]

The mildest version of this view consists only of a weak doubt about Plato's own faith in his argument. Since Plato was clearly mistaken, we must look for some logical or psychological reason to "explain away" his strange ideas. Thus, Constantine Ritter tells us that Plato himself "did not quite trust his proposal." This is Ritter's "impression," but he does not offer any internal evidence on which he bases his impression.[45]

One of the strongest expressions of this argument which recurs throughout the German tradition appears much earlier in the commentary of Karl Nohle, published in 1880. He writes that Plato "has to admit" that there is no complete equality between men and women. Furthermore, "he cannot deny" that the difference in their biological share in reproduction "hinders women from playing as great a part in the governing of the state." There must, then, have been other reasons that made the philosopher overlook these basic defects in women.[46] He assumes that Plato would have thought the governing classes much better if they consisted only of men and so undertakes his reforms only with great reluctance.

The problem, Nohle thinks, is that if only males governed

there might be fear for the children of the guardians. Since the mothers would be inferior to the fathers in education of mind and body, future guardians might be dragged down to the level of the industrial class. To prevent this, "wives of guardians" must also be admitted into the circle of rulers. But when there, they can find nothing to do because the communal arrangements abolish all housekeeping and separate married life, and the State takes over child rearing. Therefore, since no possible occupation remains for women, he must assign them the same work as men, in spite of their lack of qualification for it.

For one who admires Plato as much as Nohle does, it seems strange that he finds Plato guilty of such a major logical inconsistency. If the whole concept of justice is based on each person's doing what he is best suited for, the existence of rulers who were basically unqualified would seem a major discrepancy. I should think Plato would be reluctant indeed! As the earliest feminist commentator phrases her objections in 1913 to what she generously terms Nohle's "interesting attempt to account for Plato's wish, "[I]t seems extremely arbitrary to attribute so torturous a mode of reasoning to Plato, in the face of his express and repeated affirmations that a State is only half a State if its women are allowed to run to waste."[47]

This idea of Plato's dissatisfaction with his own proposals surfaces again years later in the commentary of the eminent German classicist U. v. Wilamowitz-Moellendorff. He tells us that the very logic of Plato's own thinking forces the philosopher to conclusions which he himself does not welcome. Plato knows that woman is the object of man's strongest desire and man wants her as his property more passionately than anything else. This knowledge forces Plato into a conclusion which is *"sehr unwelkommen"* to him.[48]

Like later feminists, Wilamowitz believes that it is the idea of the abolition of property which logically precedes the abolition of marriage for the guardians. Since such a result is a logical requirement, Plato tries to resign himself to the consequences. But, as Wilamowitz puts it, "There is evidence that he manages this resignation only incompletely."[49] Since Wilamowitz realizes that the *rule* of women is logically independent of the elimination of pri-

vate property, he looks for some other logical requirement that
led Plato to this further undesirable but unavoidable proposal.

He decides that it is Plato's belief that women possess immortal
souls and are therefore receptive to virtue that forces the unwelcome conclusions. It is virtue that determines their place in
society, and as far as they are receptive to philosophy, they must
rule. Wilamowitz does not explain why Plato himself fails to
make this argument in Book V. Nevertheless, this commentator
concludes that such reasoning must actually account for the
unwelcome proposal.

Throughout the discussion, Wilamowitz talks of *"Weiberregi-
mente"* and *"Weibe ans Staatsruder,"* that is, "women at the
helm" rather than the joint rule of equally capable men and
women which Plato actually calls for. This is partly because he
has begun his discussion with a consideration of the connection
between Aristophanes' *Ecclesiazusae,* or "Women in the Assembly" and Plato's proposals. The confusing terminology probably
stems from the fact that in this comedy the theme *is* actually
what would happen if a role reversal were to occur and women
were to take over leadership of the state. The connection
between these two works has been controversial for well over a
hundred years. In the last decade, as we shall see, an evaluation
of this connection becomes crucial to whether Plato's proposals
are also intended as comic. But although Wilamowitz would like
to minimize the importance of the reforms, he is adamant that
they must not be compared to the worn-out theme chosen by
Aristophanes which is only a pretext for entertaining his audience
with a few dirty jokes. It is "ineradicable nonsense" that Plato
was influenced by the *Ecclesiazusae,* for the two views do not have
anything in common. The important point, for Wilamowitz, is
that Plato really knew nothing about women, whereas Aristophanes knew the *"Hausfrau die in ihrem Reiche wirklich herrscht."*[50]
Evidently Plato's lack of knowledge of the housewife who rules in
her own home is responsible for the proposals that he was so
reluctantly led to make.

Thus, all those who believe Plato to have accepted his own
conclusions only reluctantly still assume that they are the result of
serious, if misguided, considerations. However, there is a con-

trasting view which even more effectively minimizes the importance of the ideas. With varying degrees of insistence, some commentators have announced that the whole discussion was intended as a joke.

One of these is I. M. Crombie, who thinks Plato's thoughts on sex relations, marriage, and the family "should be read by connoisseurs of *a priori* absurdity." He says that the most charitable comment to make on the reforms is that Plato intends "to pull the legs" of those who attach undue value to family ties.[51]

A later scholar, Paul Friedlander, also suggests that Plato introduces his paradoxes and plays with them *"pour épater le bourgeois."* By having the women exercise naked with the men in the gymnasium and by elaborating on the institution of communal marriage, Friedlander considers Plato to be introducing amusing and even grotesque details.[52] Another interpreter, H. Gauss, objects to Friedlander's making the proposals playful. But in doing so, Gauss distorts Plato's text; and Friedlander later defends his own view by pointing out this distortion. Gauss evidently considers Plato's demands for the same educational opportunities to be straightforward. Unfortunately, he writes of them that Plato went so far as to demand *"Frauengymnasia,"* women's gymnasiums, where they, like their male colleagues, devote themselves to physical exercises after having shed their clothes.[53] But Friedlander is right that Plato does not specify such sex-segregated facilities. Gauss's attempt to make the idea more respectable is reminiscent of the French commentator who describes the Greeks as exercising *"presque nus."*[54] Such reticence, however, does not alter the basic point that Plato makes. Just as the barbarians laughed at the Greeks when they first exercised nude, Plato assures his audience that the strangeness of the practice would eventually wear off. Many writers have pointed to the fact that Spartan women exercised along with men as a possible source for this idea. Although we do not know exactly what Spartan women wore for their gymnastic training, it would not doubt have shocked some Athenians if even the Spartan practice was instituted at Athens. We know that in most Greek cities, women were not even allowed to eat at the same table with a male not related to her.[55]

We also know from mosaics in Sicily that Roman women

engaged in sports in very brief costumes startlingly like our bikini bathing suits.[56] Almost nude is, of course, not completely naked, but a convincing case can be made for the fact that the former can be as distracting as the latter or more so. The important point, I think, remains that the requirement of joint nudity (not unlike the nude bathing that takes place on many beaches today) is hardly enough to discredit the seriousness of the proposal of equal education in *musike* and *gymnastike* for both sexes.

Despite his introduction of possible comic intention for Plato, it is important to indicate that Friedlander's own view differs from the major proponents of the "joke" theory. For he, unlike them, believes that Plato is in fact deeply serious behind the jest. In support of later feminist commentary, he states that it is not the institution that matters, but the principle represented by it. In principle, as many as possible should be able to share in the education provided by the state. He thinks that education in "our own society" has moved much closer to adopting Plato's paradox. He does not, then, accentuate the comic aspect solely to highlight the impossibility or undesirability of female equality.

However, the views of Leo Strauss and Allan Bloom do exactly that. Strauss describes Plato's dialogues in general as "slightly more akin" to comedy than to tragedy. And the *Republic* he finds "manifestly akin" to Aristophanes' *Assembly of Women.*[57] Bloom says that he relies heavily on Strauss' "authoritative discussion" for his own interpretive essay. And, in his notes to the text, he points out the probable allusions to *Ecclesiazusae* in Book V.

In Bloom's discussion, the judgment that the three paradoxical waves are primarily comic is inseparable from his contention, introduced above, that the proposals violate "our understanding of human nature." The first paradox of female equality he finds laughable and ridiculous, whereas discussion of the second proposal emphasized the comic element less. With the idea of philosopher-rulers the laughter and indignation reappear in a more intense form. The whole book, he writes, "*can only be understood* as Socrates' response to his most dangerous accuser, Aristophanes, and his contest with him. . . . In Book V he tries to show the superiority of the philosopher . . . by producing a comedy which is more fantastic, more innovative, more comic . . . than any work of Aristophanes."[58] In stressing the absurdity, he echoes

Strauss' vague and archaic adjective, calling Socrates' comedy "akin" to *Ecclesiazusae* in that they both propose emancipation of women and communism.

Strictly speaking, as I have said, what *Ecclesiazusae* actually proposes is role reversal with women ruling while men stay home. Praxagora, the heroine of the play, introduces a bill into the assembly for the "putting down of men."[59] This has a modern ring, evoking the excesses of some radical feminists; but there is a major logical and practical difference between gynecocracy and the identity of the role proposed for the guardians. Most of the commentators who discuss the connection of the two works, regardless of their views on the independence or reciprocal influence, do judge the theme of female equality to be similar. They fail to stress what I would consider this striking dissimilarity.

Bloom thinks that Book V surpasses and radicalizes the reforms of the Athenian women in the comedy. In the play, the women's reforms, he says, are *just,* but politically impossible. In my view, what Aristophanes has Praxagora and her comrades suggest in their gynecocracy is certainly not just, for it involves the arbitrary rule of one group over another. The misuse of male resources may in fact be possible, though it is true that contrary to the wishful thinking of some feminists, no female-dominated society has ever existed.[60] But it is surely not just in Plato's terms. And I doubt very much that Bloom actually considers most of the comic suggestions (such as the requirement that the young man sleep with the "old hag" before he can have intercourse with the young woman he desires) to be just.

The radicalizing to which Bloom refers lies evidently in the outrageousness of suggesting that men and women exercise naked together. I shall confine myself here to those arguments he offers in his original essay. As mentioned before, his views have been attacked by male and female feminists in the 1970s and I shall discuss their objections and his response to them later in that context. The important point here is that Bloom finds the public nudity of men and women to be nonsense as a political proposal.[61] The full equality of the sexes, what Bloom calls "sharing the same locker room," could not possibly work even on Plato's own terms. Men can be naked together because it is relatively easy to desexualize their relations with each other. I assume

Bloom speaks only of the relative ease since he is well aware that the sexual desire of many Athenian males was at least as strong for other nude males as it would have been for nude females.

But the difficulty comes according to Bloom because the mutual attraction of men and women must be fostered rather than discouraged if the city is to be preserved. This mutual attraction evidently could not be maintained if women exercised naked alongside men. Bloom ignores such practices as nude swimming beaches, and nude family bathing in Japan (where reproduction seems to continue despite the supposed difficulties). Nor does the increased licentiousness that Bloom thinks would inevitably result "because civilized men need some mastery over their sexual appetites" occur in all societies with different attitudes to nudity than ours.

For Bloom, however, the entire prospect of nakedness in the gymnasium is both 1) impossible in itself, and 2) symbolic in its contradictions of the impossibility of equality and ultimately of the entire foundation of the ideal State. Such a State would be impossible because its law would "at the same time encourage and forbid the mutual attraction of the sexes." In my view, what would actually be required would be the State's discouraging action on the attraction at one time, and encouraging it at another. This is perfectly possible, and in fact goes on all the time. Plato himself encourages male-male attraction as a means of understanding the desire for the good, though he discourages action on the attraction most of the time. Repression will be necessary in the just city, but then some kind of repression *is* necessary to female equality. But repression of sexuality has been and probably always will be necessary to all forms of civilization. If the city, as Bloom himself says, can, and has, forbidden homosexuality, then law and custom have also sequestered women and forbidden "undesirable" unions. The 1977 execution of Saudi Princess Mishaal for adultery is evidence of the extent to which the State can still forbid mutual attraction.

Bloom, however, finds the whole proposal of sexual equality preposterous. The erotic improprieties will be so extensive that their complications only reinforce the lack of seriousness on Socrates' part. It is not usually thought possible, Bloom tells us, to make the sexual passion respond only to those objects chosen by the city, in a way and at a time deemed fitting by the city. Although he finally grants that some training and repression of sexual desires is possible, the Platonic suggestions are outlandish. Many anthropologists would suggest that the erotic impulses of women have frequently been just as rigorously regulated. From the practices of ancient China to those of many religious sects today, extensive regulation of sexual behavior has persisted. Both Moslem fundamentalists and orthodox Jews rigorously control women's sexual behavior. Religious authorities even determine on which days of the menstrual cycle intercourse is permissible. According to reports from modern China, in order to encourage birth control, charts of the menstrual cycle of women residents were publicly posted in neighborhood health centers. Premarital sex was ostensibly almost eliminated at the same time as the age for marriage was raised.

Bloom seems to forget that the "sexual passion" of most women throughout history has been restricted in its expression to the partners chosen by fathers or male relatives, if not by the State. The way and time have been decided primarily by the wishes of the husband. I am not commenting on the desirability of State-regulated temporary unions nor supporting the view that male, female, or joint nudity is necessary to the cultivation of human physical excellence. What I am suggesting is that the variety and severity of extant customs might have given Bloom pause in his considerations of what is humanly possible.

On the whole, Bloom's account of the necessary relation between shame and sexual attraction and his total account of human sexual desire seem idiosyncratic. He certainly makes no attempt to support it with any currently available psychological data. He tells us that incest taboos are accepted without question and hardly need to be taught. Recent evidence in the United States suggests that incest taboos are frequently violated, that more than twenty-five percent of females are reported to have been sexually assaulted by male relatives. Researchers believe that young boys are also more frequently involved than is reported in sexual encounters with related females. Since reporting such incidents is still considered unmanly in this culture because of the belief that males should always desire intercourse regardless of the circumstances, we probably do not have accurate statistics on

such unwanted incestuous relations. Evidence of voluntary vio-
lations of incest taboos is of course far less reliable. Although
sociologists today believe that incest taboos are natural in the
sense that they have been evolved as adaptive for our species,
evidence still suggests that the specific forms the taboo takes has
much to do with convention. Bloom says that Socrates speaks as
if he were talking of regulations no more important than rivers
and harbors. Bloom is surely right that the matter is generally
regarded as far more important than that. However, in the matter
of incest, it does seem that justice, that is, unfair exploitation, is
the modern issue rather than violation of the natural.

According to Bloom, Plato has a hidden agenda. The real reason women are placed among the guardians is not because they
possess the same capacities as men, but precisely because they are
different. Socrates needs women guardians because they can bear
children and men cannot. Why Socrates does not tell us that he
is "fabricating a convention about the nature of women" when he
tells us at many other points when a myth or a noble lie will be
necessary to gain his aims for a just society, Bloom does not
explain.

He does, however, recognize the contradiction in Plato's comments on women, which becomes a major issue in the feminist
commentary of the 1970s. Aware that Plato finds the best women
always inferior to the best men, Bloom goes so far as to assert
that it would be highly improbable that any women would even
"be considered for membership" in the higher classes.[62]

Thus, he would seem to agree with Nohle that Plato would
have greatly preferred to have all-male rulers. The argument is
basically the same, although Bloom goes even further than
Nohle. It is not only that the guardians might be inferior if their
mothers were inferior, but rather that female guardians are necessary if there are to be any future guardians at all. The same
objection applies to both commentators. For if Plato actually did
not believe women capable of ruling, his placing them among the
philosophers would undermine his whole theory of justice, in
which each person does what he is best suited for. Although
Nohle does not seem to have noticed this lack of logic, Bloom
thinks it adds to the general absurdity and comic irony of the
project. But if what Plato has created is a society in which

women perform jobs for which they are basically unsuited, he has created a state which is not comic, but rather fundamentally unjust. And so, Bloom, like Strauss before him, must see that a decision about the capacities of women is essential to a plan for an ideal society, and therefore, despite his protestations, no laughing matter.

OTHER WAYS OF "EXPLAINING AWAY"
THE PLAN FOR GENDER EQUALITY

Other writers also look for ways of explaining why Plato came up with his paradoxical reforms. These explanations tend to minimize the legitimacy of these reforms. The line between "explaining" and "explaining away," of course, is not always easy to draw. One example of such speculation on Plato's motives is the account of the scholar-psychoanalyst, Bennett Simon. Unlike many of the previous classicists, Simon's intentions are surely not anti-female, and when not discussing the *Republic*, he explicitly expresses pro-feminist attitudes. Unfortunately, however, psychoanalytic theorizing about the underlying psycho-sexual conflicts of long dead literary figures often tends to reductionism. That is, it leads the reader to focus on the "neurotic" reasons for a theory, rather than on the possible logical and philosophical validity of the claim. Thus, Simon's account, whatever his intention, has the effect of casting doubt on the objectivity, and therefore the validity, of Plato's arguments for that abolishing of family life which makes it possible for women and men to rule equally.

Simon writes that an important aspect of Plato's design for his ideal state is the wish to protect the elite and the guardians from "primal scene trauma" and its consequences. On the basis of biographical detail, he tries to show that the arrangements Plato makes for his guardians are intended to spare them the damaging experiences of parental intercourse, which he speculates the philosopher must have witnessed in his own childhood. This hypothetical trauma led Plato to prescribe practices for the guardians which require "ordered and regulated intercourse, not 'in the dark,' . . . and as far as possible intercourse should be dissociated

from biological and social parenthood." The motivation for Plato's proposals is his unconscious belief that only new modes of
sexuality and birth that eliminate parents copulating in the dark
can eradicate the whole host of evils that disrupt societies.[63]

Simon also sees the "Allegory of the Cave" as a primal scene
fantasy. This is not the place to try to evaluate the possibility of
using ancient texts to reveal the psychodynamic issues of their
authors, and to assess the particular difficulties involved when little or no direct biographical information is available. However, I
do wish to point out that such analyses, regardless of their
authors' intentions, tend to obscure and trivialize these central
visions of Western philosophy.

Simon has little to say about the specific connection between
identical roles for women and primal scene trauma; but he does
seem to consider the minimizing of biological differences inherent
in such equality as all part of the philosopher's wish to deny the
importance of male-female intercourse. It is not clear if Simon
himself accepts the orthodox Freudian position on the importance
of those biological differences that Plato underplays. The original
psychoanalytic view would characterize a woman trying to do the
same job as a man as denying her femininity, fantasizing a male
body, being unwilling to accept her biological deficiencies.[64]

Simon does not raise these issues, but concentrates instead on
what Plato hopes to achieve by minimizing the primal scene. This
leads him to a mistaken reading of what Plato actually says.
According to Simon, fraternal love can replace fratricide only by
minimizing the primal scene. But it is not rivalry that Plato
wishes to eliminate. Plato does not abolish the family in order to
keep brothers from killing each other, but for precisely the opposite reason. It is the family loyalties that are divisive to the State.
And, of course, it is only among the guardians that he specifically
abolishes marriage, though Plato himself does speak at one point
as if fraternal love would be fostered throughout the city by his
new arrangements.[65] As some commentators have noted, Plato's
failure to provide a motive for the artisan class to feel loyal to
their guardians is a major drawback to the possible success of his
city. At any rate, it is inter-family, rather than intra-family, strife
that Plato fears. He wants to create one big family whose mythical mother and nurse is Mother Earth, and whose members are

fashioned as gold, silver, or bronze by a male god. If such a fiction is evidence of the avoidance of a primal scene, then the creators of hundreds of similar myths in many cultures may well have been equally traumatized.

This is not to suggest that Simon is wrong to raise the issue of the Greek male's fear of the female and of female sexuality. He is wrong, however, in stating that in societies in which males are considered superior, female sexuality is seen as non-existent or inferior.[66] The Greeks at any rate did not see women as without sexual appetite. K. J. Dover, who has made a careful study of the subject, notes that in contrast to the curious beliefs propagated in the English-speaking world during the last hundred years or so (conditioned by the Victorian presupposition that absence of sexual response is morally praiseworthy), the Greeks were inclined to think that women desired and enjoyed sexual intercourse more than men.[67]

The major point for our purposes is that Simon's entire discussion detracts from the significance of Plato's proposal of equality of role. One could advocate the abolition of private families, substituting male rulers and well-regulated female slaves, and avoid primal scene trauma equally well. Why Plato went to such lengths as to have male and female philosopher-rulers is not illumined by Simon's psychoanalytic speculations.

A contrary explanation of why the *Republic* advocates the emancipation of female guardians is offered by A. J. Taylor. He believes that it was the historical Socrates, Plato's teacher, rather than Plato himself, who actually advocated such reforms. In other words, it is Socrates' early childhood and not Plato's that we would have to search for explanations. Taylor says that the proposals are no personal development of Plato's thinking, but rather only the "necessary consequences" of the position of the actual Socrates.[68] Taylor cites Aeschines' work *Aspasia*, of which we have only a fragment, as evidence of Socrates' pro-female leanings. We have, of course, very little historical information about Socrates apart from Plato's portrait of his mentor. But Taylor notes that the Socrates described by Aeschines thought that the goodness of woman was the same as that of a man. Socrates supposedly supported this belief by pointing to the political abilities of Aspasia and the military achievements of the Persian "Amazon," Rhodogyne. This thesis of Taylor's is not altogether convincing if we assume that earlier Platonic dialogues like the *Apology* contain the views of the historical Socrates, while later ones are more purely Platonic. For in the *Apology*, Socrates dismisses his wife as he is about to die, preferring the rational conversation of his young male friends to the "womanish wailing" of Xanthippe. (It is, I suppose, possible to believe in the need for sexual equality and yet find one's own wife inferior. However, the situation does suggest a certain misogyny which is discussed at length by the commentators of the 1970s.) At any rate, Taylor has not proven his case that the proposal for gender equality is merely the logical outcome of Socrates' own views which Plato felt constrained to follow.[69]

We now come to the final way of explaining away or minimizing the novelty and need for Plato's reforms. This is to assert that such reforms were indeed admirable and have in fact already been accomplished. The French commentator, Maurice Croiset, writing in the 1930s, expresses sympathy with the offering of equal education to men and women. He says that this aim of Plato's has actually been accomplished in the France of his day. Considering that there were fewer women than men in higher education and that French women were unable to vote at the time he was writing, his claim seems at best premature.[70]

One of the most bizarre expressions of this view occurs in a book published in Germany in 1933, comparing Hitler's political program and Plato's *Republic*. Joachim Bannes writes that the aims of the National Socialist "freedom movement" were identical to Plato's in creating equal education and social roles for women.[71] He refers us to Hitler's *Mein Kampf*, which he assures us shows the ideological influence of Plato and demonstrates Hitler's plan for equality for women.

The only relevant reference to be found in *Mein Kampf* would seem to be a statement about physical training. Hitler writes that the emphasis on physical education must be the same for men and women, although "the aim of female education undoubtedly has to be preparation for motherhood."[72] There were, of course, no women in the elite schools of Germany in the 1930s and early 1940s. And in fact, Hitler was so irrational in his opposition to the participation of women that he avoided mobilizing them for forced labor until very late in the war. This was clearly contrary to his own interests and to the practice of both Britain and the United States. Even Socrates in fourth-century Athens is said to have suggested to Aristarchus that women be put to some productive work when an unusual situation necessitated it. When Aristarchus fled with fourteen relatives from Athens to Piraeus during a political disturbance and was left with no means to support a large household, Xenophon tells us that Socrates advised his noble friend to set the women to work, contrary to the usual Athenian practice.[73] Furthermore, Hitler in his anti-Semitism took over the idea of the Jews as a principle of femininity, demonstrating a pervasive misogyny.[74]

BIAS IN LANGUAGE:
THE CONSEQUENCES OF HIDDEN ASSUMPTIONS

There is a distinct category of commentators whose disapproval of Plato's views involves no overt statements, but nevertheless reveals a marked unconscious bias. This bias is apparent in their choice of language to state what Plato said, or in questionable translations from the Greek, or in what seem unwitting misreadings. C. H. Hoole's "brief summary of the arguments and doctrines of the *Republic* expressed as far as possible in the words of Plato" supplies an example. His renderings are expressed in the language of the Victorian gentleman. He writes: *"Woman is the weaker man;* for both sexes have the same capacities for the performance of the active duties of life, the same in kind though existing in higher degree in the male" (*my emphasis*).[75]

The striking feature here is the unconscious irony in the phrase "woman is the weaker man." It is possible that Hoole means to convey that woman is *a* weaker man, but he clearly knows that Plato admits the reproductive differences are genuine. Instead, what Hoole probably intends is only the accepted vernacular of the time. As one would say on the playing fields of Eton that Jenkins was the weaker man, that is, the less able, Hoole is here using "man" in the generic sense. His all-male students evidently found no difficulty in understanding what now appears to us as the awkwardly androcentric *"woman* is the weaker man."

Jowett's phrase, "the female sex in man," is equally awkward.[76] Many of the phrases in his translation are even more unconsciously amusing and revealing. The high comedy of Victorian euphemism appears in his rendering of the line, "then the wives of our guardians will have a fine easy time when they are in the family way."[77] Even when there is meant to be no family, Jowett still cannot bring himself to describe the women as "pregnant," but persists in using "in the family way." Regardless of what stand one takes on the importance of linguistic habits as embodiments of sexism in need of change, it would be hard to deny that this use of "in the family way" is not only unintentionally ironic, but actually misleading. At the same time as John Stuart Mill was calling for radical changes in family structure, Jowett was describing women who produce children from temporary unions and live communally as equal rulers without private families as "in the family way."

It is not surprising that Jowett uses such formulations in what has been called his idealization of Plato and his desire to make his views comfortably acceptable to his Victorian audience.[78] His "cover up" of homosexual references so that he translates *erastes* and *eremenos* as "lover" and "his beloved," in hopes of downplaying pederasty, has been criticized.[79] But the distortions that result from his attempts to obscure the radical nature of Plato's views on women are equally important. When he writes of the mating arrangements of the guardians, he assures us that "they cannot be allowed to live in licentiousness." But Plato is not here concerned with the limitation of sexual indulgence, as is indicated by the fact that men and woman outside the regulation age for breeding can do as they please. But for centuries what was called by an earlier translator "the delicate question of the community of women" has prevented writers from seriously considering the justice of equal education and social roles for women.[80]

The most flagrant example of attempts to square the Platonic view with that of Victorian Christian sexual morality is in the translation of *Republic* V, 457 as "let them strip, clothed in their *chastity*."[81] This translation of *arete* as "chastity" is clearly unwarranted since what is intended is the connotation of excellence, which stems from the proper development of both mind and body. Although the Greek gentleman, like the Victorian Englishman, would also value sexual purity and fidelity, it is precisely a new social order with different conventions that Plato seeks. The translator's reluctance to face the idea of identical standards for both sexes surfaces there. Even Cornford's and Bloom's choice of "they will clothe themselves in virtue instead of robes," does not sufficiently eliminate overtones of the old sexual morality. J. Adam, who is himself more enthusiastic about equality of opportunity for "gifted females," translates "they will clothe themselves with excellence instead of garments."[82]

T. H. Warren compares this line to Tennyson, who says of Lady Godiva, "Then she rode forth, clothed on with chastity." But Plato's meaning differs markedly from that of Tennyson, who specifically intends to praise the sexual fidelity, rather than the physical superiority, of the heroine.[83] The problem is compounded by the fact that throughout history an excellent woman has usually implied a virtuous woman in terms of sexual morality, that is, a chaste woman, whereas "an excellent man" carries no such connotation. This notorious "double standard" has been eliminated in Plato's state.[84]

Like Jowett and Warren, Cornford, in his freer translation and summary of Book V, also tries to square the Platonic proposals with prevalent English morality. Besides attempts to defend Plato against the charge of advocating infanticide, he tries to make the sexual encounters in the ideal state more palatable through his choice of words. Thus, he writes that "wives" must strip for exercise.[85] Although the Greek *gyne* means both "woman" and "wife," the choice of the latter here is misleading. Many of the commentators persistently describe these unions which would not last for more than a month as "marriages." They refer to the women guardians throughout as "wives." Plato himself does call the three-day mating sessions "sacred marriages." But he certainly does not intend, as F. M. Cornford puts it, that good warriors will be rewarded with more liberal opportunities "to sleep with a wife."[86] The crucial point is the persistent lack of symmetry; it is not "husbands" who strip in the gymnasium, but rather, men.

Alexandre Koyre, in his *Discovering Plato*, assures us that we must not imagine this communal status of women as synonymous with sexual promiscuity. He writes that "marriage exists, but is of short duration."[87] This does seem to be stretching the accepted use of the word when you remember that a woman might have as many as twenty of these "marriages" while she was of breeding age. If you were to reward her excellence as the male guardians are rewarded, she would have even more of these "marriages." Of course, as has been pointed out by commentators in the 1970s, Plato himself does not mention rewards for the women.

Nevertheless, Cornford, in his eagerness to make the Platonic arrangements less revolutionary, tells us that the unofficial unions might be permanent. And the rewards for valor are "not to have several wives at once, but to be admitted at more frequent intervals to the periodic marriage festivals, not necessarily with a different wife each time."[88] Cornford neglects to mention that in introducing this idea of more intercourse for the heroes in war Plato says that "if a man happens to love someone, either male or female" the fact that neither may refuse to kiss the hero will provide incentives for valor. Nettleship, too, tries to make Plato's views palatable to his audience. His assertion that as part of the austere life of the guardians they cannot "keep mistresses" evokes the companionate marriage of the English upper class much more than it contributes to helping the student visualize the possibility of a new order.

As we have seen, Wilamowitz speaks of *Weibergemeinschaft, Weiberregemente,* and *Weibe ans Staatsruder.* Thus, to say "women's affairs," "women's rule," and "women at the helm of the State," he uses the older form "Weibe," which refers more to wives than to females in general. Unlike the Greeks, he had separate terms at his disposal. Since the term *Frauenemancipation* was in common usage when he wrote, he might well have chosen the more neutral "Frau." Jowett speaks of the women guardians as "helpmeets," thus accommodating the independent guardian women to the Christian idea of Eve. But these women are not "wives," not auxiliary or ancillary, and the novelty of their status is obscured by these seemingly harmless word choices.

Besides the question of distortion of meaning, there is the related but separable issue which I discussed in my introduction and which needs to be repeated here. The female student who is confronted with the pronouns "he" and "his" when reading about the guardians and their education can add "she" and "hers." But the cumulative effect of the commentators' failure to include her in their terminology created a subtle feeling of exclusion. At the very least, it fosters among women readers the sense of the unimportance of the entrance of females into the guardian class. The choice of pronouns de-emphasizes the plan for "Philosopher-Queens." The term itself as a coordinate with the ubiquitous "Philosopher-King" has only recently been used at all.

Almost exclusively, we find such formulations as that of Charles Bakewell. After telling us that Plato is in advance of his time in including women, he goes on to describe the guardians as "these best of men."[89] Bakewell, while stating that Plato does not appreciate that abolishing the family would at the same time be destroying virtues fostered in family life, mentions female guardians. But he then describes this ruling circle as a "very small group of carefully chosen men." He summarizes the character and ability of the guardian with the description, "a man of quick mind, . . . gentle and just in his dealings with men."[90]

I contend that more than linguistic convenience is at issue here. For it is striking that Bernard Bosanquet, who is more enthusiastic than most for what he calls the "violent revolution" which Plato demanded in advocating an equal share for women in the pursuits and the education of men, makes some effort to alter his terminology. Among books and articles focusing solely on the theory of education in Plato, he alone writes that the reforms would produce "a hearty, active, and disciplined young *creature*" (*my emphasis*).[91] Instead of Nettleship's and others' talk of educating the young lad, "the public school boy," Bosanquet's language incorporates the realization that ideal education was also for the best women. Here, the failure to alter the linguistic convention may not involve any intentional distortion. But it surely perpetuates that omission of half the human race from serious consideration that, almost 2,400 years ago, Plato wanted to rectify.

AS LONG AS THEY DON'T GO TOO FAR:
THE WARNINGS OF THE SO-CALLED FEMINISTS

We now come to that category of commentators who, at least in expressed intent, eagerly desire some kind of equalization. There is no sharp differentiation between some of these writers and the ones I have already considered. In their work, a few lines will appear that express enthusiasm for female emancipation or what they sometimes call feminism. One is then lulled by a false sense that there, at last, is a scholar who believes that women are capable of the same tasks as men. However, on careful reading it soon emerges that such a conclusion must be carefully qualified. The final word is that equality is a good idea, as long as women don't make excessive demands. Even those who openly and repeatedly express enthusiasm eventually warn that equality is desirable only so long as women (as we would now put it) "know their place."

Thus, Richard Crossman professes himself an advocate of women's rights and on the whole approves what he terms Plato's "feminism." But, as we have seen, he fears that much will be lost if egalitarianism "goes too far." Most typical of this view is the argument to be found in the one book devoted entirely to the subject of Plato's ideas on women. In *Les idées de Platon sur la condition de la femme*, Jean Ithurriague repeatedly expresses his feminist sympathies. He quotes with approval an 1866 statement from the suffragist Susan B. Anthony that "equality of intelligence and virtue between the two sexes is indisputable; why make a difference between them?" Ithurriague sees Plato as only one in a long line of feminist advocates, far from a revolutionary or an "illuminé." Such ideas he tells us were in vogue in Athens in Plato's time in poetry, the theatre, and among philosophers. Practices in Egypt and Sparta led the way to reforms favorable to women. He even goes so far as to contend that "if the Orient made women into an inferior type, Egypt and other primitive peoples placed her on the same level as man and conceded her the same rights and privileges." But Plato was the precursor and *"le plus grand des féministes."* After him, Ithurriague tells us, women will no longer be thought of as she was before him. And despite the vicissitudes of an unequal struggle, the basic idea of the equality of women and men will make its way, taken up again later and illumined with a new light by Christianity.[92]

In this supposedly linear progress, he devotes three short paragraphs to Aristotle. He admits only that the Stagyrite was without Plato's "largeness of spirit and liberalism" on questions of women's role. Reinterpreting what few, if any, commentators today would deny was a disparaging attitude toward women, Ithurriague defends Aristotle. Although Aristotle reasons like many ancient and modern conservatives (*"hommes prudents"*), he safeguards the dignity of women and adopts the moral equality of men and women. This is not the place to discuss Aristotle's views, but it is worth noting that Aristotle did not in fact believe that a woman could be virtuous in the same way as a man. He believed rather in woman's natural inferiority and natural role as subject to her husband. The relevant point here is that Ithurriague's sanguine view that progress has been constant beginning with Plato and that prejudices are "fading away" is unwarranted. Even if one were to accept his view of Plato as an unambivalent proponent of female equality, we would then have to say that it is the counter-influence of Aristotle that has prevailed until fairly recently.[93]

Ithurriague's own view in the 1930s was that we were not far from complete equality. It becomes clear, however, that the equality he approves is not the position of Book V of the *Republic*, but the assigning of tasks "fitting to their sex" which he finds in the *Laws*. In his final summation, he pronounces Plato's doctrine to be unequivocally that the actual inferiority of women is due solely to the defects of their education. Ithurriague overlooks the contradictions in Plato and is unaware of any inconsistency in his own opinions. One must give women an education identical in all respects to that of men. By nature she is the equal of man, and capable like him of performing *"offices les plus délicats et . . . fonctions les plus difficiles."*[94]

At the same time, a certain crucial qualification on his part emerges. He finds Plato to have been "preaching wisdom" when he urges the legislator in the *Laws* to confide to women only the functions conforming to their character and their sex. He writes, "The great philosopher of Athens has generously opened the road to liberation for women while pointing out to her her duties and without hiding from her the *boundaries that the weakness of her sex sets* to her claims" (*my emphasis*).[95] Thus, Ithurriague, after tracing the origins of Plato's views describing the subjugation of Oriental women and the oppressive situation of women in classical Greece, concludes his noble sentiments with a note of caution. In woman's attack on behalf of her just claims, he puts it, one may fear that she will go beyond her objectives and "call down on herself, by abuse or excess, legitimate reactions." Ithurriague fears that unreasonable ambition might lead women outside their natural paths, "estranging her from the duties that belong to her alone, from the functions that nature and reason reserve for her." One would not dream of haggling with her or refusing her this right which she obtains by her intelligence and her energy. This self-proclaimed feminist ends his study by informing us that woman is entitled to her rights so long as "she knows how to remain within the limits fixed by a sound equity, if, in short, she knows how to remain a woman, mother, wife."[96]

Once again there is the unsupported appeal to the truly natural. But of more concern is the paternalism and warning of a possible backlash from this professed champion of women's rights in the early 1930s. Such a double message can surely do as much harm as the outspoken anti-egalitarian views we have considered.

The final self-proclaimed feminist to be considered is F. A. Wright, whose work ends with even more virulent judgments. This English scholar, author of a book on "feminism" in Greek literature, finds both strength and weakness in Plato's feminism. The weakness, as we have often heard before, stems from Plato's inclination to disregard some of "the invincible facts of human nature."[97] Wright calls Plato "essentially a masculine genius." Like Wilamowitz, he believes that Plato's feminism and his educational reforms are weakened because they stem from ideal theory, rather than any actual experience. Nevertheless, Wright is enthusiastic about certain aspects of Plato's feminism.

He approves Plato's treatment of the question of military service for women. According to Wright, if a man is unwilling or unable to defend his country, he certainly has no claim to citizen rights, nor does a woman. Therefore, he writes in 1923 that it may reasonably be argued that the qualification for a vote is neither property nor sex, but the proof that the individual has passed through the period of training necessary to qualify him as a defender of the fatherland. A soldier needs only courage, strength, and skill, all three of which Wright believes women to possess. In fact, in the passive courage which a modern soldier chiefly needs, women possibly "have a slight advantage over men and they usually recover more quickly from wounds." Modern warfare requires chiefly endurance: the power to stand exposure to the weather, insufficient food, lack of sleep and comfort, marching capacity. He writes: "No one who knows the vagabonds and strollers of our English roads will say that women are not capable of supporting all these hardships as well as men. The female tramp is every whit as sturdy and hardy as her male companion."[98] Even the skill to handle a gun and the power of shooting straight are matters almost entirely of training. And he believes that the natural qualities that facilitate such training, a steady hand and a sharp eye, are by no means predominately male characteristics. It is a picture of female physical prowess worthy of the most militant contemporary feminist. Unfortunately, there is always the danger that such generalizations, based on the flimsiest of evidence, can easily be turned against women's aspirations.

Another aspect of Plato's program which Wright approves are the reforms in feminine education which he believed strongly were in the process of being realized. He notes that the educated woman was even being allowed to become herself a teacher and rank with male colleagues. His enthusiasm is so excessive that he writes that in the inner circle of Plato's Academy, "the first University College of which we know, *men and women met on equal terms and shared responsibilities and privileges*" (*my emphasis*). This singular view he supports only by referring to the two non-Athenian women reported by Dicaearchus to have attended the Academy. Considering that there is no evidence of other female attendance and that not a single Athenian woman appears as a participant in any of the dialogues, this conclusion is highly suspect.

So, too, is Wright's belief about the source of Plato's contempt for the society of his native city. According to Wright, Plato correctly saw that "the main cause" of the unfortunate condition of his state, was "the indifference to women and children which the ordinary Athenian prided himself on displaying."[99] How sharply this view contrasts with the opinions of those commentators who believe Plato's reforms for women were a mere unwelcome afterthought!

Such undiscriminating zeal often turns out to be a mixed blessing. And such is the case with Wright. He concludes his chapter by declaring that although Plato is sometimes wrong about women, he clearly hits the truth about one of the natural weaknesses he ascribes to them (in the *Laws.*) Plato is on target when he tells us that *secretiveness* is the one quality which is peculiarly a woman's, and not a man's, characteristic. This quality is the result of many centuries of self-suppression and gives a certain "aggravating charm" to the female mind and usually does no particular harm.[100] One might suggest that if it is the result of the habit of centuries, then its innate naturalness would at least be questionable, but Wright does not raise this issue.

On this shortcoming of women, he is unrelenting. In his adamance, he even seems to desert the subject of Plato in order to inform us that women's secretiveness is the chief reason for their comparative failure in literature. It is "sincerity in writing" which is literature's saving grace, and if a book is not frank, it should never be written. Most women, he says, fail in frankness toward themselves and their readers. He writes: "George Eliot, Ouida, George Sand . . . dissemble their facts as much as they dissemble their names. Like ostriches, they hide their faces under a cloud of words."[101] This judgment, which implies that like the children of irregular unions in Plato's ideal State, a book like *Middlemarch* "should never see the light of day," comes from an avowed and enthusiastic feminist. One can only rejoin: if these are our friends, God save us from our enemies!

THE EXCEPTIONS: EARLY GENUINE ENTHUSIASM
FOR THE EGALITARIAN REFORMS

In all this litany of hostility to identical roles for women, feminists do possess some genuine friends. Two male scholars stand out as notable exceptions. One of them, the distinguished historian and pupil of Bentham, George Grote, was born in the eighteenth century and thus belongs chronologically more to the earlier tradition of great German scholars from Schleiermacher to Ast whose major focus was on establishing the exact text and the authenticity of the corpus. The first edition of Grote's *Plato and the Other Companions of Socrates* was issued before the period under consideration, but his comments were still influential when Pater was proclaiming the superiority of Christianity over the Platonic reforms.[102] The thrust of his lengthy discussion of Book V (along with a thorough, accurate paraphrase) is to convince his readers of the "extraordinary variety and discrepancy of approved and consecrated customs" that have existed in the world.[103] He takes a cultural relativist position throughout, giving examples of actual practices in ancient times which would seem even stranger to his readers than the suggestions for Plato's commonwealth.

Grote considers Plato to "dissent altogether" from the common man's opinion that women are naturally unfit for ruling. He points to Plato and Aristotle's opposing views on the subject. Then he uses the discrepancy between them to illustrate the uselessness of arguments based on the word Nature. Grote believes that when we see two such distinguished thinkers completely at issue as to what Nature indicates "in this important case," we realize that "each of them decorates by that name the rule which he himself approves."[104] The same might be said of the conflicting views on women's natural capacities that have appeared in the more than one hundred years after Grote's pronouncement.

Grote makes an effort to talk about the "distinguished persons in the regiment (*male or female, as the case may be)*" (*my emphasis*). He writes of the education of boys and girls, using pronouns carefully and emphasizing repeatedly how strongly Plato was attached to his doctrines about the capacity of women.[105] He even uses the modified views in the *Laws* as evidence of how unchanged Plato's opinions were about "the mischief" of separating the training and function of the two sexes, and of confining women to indoor occupations, to what is called in the later book, "a life of darkness and fear." In Grote's enthusiasm, he deemphasizes the traces of misogyny which commentators in the 1970s find not only in the *Laws* but in Book V and other places in the *Republic*.

He does not, however, try to gloss over the fact that in the ideal State, as he interprets the text, the best women will be on a level only with the second best men. The heaviest and most difficult duties, "those which require the maximum of competence to perform, will usually devolve upon men."[106] But he is eager to understand where Plato got the idea that even in cooking and weaving men were superior to women. In Greece, weaving was generally a woman's occupation, though we cannot be sure whether it was exclusively so. In Egypt, however, weaving was done by men; Grote wonders whether Plato perhaps saw finer Egyptian webs. If so, he would use this knowledge as ammunition against those in his audience who might claim that women have special aptitudes for certain occupations.

He wants also to show that there were precedents in the ancient world for extremely competent women. He regrets that Plato probably didn't know of the exploits of the brave and skillful Artemisia who, according to Herodotus, distinguished herself in the expedition of Xerxes against Greece. Plato could have strengthened his argument by the pertinent example of the "courage, vigor, and prudence" of Zenobia if he could have quoted the original letter addressed by the Emperor Aurelian to the Roman Senate.[107] Plato turns to contemporary factual examples of the Scythian and Sarmaritan women to show that women are capable of efficient military service. But, according to Grote, he might well have used ancient legends which abounded in tales of aggressive women. The goddess Athene, patroness of Athens, was the very impersonation of "intelligent terror-striking might," constraining and subduing Ares himself. In a statement as forceful as any combative contemporary feminist, he reminds us that the goddess Enyo presided over war as much as did Ares. He points to Artemis who, though she only fought wild beasts, was equally formidable—"indefatigable as well as rapid in her movements—and as unerring with her bow, as Athene was irresistible with her spear."[108]

The point throughout is to show that there were abundant examples to embolden Plato in his affirmations of the female's capacity for warlike enterprise and laborious endurance. Grote, again like certain overzealous modern feminists, even recalls the legendary Amazons as examples that Plato might have seen as supporting his views. Although we know the Amazons to be legendary, Grote reminds us that the ancients believed their existence to be historical fact. They were thus influential on the Greek imagination, particularly because they were so familiar to the public through paintings and sculpture. The Amazons were in fact an extremely popular subject for sculpture. We learn from Pliny that since all the most distinguished sculptors executed versions of them, this was the only subject upon which a direct comparison could be made. Grote argues that the idea of women performing traditionally male roles would not have seemed out-landish to Plato. Although feminists today might interpret the statues as embodiments of the masculine fear of female power, Grote sees mythological examples as suggesting rational possibili-ties to the philosopher.[109] Grote points to a passage in the *Laws* to show that Plato complains bitterly of the repugnance felt even to the discussion of his modified proposals for sexual equality. Although it was contrary to current Athenian practice, Grote believed there were numerous reasons why it seemed both possible and desirable to the philosopher.

The chief purpose of Grote's discussion is to explain why Plato thought women could participate in active pursuits and why he might indeed be able to convince the more open-minded of his hearers. Grote goes to great lengths to show exactly how the usual relations of the sexes would be combated by Plato, giving the proposals the serious attention they deserve. He describes enthusiastically the muscular development and the rough and unadorned bodies of the female guardians. He speaks of the indis-criminate companionship, with perfect identity of treatment and manners between the two sexes from earliest infancy, the training of both together for the same public duties under constant super-vision. The possibility that neither Strauss nor Bloom can countenance as anything but an ironic joke, Grote goes to great lengths to make convincing.

He concerns himself with the reforms in sexual practice that Plato suggests. He even tries to render imaginatively, through col-orful descriptions, the way the strict regulation of exercise and diet, combined with monastic censorship, would place the sexual appetite under the ruler's control. He reminds us that in their proposals for social change, not only Plato, but Xenophon and Aristotle, looked to the example of Sparta. The Spartan way of life, strictly controlled and markedly different from the Athenian, was much admired by all the Greeks. Grote even discusses the question of abortion and infanticide, a practice we know existed in Sparta, without making any attempt, as many commentators have, to cover up what both Aristotle and Plato considered acceptable treatment of undesirable infants. Without condoning the specifics of the philosophers' views on the subject, Grote wishes to show the rational intent behind them. In doing so, he

uses language consonant with that of current pro-abortion advocates. The rationale behind the philosophers' proposals is that
"procreation ought to be a rational and advised act."[110] It should
be governed by a forecast of the consequences not only to personal happiness, but also to the good of society.

Thus, Grote, unlike the overwhelming number of other commentators, 1) summarizes Plato's views sympathetically and
accurately; 2) chooses his language carefully to avoid minimizing
the novelty and importance of the proposals; and 3) disparages
any appeal to what is "truly natural" as a legitimate ground for
denying identity of role to women. His final conclusion is that a
more egalitarian society is possible, but he finds a major difficulty
with such utopian views. The problem is where will the motive,
the demiurgic force, for instituting such reforms come from? Plato
does not provide any source which will give such reforms their
first impetus.[111] And, in my view, this question must still be of
primary concern to feminists today.[112]

There is also one other commentator who presents an unbiased
account of the proposals in Book V and in fact expresses even
more outspoken enthusiasm for the "emancipation of women"
than Grote. This is the viewpoint of Theodor Gomperz, whose
four-volume work, *Greek Thinkers*, first appeared in Leipsig in the
early 1890s.

Gomperz is not blind to Plato's prejudices and discusses the
"mere pride of birth and rank" which influence him in the contempt for the lower orders which Gomperz, like so many of us,
disapproves. Prophetic of the attack on Plato's overvaluation of
unity, he notes the fact that Plato is free of the anxiety that has
troubled some of the best men of the nineteenth century. That is,
he underestimates the dangers of uniformity, of what Gomperz
describes as "the Chinese ideal of making all people alike."[113]
But, unlike Jowett, he does not use our Western liberal preference for individualism or diversity as an apology for maintaining
separate and distinct occupations for women.

Instead, he stresses, like Grote, the examples known or
believed to have existed of "community of women" and emphasizes that the paradoxes of today are the commonplaces of
tomorrow. He calls for empirical tests of social reforms. With a
refreshing sense of possibility lacking in all those writers who find

it a violation of women's nature to perform certain tasks, Gomperz alone calls for empirical trials. He says that we require of deep-reaching innovations that they shall establish their viability and usefulness not solely by reasoning, but by actual experiment.[114]

Furthermore, he criticizes the argument of Aristotle that the world is now very old and had the realization of reforms like Plato's been possible they would surely have already occurred. With extended ethnographic and historical perspective such an argument is now far less appealing, Gomperz thinks. But he was writing about human possibilities at a time of great optimism; such optimism has undoubtedly been tempered in the twentieth century. Nevertheless, his warning against Aristotle's position on social change still applies. Such reasoning, he writes, is "the standing and staple argument of all conservative minds against subversive innovations."[115] And here again, Gomperz was prophetic. In Plato scholarship, such denial of female possibilities became dominant in the century following his work.

Unlike most commentators, Gomperz judges that the rationalistic utilitarian element is only an afterthought for "the aesthetic and ethical preference" which supplies the real motive power for the Platonic reforms. It is hard to resist the conclusion that it is Gomperz's zeal rather than Plato's that makes him overrate the Athenian's profemale sympathies. Gomperz writes that Plato desired the full and many-sided development of women's talents. He dreamt of their elevation from profound ignorance and subjection, bordering on servitude, to the power of knowledge and proud independence. Plato "felt the charm of the ideal type of woman which he had in his mind's eye," and which was rudimentally exhibited by Spartan women with their fine physical development and celebrated beauty. The proverbial boldness that came of Spartan semi-emancipation Plato wished to ennoble by a better education and to transfigure into "self-conscious dignity."[116] Gomperz imagines such considerations outweighed the rationalistic considerations Plato uses to support his proposals. Gomperz has perhaps imagined too freely. Self-conscious dignity and a dream based on a guiding vision of women is hard to reconcile with those traces of misogyny which are exhibited throughout the dialogues, or with the breeding arrangements, which some find "repulsively utilitarian."[117] Glowing statements about the physical and mental virtues of women simply do not exist in Plato.

To the modern-day feminist, Gomperz's enthusiasm is welcome with all its excesses. In considering the emancipation of women, he describes himself as turning from critic to eulogist. In following in Socrates' footsteps, Plato "has given utterance to the pure and complete truth, almost without admixture of error."[118] As we shall see, that small reservation that Gomperz sustains becomes the major complaint against Plato of the critics of the 1970s. Gomperz's own enthusiasm for Plato and for the idea of equality for women is almost unbounded. Gomperz does not gloss over the fact that the female is described as the relatively weaker sex. However, he explains that this relative weakness only appears on striking an average, since an arrangement of all men and all women by order of capacity would yield a highly diversified series. And qualitative differences that would affect roles do not exist.

Gomperz then launches into what can only be seen as a much needed corrective to this aspect of Plato's view. He writes:

> Even in respect of that average inferiority, it cannot as yet be regarded as established that, where intellectual gifts are concerned, it is an ultimate unalterable fact. On the other hand, the possibility is not excluded that a free field for the development of women's talents might bring to light average differences of even qualitative order. Only so much is certain, that these differences could never suffice to justify the limitations of callings for one half of the human race.[119]

I quote at length, because this is a view which does not surface again for close to eighty years.

Gomperz provides an eloquent reply to all those who have doubted women's capacity for genuine accomplishment. His answer to those who have observed in the past that intellectual creations of the first rank which demand exceptionally sustained concentration—in poetry, music, philosophy, or history—have not been produced by women, is convincing and still relevant to those who persist in such opinions today. This empirical rule, he says, has merely provisional validity and may at any moment be broken through by a brilliant exception. In narrative literature, he insists, women have in the last decades of the nineteenth century produced works that rival their male counterparts.[120] Further, women's presumed inferiority may well be due to the pressure of unfavorable circumstances rather than to any deficiency of talent.

Gomperz has his own vision of the charm of the new woman: "Their cheeks are bronzed with sport, they deliver lectures and take part in public meetings, they paint pictures and write books; many professions, in North America almost all, are open to them; and they are leaving farther and farther behind them the stage in which they were banished to the washtub and the needle, the kitchen and the nursery."[121]

In the light of "the feminine mystique" of the later forties and fifties, Gomperz's optimistic appraisal of developments in the United States turned out to be unwarranted. In his own country, the later acceptance by many of the Nazi view of women's role—"Kinder, Küche, Kirche"—show that he was far too sanguine about women's prospects.

Gomperz did see the interconnection between the retention of private families and the possibility of realizing Plato's ideal.[122] Unlike later feminists, however, he makes no suggestions for changing roles within the family, nor does he discuss the possibility of eliminating the nuclear family. Instead, he accepts the fact that, given the modern way of ordering the family, the division of labor which Plato generally supported but rejected in regard to the sexes is likely to obtain in most—though not necessarily in all—cases.

Therefore, though he applauds the bronze-cheeked lecturers, he explains that "nothing can be more natural" than that mothers, being kept at home by the care of their children, should devote themselves to household duties and other tasks like nursing which are suited to their degree of physical strength.[123] The naturalness to which he refers seems to mean only that such arrangements are reasonable; his words lack those overtones of biology with which we are now so familiar. For he stresses that in the highly civilized nations at the time he was writing the development was in the direction Plato desired. Like Ithurriague, he considers that a considerable part of Plato's demands have actually been fulfilled. But he does not accompany his rosy picture of progress with any such admonition to women not to overreach themselves. It is true that his view gives a sense of the inevitability of certain family arrangements. He makes no visionary prediction of men sharing in child care; nor does he suggest communal care of infants or the ill aged. Still, his voice is rare in a chorus of nay-sayers. (Even John Stuart Mill, whose pedigree as an early feminist is strong, has no greater confidence in the possibility of married women with children performing exactly the same tasks as men.)[124] In his Plato commentary, Gomperz may not proclaim the likelihood of complete realization of gender equality, but he at least allows for the possibility. And his message throughout is that women have done good work and achieved notable success in many spheres, whenever the accident of birth or the play of circumstances has presented them with the opportunity.

The last commentator I shall discuss is Adela M. Adam, the *only female* to write about the relevant section of Book V before the New Wave of commentators in the 1970s. Like Gomperz and Grote, she does not describe herself as a feminist. She does not even express an enthusiasm or crusading spirit comparable to theirs. But in her little-known book, published in 1913 to satisfy a demand she sees for "a clear account, intelligible to the plain man, of what Plato did in the moral and political sphere," she clearly favors many of the changes Plato proposes.[125] She shares with later feminists the belief that, despite the philosopher's intense conservatism in some respects, on the question of the education and duties of women "he was perhaps the most daring innovator the world has ever seen."[126]

For the first time, she calls attention to a discrepancy between Plato's professed program and the automatic bias of the Greek male. No previous commentator had noted this, nor does it become a major issue until sixty years later. A. M. Adam puts it forcefully: "It is easy to see that his intellectual conviction outruns his instinct." In discussing the *Laws*, she indicates that Plato "whenever he remembers his principles" actually means women to take a wider share in government.[127] This shows her awareness of the tension between Plato's professed desire for reform and other competing assumptions.

She also concludes, as does the most recent feminist writer on Plato's theory of education, that as the philosopher progressively developed his scheme he was plainly thinking of men guardians only in the *Republic.* He only remembers women when "he sharply reminds himself . . . that the fair images of Philosopher-Kings that he has been making represent also Philosopher-Queens."[128] To my knowledge, this is the first use of that corresponding form, "Philosopher-Queen," a term which might well have appeared earlier had there been many women scholars commenting on the text.[129] To guarantee the intended joint rule, such an expression is surely necessary, but so far as I can determine, the phrase, or its precise equivalent in any other language, does not occur before 1913. Various points of A. M. Adam's interpretation will be questioned later. She accepts that in Plato the best women are excelled by the best men; she doesn't even reserve the doubt expressed by some that it is only "highly unlikely" that the best *individual* could be female. In her attempt to garner enthusiasm for Plato's educational reforms, she may exaggerate in stating that women are to share with men the exact same responsibilities for bringing up children. But in general, she describes Plato's views in the *Republic* and the *Laws* more accurately than many of her male counterparts, and she repeatedly emphasizes their importance.

Nevertheless, Adam is not a feminist in the same sense that most of the commentators of the 1970s and 1980s use the term.[130] For her final word is that Plato's "half-unconscious" reservation of certain duties for women foreshadows very nearly the course that events are likely to take. And she makes no objection to this course. As the State takes over more and more the care and education of children and the morality of the sexes, women will increasingly take these positions. Nursing and social welfare are the kind of jobs that will always absorb the energies of most women "who have time to spare from their own families." It is only "when a woman *shows a special aptitude* for serving her country in some other way" (*my emphasis*), that Plato's claim that her power should be used is triumphantly vindicated. In other words, A. M. Adam does not call for the employment of women in non-traditional occupations, nor does she believe that this is the path women's struggles ought to take. She expresses no concern that Plato spoke of equality only for an elite group. She, too, assumes that only "gifted women" (as her better-known scholar husband first described them) would be interested in roles equal in status to men. But despite her reservations and her own modest ambitions, her views stand out against those of most of her male counterparts. She stresses that whatever gifts a woman has Plato rightly wishes to be turned to account for the common good. And she states unequivocally, "He sees that the work of bearing children to uphold the State in the next generation cannot possibly occupy a woman's whole life."[131]

2

The Resurgence of Interest in Philosopher-Queens

THE QUALITY OF THE NEW SCHOLARSHIP

After years of neglect and hostility to the proposals in Book V, a sudden interest developed in the issues. From 1970 onwards, numerous articles appeared in diverse publications. The contrast between the previous marginal treatment and the new attention and recurrent discussion is striking. No doubt this new interest is partly attributable to the appearance on the scene of female commentators. There *were* isolated women classicists writing on the *Republic* earlier, but unlike Adela M. Adam, these few women scholars, like their male colleagues, paid little or no attention to the question of female equality. Thus, for example, in a 1950 book concerned solely with Plato's theory of Philosopher-Kings, Rosamond Sprague never even raises the question of the possible effect on the theory of the presence of Philosopher-Queens, nor even acknowledges their proposed presence.[1]

The cause of the flurry of interest, then, is not only the advent of female scholars. More important is the development of an organized women's movement with vocal representatives within universities and the concomitant desire by feminists of both sexes to understand past inequities and redress previous wrongs. Today, it is more difficult for scholars, regardless of sex, to reveal anti-female bias without a defensive posture. Women scholars who previously might have preferred, whether consciously or not, to ignore the issue so that they would in no way stand out from or alienate their male colleagues, are today freer from such concerns. The new climate for younger scholars has eliminated some of the need for such unconscious self-censorship and protective coloration.

An interest in the history of feminism has arisen and such investigations have become more respectable. Unfortunately, concern with women's issues has also become more fashionable in some circles. People sometimes chose to write on the topic because it was timely whether or not they had any background or preparation for such studies. Consequently, there is a great discrepancy between the thorough, painstaking works of past scholars and the open partisanship of some current discussions of the *Republic.*

One serious failing which I find in many of the post-1970 articles is their discontinuity with the work of the past. Many display a basic a-historicism in their approach. At the same time, they also fail to refer to the efforts of their contemporaries on the same topics. Without investigating, many write as if they have suddenly discovered what no one else ever noticed. This stance is markedly different from that of previous commentators who, when dealing with most issues in the *Republic,* foster the sense of a continuing dialogue. Earlier scholars usually show great respect for the work of others, even when they disagree sharply.

Along with the disadvantages of ignoring past scholarship, there are undeniably also certain advantages. Writers can no longer presume their audience to have a general acquaintance with Greek, Latin, ancient history, or even major Western literary works. They therefore have a chance of reaching more readers if they eschew footnotes and other scholarly apparatus. Thus, even when the writer herself has not looked into previous work, her popularization of the issues might still be beneficial. Some of the articles of the 1970s, though adding little to the on-going scholarly enterprise, have no doubt provided a service to interested readers who have neither the background nor the inclination to deal with the details of previous interpretations. A further advantage for the young scholar of today who is willing to ignore past views is the elimination of that paralysis which can result from being overwhelmed by the best of, or at any rate the bulk of, what has already been thought and said.

Whatever the advantages, the danger remains of producing work representative of two unfortunate extremes. Much of the publication of the 1970s alternates between two opposing shortcomings. One the one hand, we find large-scale conclusions which in effect amount to "rediscovering the wheel," and on the other hand, narrow logical analysis which is trivial, will be read by few, and has no influence. Among the articles I shall now examine in detail are pronouncements made as if they were original discoveries, when in fact they are only restatements with a history in the scholarly literature of rebuttal and reinforcement. Others offer narrow linguistic analysis which, even when correct, adds little to the understanding of Plato or to the discussion of the best deployment of women. Scholarship which avoids these extremes, which shows familiarity with previous work in many languages and sheds new light on important issues, is relatively rare.

Besides the a-historicism, there is also a tendency to use language far less precisely than do the scholars of the previous hundred years. Of the commentators I have already discussed, few, with the notable exception of Walter Pater, can be accused of general vagueness of thought or language. The great Germans—Zeller, Ritter, Friedlander—on the whole reason clearly and use concepts with admirable precision, except perhaps in those few instances where unconscious prejudice intervenes. Many of the committed feminist commentators use language imprecisely and do not carry through on the philosophical and logical implications of their assertions. Admittedly, a delicate balancing act is required to avoid pedantic trivialization, to offer important new insights, and yet to use language, logic, and factual detail carefully.

This ideal of scholarship has been difficult to meet in the last ten years. Some of the reasons for the difficulty relate directly to two important issues Plato himself addressed. The first involves that democracy he deplored, for, along with the enormous benefits democratization has conferred on those of us of the lower bronze class, it has also necessarily weakened the structures which supported the great scholarship of the past. The second issue is that of the equal education for qualified women, which Plato was the first to advocate. It, too, has had an indirect, but nonetheless, negative impact on the former conditions for scholarly excellence. No matter how imperative and just these two connected reforms, their increasing realization has involved certain "trade-offs."

The learning of the great classicists was primarily acquired at elite schools. The time required for their scholarly pursuits was provided by institutions which did not demand that the scholar meet classes and deliver prepared lectures several times a week, as is often the case in the universities of today. In the more hierarchical pre-1970 societies, professors were accorded respect and recognition in many segments of the community. Now, scholars often must work without strong institutional support, with the threat of "publish or perish," or more pointedly, "tenure or trauma." The community's evaluation of the scholar in America, at any rate, has measurably changed. Whereas being a professor was considered among the top status jobs in polls of the 1950s, recent studies show the public's rating of the university teacher has dropped markedly.

Formerly, a scholar could count on his wife to tend to his needs, protect him from interruptions, and value his work, whether she understood it or not. Far fewer scholars today can claim such a devoted spouse. A scholar's wife, even if her inclinations in this transitional period were to follow the older pattern, has been influenced by the media and other social pressures to consider it undesirable to live vicariously through her husband's work. Thus, even if she is not economically constrained to work, nor motivated toward an independent career, she is still unlikely to perform the old jobs as willingly as the "helpmeets" whom Jowett praised. (The female scholar, of course, has always had to function without such a wife.) Such helpmates formerly played a crucial role in providing the atmosphere for scholarship. The value of a spouse's services and support, whether provided without enthusiasm or freely offered, cannot be overestimated.

There are other problems specific to the female scholar who is beginning to attain a greater measure of equality in the university. Side by side with her new status is a new psychological burden. Women in the United States, at any rate, are influenced by the myth that they can "have it all." They are led to believe that they can enjoy the satisfactions of child-rearing, domestic activities, and some of the leisure activities of an earlier middle-class mother while excelling in intellectual pursuits. All of this is assumed to be possible without any cataclysmic changes in the social structure.[2] British and American female scholars, hoping to produce a body of work like Taylor's or Bosanquet's, also experience other strong pressures. They are expected to provide for the emotional and intellectual needs of 2.2 children, maintain their sexual attractiveness, succeed at work so that the laurels of the guardians in Plato's scheme will be awarded to them, and perform at least half of the manual labor necessary for maintaining a household.[3]

Nor do single scholars, male or female, often have the same background of support and intellectual conversation once available in the rooms at college or dinner at High Table. The trusty servant and university-connected amanuensis are not available. Scholars may have the compensations of computers, typewriters, and interlibrary loan facilities, but they rarely have a partner of the same or opposite sex who is willing to take on the chores which would leave him or her free for months of uninterrupted study.

Still, in some fields, first-rank scholarship has been produced in the 1970s, and it is surely unfair to juxtapose the life work of a Victorian scholar against a brief article in a little-known journal. Furthermore, even if the proliferation of periodicals and low-cost editions has resulted in a "rush to print" and a lowering of standards, these results must be balanced against pronounced benefits. For we cannot forget that such changes have also been responsible for the possibility of participation in the life of the mind by a far larger percentage of the population. Concurrent with this broadened participation has been that equalizing of opportunity and expectations for females which has led to the raising of new questions for the first time in twenty-three hundred years about the Platonic proposals.

THE FIRST AWARENESS OF PREVIOUS BIAS

An important characteristic of the post-1970 scholarship is the dawning realization of the previous hostility to the idea of sex equality in the *Republic*, along with attempts to account for this hostility. Christine Pierce opens up a Pandora's box—to use the misogynist myth for my own purposes—by calling attention to that hostility for the first time in print. She finds that much Platonic scholarship has been a set of "variations on the theme of women's essential inferiority." Commentators have faulted Plato for failing to consider the necessary consequences of that inferiority in developing the social, economic, and political structure of a society. Pierce notes that few have been aware of what an ingenious critique Book V offers of the main assumptions used repeatedly in arguments against equality. Pierce focuses on this Platonic critique of the ideas of "women's place" and "man's competence," introducing a new theme which, with its variations, appears repeatedly in the scholarship of the next ten years.

Covering approximately ten scholars who have been hostile to Plato's proposals, she begins the process of countering their incredulity and disapproval. Pierce is particularly effective in answering the arguments of Leo Strauss. Her aim is to undermine his contention that Plato wished us to realize the impossibility of the creation of a just city and used the clearly false notion of the equality of the sexes as one of the indications that the *Republic* is indeed an impossible abstraction.

Like most feminist commentators after her, Pierce also finds the interpretation of Allan Bloom (who accepts the Strauss thesis) particularly offensive. Opposition to Bloom is likely to continue, particularly if he persists in defending and expanding his objections to sexual equality, as he has been inclined to do in the fifteen years since the publication of his highly influential "Interpretive Essay." Pierce marshals several arguments against Bloom's belief that Plato in fact did realize women's inferiority, but merely fabricated a view of their competence to cover up the truth that women are placed among the guardians only for reproductive purposes. Without realizing that Bloom is not alone in this view, she offers an interesting rebuttal, one not stressed by scholars who have tangled with Bloom after her.

Instead of the more basic argument I have outlined above against Bloom (that Plato's entire concept of justice would be undermined if women were allowed to do work for which they were not suited), she suggests another line of reasoning. She says a myth to support assigning the same social role to women would not only have "devastating social consequences."[4] By subverting competence, it would run counter to the obvious and, to her, plausible purpose of Plato's other myths. She correctly observes that the allegory of the metals is designed to help people face up to an accurate assessment of their abilities. But a fabrication about women's nature would have a very different function, since it would lead people to believe women are capable, when they are not.

In criticizing previous commentators, Pierce reminds us that philosophers have often been accused of defending as eternal truths the customs and assumptions of their own societies. Plato and Aristotle argued in defense of slavery, and Kant considered Euclidean space a logical necessity. She offers tentatively that this same tendency may pervade philosophical scholarship, "the tendency to superimpose the mores and beliefs of one's own society on figures of philosophy's past."[5]

Thus, Pierce effectively introduces the idea that an examination of previous views on the *Republic* may show the extent to which beliefs about the intrinsic inequality of the sexes has permeated our own society. She also issues an important *caveat*. She warns that anyone who thinks the solution to current problems in sex equality can be worked out mechanically, i.e., "without changing hearts and minds," can be seen to be mistaken if they consider Plato commentators. She writes, "The length to which 'pure' scholars, rational men are driven shows that accepting women as persons requires more than philosophical justification."[6]

In the final analysis, Pierce considers the passages in the *Republic* about men and women having identical natures and meriting identical roles to be "clear and straightforward." Therefore, the commentators' questionable interpretations *may* be due to the intrusion of their own outlooks. On the other hand, my contention is that the passages themselves are not entirely clear and consistent, as the discussions of commentators after Pierce amply show. In my opinion, these very inconsistencies and ambiguities foster the projections of scholars' own attitudes onto the work, a practice as characteristic of the feminist commentators who follow Pierce as of the hostile interpreters of the past hundred years.

INCONSISTENCIES IN PLATO:
WAS HE A FEMINIST?

A second major characteristic of the new scholarship is the focus
on the web of previously unnoticed inconsistencies in Plato's total
view of women. Commentators distinguish at least four different
ways in which Plato's views are inconsistent or contradictory.
And they take their stand on whether Plato can accurately be
described as a "feminist" depending on how they view these
inconsistencies. Those who see the inconsistencies as trivial
embrace Plato as their champion. But there are many others who
find the contradictions irreconcilable and adamantly reject any
classification of Plato as a woman's liberationist.

For the first time, commentators call attention to the sharp
discrepancy between the misogyny scattered throughout the dialogues and Plato's claim that both sexes have the same nature.
This discrepancy they find even within the *Republic* itself. They
also note the contrast between arrangements for women in the
ideal city and those in the second-best (or more correctly, third)
actual city of the *Laws*.[7] This contrast, unlike the others, has
been mentioned frequently by previous scholars. To a man, they
have, of course, preferred the arrangements in the *Laws*.

Feminist commentators discover a third pattern of inconsistency between the attitudes revealed in the myths of the
Symposium and the *Timaeus*, when contrasted with the strain of
relative egalitarianism of the *Republic* and the *Laws* taken
together. Establishing this inconsistency involves an exploration
of that question, which has long been of interest to scholars, of
the relation of the Platonic myths to the philosopher's actual
views. Here, the issue is his true view on women's nature; and a
consideration of the myths in this connection becomes important
for the first time in the commentary of the 1970s.

The final ambiguity writers deal with is the more subtle, but
equally troublesome, question of how to reconcile Plato's belief
that men and women are equal in nature and yet women are
always inferior in capacity. The adequacy of the previously propounded solution that the two sexes are not different in kind, but
only in degree, becomes a major point of controversy in current
scholarship. The problem becomes how one can speak of Plato as

a feminist—as most previous commentators have—when he proclaimed the class of women inferior.

By the mid-1960s, H. D. Rankin had already introduced the question of troubling inconsistencies, although feminist commentators do not seem to be aware of his efforts. In his book on Plato's treatment of the individual, Rankin does not specifically identify himself as a feminist, and speaks more dispassionately than later writers. But he notes with regret that there is "little stability" in Plato's attitudes and focuses on several kinds of inconsistencies, including the fact that throughout the dialogues places exist where women are classed as natural inferiors, with children, slaves, and foolish people in general.[8]

Rankin supports Plato's purpose, which he sees as the attempt to make the women guardians independent and as free as possible, "subjects" rather than objects. He refers to Simone de Beauvoir's idea that relations between the sexes suffer because women have seen themselves both as "subjects" and as "objects" and regrets that de Beauvoir did not discuss Plato's ideas on the topic. He writes that "it is not surprising, and not at all undesirable, that they should seem temperamentally similar to men." I am assuming that he means here that neither Plato nor Rankin regrets the loss of sharp distinctions between the personality traits valued in men and those valued in women. This contrasts markedly with Jowett, Wilamowitz, et al., who deplore the loss of "femininity" in the guardians. Rankin, using existentialist terminology, instead applauds the great advance of the idea of female guardians over previous notions of "women's situation in the world." He laments (as some later enthusiasts neglect to do) the sad discrepancy between the *phylakes* and the traditional subservience which Plato evidently imagined for the lowest grade of women in the *polis*. Although he says we should not overlook the inconsistencies, Rankin finds that Plato's ideas, on the whole, compare favorably with twentieth-century attempts "to rationalize the balance of rights" between the sexes.[9]

In the commentary of the 1970s, the inconsistencies take center stage, with writers falling into two opposed camps. There are those who defend Plato vociferously and others who see him as just another woman-hater, part of a chain of philosophers from the pre-Socratics to the mid-twentieth-century metaphysician

Paul Weiss, who advises in his book on the philosophy of sport that women be viewed as "truncated males."[10]

In the first group are writers like Abigail Rosenthal who declare that the feminism of Plato is exemplary and unparalleled in philosophy or political theory.[11] Martha Lee Osborne also falls into this group. In her title, she unequivocally states that anatomy does *not* spell destiny in Plato. Biology, she says, is irrelevant to Plato's views because he is a metaphysical idealist in whose work "the soul is celebrated at the expense of the body."[12] Therefore, one would expect that in utopia the destiny of women as well as men would be determined by their sovereign souls. Plato's view of the place of women in an *ideal* society did not change at all.

One of Osborne's chief aims is to refute the dubious attempt of Anne Dickason to explain the differences between the *Republic* and the *Laws* on the basis of the alleged biological views in Plato's myths.[13] She justifiably objects to the use of the famous myth on the origin of the sexes advanced by Aristophanes in the *Symposium*, as if it were Plato's own view. And she likewise rejects Dickason's use of the speech of Timaeus on women's inferiority, showing that here again one cannot ignore the dramatic nature of the dialogue or neglect the possible relevance of the fact that the speaker is Pythagorean. In the end, Osborne insists that what is remarkable about the city of the *Laws* is not how far short of the ideal it falls, but how close it comes.

Christine G. Allen also argues that Plato was "thoroughly consistent in his theories on women."[14] She finds a single view underlying all this work, but contrary to Osborne she thinks one can use selected myths to resolve any apparent inconsistencies. Her theory is that Plato always believed not only in the equality of souls, but in their pre-existence and immortality. Her argument rests on the evidence of certain "central" myths, though she is aware that some of the myths must be disregarded. That is, she takes over the idea of "levels of myths" from Friedlander, borrowing his tripartite scheme in which the higher levels "render intelligible the mysterious aspects of life" and "create a new kind of truth."[15] But she then takes the *Timaeus* myth of incarnations and upward striving of the soul *literally*, to show what Plato "really thought" about women. In my opinion Allen's belief that

Plato's consistent view was that women are equal to men in their immortal souls but only an "inferior kind of incarnation" presents great difficulties. Statements in the *Republic* that the *physis* of men and women is the same, and that some women have natural aptitudes superior to some men for some jobs, simply cannot be reconciled with her theory.

The classicist Dorothea Wender also belongs in the Plato-as-feminist camp, but she does not attempt to reconcile inconsistencies. Instead, she tells us that although Plato was indeed a paedophile and a misogynist, he is also a feminist whose proposals are "delightfully radical!"[16] In order to describe Plato as a feminist, she must, however, arbitrarily adopt a definition which differs from that in most dictionaries, or from what I consider a general understanding of the term.

For my purposes in this study I have assumed that a feminist must at the very least 1) consider it an important and disturbing fact about all previous social organization that women have been oppressed, and 2) propose that henceforth complete gender equality should prevail. I have intentionally not attempted to formulate any more complete definition here, choosing instead to focus on how recent writers on Plato have construed the term. The various shades of opinion among feminists have been well categorized by Alison Jaggar, who describes the different programs embraced by liberal feminists, radical feminists, Marxist feminists, lesbian separatists and Socialist feminists.[17] All of these would find Wender's definition unsatisfactory.

In her otherwise informative and amusing article she chooses to define a feminist as anyone who believes that women should be given a better place in society, legally, politically, or professionally. To be a feminist, one need only profess that women are entitled to a position which "more closely approximates that held by men of the same class." A feminist, according to Wender, need not necessarily believe that women are equal to men *"in any way"* (my emphasis).[18] This seems an odd use of the term. One can hardly deny that it is often used vaguely, although rarely I think to refer to the indefinite, and even contemptuous, meliorism that Wender allows. For she describes Plato as a feminist, even though she maintains a view echoed by later commentators: "Plato does not promise that women are equal to men—he cannot; it seems to him they are not."[19] Nevertheless, she describes him as a feminist since he does propose complete equality of opportunity. In fact, with the abolition of all domestic work, he goes even further in this direction than many feminists today would go. Although he weakens the feminist program in his second-best state, the treatment of women still remains the most radical part of the proposed constitution. There is also evidence for feminism in the other dialogues. In short, Plato did not like women, but he favored their emancipation.

In examining what might be called the New Wave of Plato commentary, it gradually becomes apparent that, like the proverbial glass of water that can be seen as half full or half empty, Plato's proposals can legitimately be viewed in opposing ways. Those who stress the egalitarian strain see the glass as half full. That is, though now aware that the philosopher's proposals are incomplete, they believe we ought to accentuate the positive. Thus, W. W. Fortenbaugh, in reacting to the denunciation of Plato by a fellow classicist, offers a warning. He writes that we can only obscure the significance of Plato's approach by "an excessive concern with the possibility of latent misogyny."[20] It is important to remember that in the previous hundred years of commentary not a single word has been said about *any* anti-female attitudes in Plato. Although some writers did refer to the unequal status of Athenian women, they judge Plato to be admirably aware of female suppression and even excessive in his zeal to remedy their deprivation. Thus, the sudden pointing to what has always been there to see, like the revelation of the ruler's nakedness in the tale of the emperor's new clothes, has much value.

Brian Calvert is a feminist who wisely takes this dual possibility into account in his interpretation. In the end, he believes that Plato was primarily pro-female and reads the passages in Book V as the strongest expression of Plato's sympathy with the feminist cause. Writing in the context of the new scholarship, Calvert sees the need to refurbish Plato's image. He attempts to clarify how we should understand those passages which cast doubt on whether Plato should be regarded as a champion of the equality of the sexes. Plato, he says, was operating on two levels at the same time. In the dialogues, these two become "unconsciously mingled." It should not be surprising that someone who is trying to

formulate and give moral justification for a revolutionary idea
should find it difficult to liberate himself from the traditional
views. Calvert finds that on the rigorous and philosophical level
Plato is completely egalitarian. There is "a lot of backsliding,"
however, in which he is guilty of the most obvious male
chauvinism.[21]

This defense strikes a completely new note in the history of
Plato studies. It is a view which could only have surfaced at a
time when the Freudian notion of unconscious motivation is a
commonplace and when agitation for women's rights and "consciousness raising" for men had already occurred. Although I
would argue that even on the philosophical level the description
of female nature as "equal in kind but not in degree" is not rigorously egalitarian, Calvert surely deserves enormous credit. As a
male philosopher in a field which has systematically excluded
women for centuries, his awareness of and desire to explain
inconsistencies is highly praiseworthy. I wholeheartedly applaud
his recognition of the difficulties men face in freeing themselves
from pervasive sexist attitudes absorbed, as it were, with their
mother's milk!

Besides these serious attempts to defend Plato and argue for the
strength of his feminism, numerous well-intentioned, but poorly
argued and confused pronouncements on Plato's glorious advocacy
of women's rights have appeared. Among the excesses are the
statements of the editor Joseph Ghoughassian who says that feminists may rejoice in what Plato said about their fortunes. In fact,
it is his work that has kept the feminist program alive and is
actually *responsible for* our current ability "to rethink the roles and
images of the sexes." If it weren't for Plato, the Aristotelian view
would have eclipsed "the rebellious consciousness of the feminist
movements that surfaced throughout the centuries."[22] No attempt
is made to show any causal influence for Plato's work on such
movements. In fact, I have been unable to locate any evidence
whatsoever that the passages in Book V to which Ghoughassian
refers had any influence at all until quite recently on the thinking
of men or women, except perhaps the negative one of keeping
the *Republic* from being translated.

Ghoughassian thinks we should excuse Plato for thanking the
gods that he wasn't created a woman because he left a "vast liter-

ature on women" to later generations. Of course, Ghoughassian is misinformed. We have no record of Plato expressing gratitude for not being born a woman. He is probably referring to the account of Diogenes Laertius of a story attributed by some to Thales, but by other biographers to Socrates. Furthermore, there is of course no vast literature on women left by Plato. There are numerous other confusions and misstatements not worth dwelling on except to point up the dangers of searching for confirmation in ancient thinkers for currently fashionable views which coincide with one's own.[23]

At the same time that Ghoughassian is touting Plato's influence, another editor is including him as an *unsung* champion of women. Noting that Xanthippe is practically a synonym for a shrewish wife, Mary Cohart finds it particularly ironic that Plato attributed his own ideas on equality to Socrates.[24] She makes no attempt to assimilate any of the scholarship on the actual views of the historical Socrates. This lack of concern for accurate historical research reaches absurd heights in a popular book called *The First Sex*. In the author's attempt to show that a matriarchy once existed, she distorts history to a bizarre extent by making it seem that the projected city in the *Laws* actually existed. She cites the Platonic proposals for female guardians, magistrates, and priests as if such a society had actually existed in the ancient world.[25] Such disservices to scholarship are all the more alarming since, unlike most of the scholarly articles I am considering (which are on the whole accurate and carefully reasoned), these textbook introductions and popular works of propaganda are more likely to reach a wide audience.

In opposition to this group of informed and misinformed writers who applaud Plato's feminism, is an equally diverse and vocal group of dissenters. These range from those who consider Plato among the worst of male chauvinists to others who would grant him some credit, but believe that on balance he does not deserve the accolades he has been receiving in the last ten years. The scientist Richard C. Lewontin, who has devoted much thought and energy to women's rights, even describes Plato's discussion in Book V as the earliest one in which intellectuals explain to one another why affirmative action just doesn't work in the academy.[26] He says that Plato ran an academy even more male-biased than its modern equivalent. As a means of highlighting the faulty arguments of male academics today, Lewontin says of Plato, "I suppose he searched for women candidates but none were suitable."[27] With admirable intentions, he misinterprets the nature of "marriages" between the guardians. Unfairly, but probably only half-seriously, he tells us that in reading the description of guardians and their wives he is reminded of his housemaster and his wife, "an educated and cultured woman who presided at the tea table while talking of Michelangelo."[28]

Behind the sarcasm, Lewontin clearly considers it important to claim Plato as a forerunner of those contemporary academics who, while paying lip service to meritocracy, continue the present discriminatory situation and mistakenly believe it to reflect the actual lack of merit among women.[29]

Martha Nussbaum, though she is well aware of current discrimination, defends Plato eloquently. She says that Plato did not favor "affirmative action" only because Athenian society was so profoundly unequal that women could not be expected to overcome their disadvantages. Republic VII, she points out, contains a devastating indictment of this society "not least of the way in which it neglects and/or corrupts the capabilities of its women." The only way to rectify the situation would be to rear human beings *de novo* in a way in which they had never been reared before. Then the remaining differences in physical function would no longer be judged as linked to intellectual capacity. And in working toward such a society today she thinks women can demand consideration on an equal basis, "asking those who assess our credentials to 'look to that city and constitute themselves as its citizens,' Rep. 592B." But Lewontin still prefers to see the glass as more than half empty and refers to Plato's use of the "sex-biased form 'guardian's women'" as an indication of the asymmetry Plato assumed between the sexes.[30]

Another of those who disparage Plato is Elizabeth Janeway, the author of a popular feminist book intriguingly titled *Powers of the Weak*. On the subject of Plato, she is a purveyor of misinformation. Unlike Lewontin, who shows an impressive knowledge of the *Republic*, she seems to have no direct acquaintance with Plato's work at all, but nevertheless describes him as a major villain. Without referring to any Platonic text herself, she quotes a sec-

92

ondary source on slavery and political power, offers an out-of-context paraphrase, and evidently finds Plato virtually indistinguishable from Aristotle in calling for the obedience of the masses.[31] She mentions the concept of Philosopher-Kings. But then, although her book is about the age-old powerlessness of women, she completely neglects to mention that Plato wanted to include an equal number of women among the powerful.

In contrast, the knowledgeable classicist Sarah Pomeroy bases her dissent on careful textual analysis. She concludes that although Plato may seem revolutionary in comparison with the prevailing Greek misogyny, scholars who have hailed him as a believer in the equality of the sexes are mistaken. The truth is that he never intended women to be equal in status. In fact, one can tell from Plato's diction that he is "incapable" of seeing women as equal. In elaborating on what she refers to as Plato's lack of capacity, she states that "he could not, or did not wish to free himself from the Athenian prejudice which treated women legally as perpetual minors."[32] Pomeroy offers no further clarification of the distinction between incapacity and unwillingness or disinclination. According to her, Plato "couldn't conceive of women living without male tutelage." Furthermore, Plato "tends to" classify the women with the children, since in seven out of nine passages, possession of women and children are considered simultaneously.

In Pomeroy's eagerness to emphasize the anti-feminist aspect, she downplays the evidence for the existence of contradictory tendencies in Plato. She does not allow for Plato's being in two minds on the subject, as he was on other issues.[33] She does not emphasize the possibility of a philosopher consciously and genuinely choosing one attitude toward women, while unconsciously clinging to an alternative view. In short, she seeks no explanation like Calvert's for Plato's wavering and ambivalence. She seems unaware that her claim that Plato *could not conceive* of complete equality requires stronger evidence than she presents. Her mere indication of contradictions, which show that Plato in fact *did not* consistently maintain a plan for complete equality throughout the relevant passages, is insufficient to support her charge.

This is not to deny the existence of those contradictions that male commentators overlooked for hundreds of years. In the 1970s, several commentators have found many residual inequities which escaped previous writers. For example, Pomeroy is not alone in pointing out that Plato nowhere describes the predictable consequences of wife-sharing, which would be the "sharing of husbands." Many now notice, too, that rewards of more frequent intercourse are offered solely to the bravest men, displaying unequal treatment. But of course none of these anomalies demonstrate that Plato could not conceive of another kind of woman. As many of the earlier commentators pointed out, he had legendary models in Amazons and goddesses who lived without male tutelage. And the fact remains that he actually did conceive of the idea of women guardians who perform the same tasks as men.

Much of Pomeroy's argument turns on the use of the Greek word *koinōnia*, a term which refers to common, or public, affairs, property, or acts. She chooses to stress that Plato describes the common holding of women as *koinōnia*, which is the term used for property in Athenian legal documents.[34] Although this legal use is undoubtedly frequent, Pomeroy perhaps overstates her case. The adjectival form appears at the outset of the discussion in the proverb used by Euripides and others: *koina ta philōn* (*Republic*, V, 449c), which translates as "common are the things of friends." As is the case with *ktesis*, and for that matter "acquisition," "having" or "possessing" in English, you can both acquire and possess knowledge as well as objects. Ideas, as well as property, can be common to friends. Aeschylus says, "Fortune is a common thing."[35] Fortenbaugh, who challenges Pomeroy's view, is right that there are many kinds of *koinōnia*, and that Socrates must make clear what sort of commonality exists between male and female guardians.[36]

To be entirely fair, Pomeroy would have to admit at the very least that Plato uses the term in more than one sense. As Fortenbaugh says, the sense of legal possession does not appear in Socrates' important final summary. There, he is clearly referring to the *koinōnia* of men and women to education, children, and guardianship. Women will watch and hunt together with men, generally sharing (*koinōneia*) all things in every way. This does seem to be a *koinōnia* of partnership rather than an arrangement of captive property.[37]

My point is not that Plato never lapses into language and policies which countervene his plan for complete identity of role. I am not even sure what it would mean to say that such backsliding was inevitable, that he was "incapable" of doing otherwise. Nor do I wish to detract from the credit due Pomeroy for pointing out the pervasiveness of misogyny in the classical philosophers. I want only to suggest that Pomeroy is overzealous in her attempt to discredit totally Plato's praiseworthy attempts at equalizing the roles of the best and the brightest of both genders.

Marylin B. Arthur is equally eager to combat the idea that Plato's proposals are an example of liberated thinking. The equality of the sexes really "entailed" the very different idea of "holding wives and children in common." Women, she says, were to be held in common by the men of the class as a whole; they are thus "the exchange objects." Like Pomeroy, she refers to the idea of *koinōnia* and tells us that the proverb "friends' possessions are held in common" refers to a system of free exchange within a restricted group. Arthur compares such a system of free exchange unfavorably with Homer's picture of married life in the *Odyssey*. She describes Penelope and Odysseus as sharing their thoughts as they share their household.[38] I cannot see how the relationship of Penelope, who sat spinning and warding off suitors while Odysseus roamed, can serve as a prototype for any kind of desirable marriage. As the historian M. I. Finley reminds us, more often than not, Penelope was omitted from Odysseus' image of the home he longed for. According to Finley, Homer fully revealed what remained true for the whole of antiquity, that women were naturally inferior and therefore limited to producing offspring and performing household duties, while meaningful attachments took place between men.[39] The relation between Odysseus and Penelope is certainly not a relation between equals. For me, the Platonic plan of men and women ruling equally, studying and exercising together, still seems preferable to the model of Penelope waiting patiently while Odysseus wandered.

Julia Annas also tells us that it is quite wrong to think of Plato as the first feminist. His arguments are unacceptable to a feminist and the proposals made in Book V are irrelevant to the contemporary debate. She is not satisfied with Plato's assertion that there is no civic pursuit belonging to a woman as such, or to a man as such. Since he offered no trace of an argument against the existence of "specifically male competences," his presentation is decisively lacking.[40] For a feminist, this issue must be uppermost.

Annas' view is that anyone acquainted with the modern literature will realize that those objecting to the idea that men and women should share all roles are "not very worried" about whether there are some jobs that only women are suited for.[41] Since these are less well paid and less prestigious jobs, the antifeminist is not concerned with them. Opponents of feminism are interested solely in those jobs for which only men are suited. But Annas neglects the fact that in hard economic times men *are* interested in jobs traditionally held by females, and furthermore, many females need and desire blue collar jobs. A feminist emphasis, it seems to me, must involve the breaking down of all gender designations as guarantees of or barriers to job competency.

As we have seen, Plato's discussion is directed toward showing that women have no special competence in, for example, cooking. In the modern world, cooking at the professional level has been traditionally male and feminists are still working to open up opportunities in this field. The decisive issue does not seem to me to be the need for arguments against special competences for either group. It is true that Plato offers his male audience empirical examples to show that women have no monopoly on ability in any area. One can sympathize with Annas' perceptions, since Plato's tone of "men can do anything women can do—better" (to invert the heroine's claim in the musical comedy song) is undeniable in Book V. Nevertheless, she undervalues the importance of his overall attempts to demonstrate that biological differences are irrelevant to all but reproductive activities.

In my view, the question of whether women have innate special excellences is very important indeed; the fact that Plato denied the existence of such excellences has great significance. For the history of Plato scholarship shows how frequently the argument of women's special abilities has been used as a justification for keeping them out of traditionally male fields. Whatever the logical weaknesses of such arguments, their repetition has had a deleterious effect. A condescending insistence that women are specially endowed for jobs connected with child care or nurturing has conveyed the message that since ladies do these things so much better than men they ought to stick to those areas. Plato's attempt to disqualify such arguments is therefore more important to feminism than Annas allows.

She believes that historically the main objections to attempts by women to enter hitherto male professions, or obtain allegedly male rights like the vote, have been based on the argument that there are certain activities for which only men are suited. The argument today is that the difference in men's intelligence militates against women having serious careers comparable to men's. But in my view, the argument also still revolves around whether women have special abilities.

Anthropologists, sociobiologists, and other social scientists continue to assert that women are biologically primed for nurturing roles. They should therefore choose careers which will utilize their allegedly innate skills in interpersonal relations. As I shall discuss in my final chapter, some modern thinkers now call for the placing of women in roles where their supposed collaborative style and special peace-keeping abilities are essential. Thus, the assertion of special competencies is used to suggest that women in positions of power would perform better in solving national and international disputes and even be more effective in preventing nuclear war and guaranteeing the survival of the human race. Whether or not one finds such arguments convincing, the discussion is certainly relevant to feminism. Although Annas is correct that claiming specific competences for men undermines women's demands for equality, Plato's arguments against specific competences for women are surely equally relevant to the continuing debate.

Many current feminists would insist that fathers must be seen to be equally competent for the task of caring for children. The suggestion that women are biologically, psychologically, or intellectually better suited to raising children is an important stumbling block to the restructuring of family life which many feminists see as essential to their gaining full equality.

Annas' article is carefully argued and, unlike many others, draws on the work of previous commentators, carrying on the tradition of scholarship as a continuing dialogue. But in the end, her demand that Plato, in order to be a forerunner of women's liberation, must have precisely the same concept of justice as fairness as she (and many, though not all, contemporary feminists) seems to me unreasonable. Annas says that Plato is not at all concerned with women's desires or needs. He doesn't care whether their present roles frustrate them "or whether they will lead more satisfying lives as guardians than as housebound drudges."[42] Plato's arguments are authoritarian rather than liberal and far from the arguments that women should have equal opportunity because otherwise they lead stunted and unhappy lives and lack the means for self-development.

But this is to say that, given Plato's views of justice for human beings, Plato *a priori* could not have been advancing feminist aims. It is to define feminism so that only the moral aim of "self-development" or her own view of justice as fairness is compatible with it. This is not only far from Wender's extremely broad definition of the term, but also contrary to other more limited, but equally valid, concepts of feminism, including those compatible with various versions of utilitarianism.[43] Plato does not directly address the question of whether women will be happier as guardians, any more than he asks directly whether men will be happier. In fact, he knows that, given conventional views of what provides satisfaction, a good deal of persuasion and reinforcement will be necessary to convince men to embrace such an austere existence. Plato assumes that if all citizens of the *polis* are doing what they do best, they will, by being useful and living harmoniously, attain the highest happiness.

Why can't genuine feminists base their convictions on the belief that the subjection of women is wrong because in the long run it is harmful to all humanity? Surely feminists *can* hold a consistently utilitarian morality. They can maintain that the ultimate reason it is wrong to deny any group the development of its talents depends on the consequences produced for society as a whole. It is consistent with feminism to maintain that unequal treatment of the sexes is harmful, not only because of its effect on women, but equally because the oppressor suffers from a diminishing of his human possibilities and the deprivation of the benefits of a truly equal sexual mate. The black American writer James

Baldwin argues similarly against racism when he stresses what is lost by whites, and thus by society as a whole, through racist practices.

Annas' charge that on a utilitarian argument as soon as more efficient means to the desired end are found "women can at once be thrust back into the home" is not justified.[44] Plato's metaphysics is grounded in the very different belief that developing one's nature to the utmost will alone provide for the best state. So that a woman not using her natural capacity would necessarily produce a less desirable state than one in which all act according to their nature. It could not then be true, as Annas puts it, that the moment the state "did not need extra women public servants, there would be no grounds for letting them have the jobs." Instead, new jobs which use their capacity and further the purposes of the state would have to be found.

Annas raises the question of the fate of the many potters' wives who might want to be potters in the ideal state. "Presumably," she writes, "the Guardians (male and female) would only tell them to stay at home and learn *sophrosune* in carrying out their appointed tasks."[45] But such a presumption cannot be based on an attempt at sympathetic understanding of Plato's view of justice. Plato's disdain for the artisan class is lamentable, and he surely tells us little of the arrangements for the lower classes. It is true that he only mentions women's abilities in connection with those who would be Philosopher-Queens. But if we are "presuming" on the basis of his total view, we would have to presume that potters' wives would also have to do whatever their nature fitted them for. If they had an aptitude for pottery and instead did only weaving, this, in Plato's view, would be unjust.

There is no doubt that Annas is correct that Plato's argument is not couched in the modern terms of "women's rights." But the granting of what we call "rights" would be considered by him to be ultimately justifiable only in so far as it ensured the smooth running of the whole. And it strikes me as still a meaningful question to ask any moralist what the ultimate justification of a right is. That is, the question still remains of what arguments justify the statement that it is wrong *in itself* to deny women equal rights. The superiority of Annas' own doctrine of fairness over Plato's concept of justice is not self-evident.

Another feminist, Lynda Lange, also joins the camp of those who deny that Plato deserves the appellation of feminist. She focuses on "the inadequacy of his views from the standpoint of feminism today." Plato did not intend that the guardian class be equally divided by sex. She even claims that Plato's recommendations do not "necessarily imply" that *any* of the guardians will be women.[46] Like many of the writers in the 1970s, Lange's main interest is to show, as the title of the book in which her essay appears indicates, the "sexism of social and political theory." In the process, she ignores the historical importance of Plato's enterprise and misinterprets his philosophical aims. For surely to understand the *Republic* is to realize that the philosopher-rulers, who alone see the truth, must be born of the best-endowed and the best-educated of both sexes. How, then, could there be no female guardians?

Lange is also guilty of neglecting the previous scholarly literature, so that she announces, as if it were her own discovery, that Plato uses the language of property relations for the common "ownership" of female guardians. In fact, she even states that Plato does so "consistently." She does not refer to the Greek text nor to the problem of the translation of *koinōnia*. Nor does she allow for any of the contrary formulations discussed by Pomeroy and Fortenbaugh (and apparent even in translation). Her aim throughout is to outdo Annas in her condemnation of the Athenian philosopher for not basing his discussion of women guardians on the fairness of the matter. Lange's discovery of the obvious, that Plato's recommending equal education is ultimately derived from his concept of justice, seems sufficient to automatically discredit him. That he followed his own agenda and not that of the contemporary women's movement dismays her. "If Plato were a feminist but merely inconsistent, it strikes me as unlikely that the inconsistency would be quite that gross . . . " she writes.[47]

Another representative of the view that Plato is no friend of women is the strangely muddled position of Arlene Saxenhouse. Her approach is different from all others, however, and I think few would describe her own argument as feminist. It contains, without specific acknowledgement, several of the strands of the Bloom-Strauss position. She gives her own version of the argument that Plato actually wanted to show that the *Republic* is unrealizable. Plato's recommendations for women were not intended to foster their emancipation, but rather to forewarn of the injustice that politics imposes on "the philosopher himself."[48] And the injustice of Socrates consists of his disregarding the sexual qualities of the female. In a restatement of Bloom's charge that Plato "forgets the body," she writes that women guardians are "almost without body" and free from eros. She conveniently ignores the fact that Socrates gives the eros of women over forty free rein, and that he makes careful provisions for the development of women's bodies in the gymnasium.

But Saxenhouse intertwines the argument of Plato's lack of appreciation for women's unique physiology with the contention that he wanted to show the impossibility of the just state. Her own view of women's physiology is a version of the belief we have seen expressed before by male commentators, the belief in "special excellences." She deplores Socrates' neglect of the peculiar biological qualities "that women alone have and that make them superior" in their ability to bear children.[49] She tells us that even women least skillful in this task do it better than men! I shudder to think how she would describe all those women today who either do not possess or do not exercise this skill in which their superiority supposedly lies. For she objects to Plato having reduced motherhood to a "bare minimum," to nursing. This reduction ultimately accounts for his judgment of their inferiority. The actual purpose of Plato's proposals is, she tells us in a confusing metaphor, "to cast a philosophically significant shadow" over the whole enterprise of the ideal city. Evidently, politics is fundamentally imperfectible, always to be plagued by conflict. And the implication is that women ruling, rather than being mothers, is against their nature.

It is the process of giving birth that she wishes to glorify. She tries unconvincingly to unite the female with the philosopher because of the "generative powers" of both. Without any references to the text, she argues that both the female and the philosopher are cast uncomfortably into a political community that concentrates on war. By forcing women into politics, Socrates turns them away from the generation of life to a concern with death. She wants us to see the pursuit of knowledge, rather than its attainment, as feminine or generative. Why pursuing is parallel to giving birth eludes me. In general, Saxenhouse fails to make her case for the equation of the masculine political world with death and the feminine philosophical world with life in the *Republic*, despite her reliance on metaphors of Socrates as midwife and philosophy as giving birth to ideas. In Plato's just society, the philosopher-rulers of both sexes must wage war effectively against their external enemies. And the arguments of Book V are advanced, not through metaphors, but by clearcut discursive statements comparing male and female dogs to male and female human beings.

Like many of the earlier male commentators, she stresses that males need females in order to give the city sons. But she offers her own addition that the female needs the male in order to fulfill her nature as the bearer of children. Of course, it is Saxenhouse and not Plato who confines women to this function. She thinks that Plato intends for us to find laughable the attempt to turn a female into a male, just as it would be laughable to turn the philosopher into a politician. Both would be perverting the natural.[50] Thus, she ends up with that view of some previous male commentators that the mainstream feminists have so vociferously denounced, the view that Plato's proposals are not intended seriously. She does not even acknowledge that the text itself states that it is precisely treating women differently from females of other species (in which leadership is shared) that "perverts the natural." Her fear of androgyny, what she calls the "de-sexed female," leads her to join those who doubt Plato's seriousness.

It is tempting to compare Saxenhouse's position to that of the well-known female opponent of the Equal Rights Amendment in the United States. This political figure advocates that all women stay home with their families, while she herself makes a career of traveling extensively, giving lectures designed to convince women that it is their nature to strengthen the family and avoid public life. Like the Cretan who says that all Cretans are liars, Saxenhouse works in political philosophy, attempting (though perhaps unsuccessfully) to argue abstractly and combatively while maintaining that it is women's nature to be gentle and generative of children rather than ideas. What her case surely demonstrates is that gender, even in a society where the sexes are still raised very differently, does not determine (even when gender-based self-interest might be expected to operate) one's position in a given controversy.

PRIVATE WIVES AND SEXUAL EQUALITY

Susan Moller Okin takes another view of Plato's intentions. She attempts to prove that Plato's plan to abolish private wives left him no alternative other than to provide for gender equality. Her analysis includes an admirable discussion of the inconsistencies of Plato's views within the *Republic*. But to make her case that abolition of the private sphere is prior to the instituting of Philosopher-Queens, she concerns herself more with the discrepancies between the *Republic* and the later *Laws*. She gives an excellent account of the arrangements for women in the latter, pointing out that women there perform in positions "not of the highest rank, all those domestic, nurturing, child-oriented tasks to which women have always been assigned."[51] Needless to say, she notes this assignment with none of the enthusiasm expressed by Rabbi Frank, who made the identical observation, but lauded Plato's return to common sense.[52] She, on the other hand, decries the philosopher's failure to institutionalize what he has proposed for women in general terms.

Contrary to the usual view, she surprisingly concludes that Plato's general aims actually grew "increasingly radical" from the *Republic* to the *Laws;* the Republic itself she has previously termed an "extremely radical dialogue."[53] She finds Plato's "general proclamation" in the *Laws* to be that boys and girls should have the same education and training, that women should share with men in the whole of their mode of life. But, she objects, Plato then "fails to apply these precepts in many of the most crucial instances."[54] And for this failure Okin has her own dubious explanation.

To understand her position, it will be necessary to include some discussion of the arrangements in the *Laws*, although they are not of direct concern in the present study. Despite the incisiveness of much of Okin's account, I believe she is mistaken in dwelling on a supposed necessary relation between the abolition of the family and private property and the establishing of gender equality for the guardians. She is quite right in that the discrepancy between the expressed egalitarian aim and its actualization is most pronounced in the *Laws*. According to her, the difference between the two works in regard to women's role hinges entirely on the question of the family in each. In the *Republic*, the abolition of property and the family for the guardian class *"entails the abolition of women's traditional sphere"* (*my emphasis*).[55] Only because Plato has eliminated the family does he reduce the differences between the sexes to their role in procreation. But in the *Laws*, the reinstatement of property requires monogamy and private households. And this restores women to their role of "private wives" with "all that this *entails*" (*my emphasis*).[56]

This question of the logical relationship between the two reforms has been discussed far more often than Okin realizes. She does see that by following her reasoning we end up with strange bedfellows, for she finds herself agreeing with the notorious misogynist Rousseau about the connection. In *Emile*, he wrote, "Having dispensed with the individual family in his system of government, and not knowing any longer what to do with women, he [Plato] finds himself forced to turn them into men."[57] For Okin the relation between the two innovations is as Rousseau saw them, but with an important modification. Rousseau, she says, should substitute that Plato has turned women into "people," rather than into "men." For Rousseau "in many important respects only men were people."[58]

As we have seen, not only Jowett, but even Saxenhouse and the Italian feminists have taken Rousseau's objection seriously, worrying whether Plato has in fact done women a disservice by turning them into men. The relevant point here is that Okin agrees with Rousseau about the causal effect of one reform on the other. Though she seems aware of only a very few, she notes that those commentators who have considered the connection disagree with her. Pierce stresses the independence of the two proposals, whereas Strauss finds a causal link, but doesn't declare himself on the direction. The third scholar she mentions, A. E. Taylor, she correctly notes finds the connection to occur in the reverse direction.

However, her understanding of Taylor is based on a serious misreading. She is right that he sees the desire to emancipate women as leading to the abolition of the family. But she is unfair to this great scholar in insisting that Taylor asserts this "rather dogmatically," without giving any reason.[59] For on the very page to which she refers, Taylor states his reasons clearly. As we have previously discussed, Taylor believes that it is the historical Socrates who is the original feminist. He writes: "[T]he general principles which underlie the treatment of the position of women . . . are no personal 'development' of Plato's; they belong to the actual Socrates. . . . Hence the thought that the duties of statesmanship and warfare should be extended to women must be regarded as strictly Socratic, and the rest of the proposals . . . are no more than necessary consequences of this position."[60] In Taylor's view, then, Plato was saddled with the liberationist philosophy of the actual Socrates and therefore required to make the other accommodations.

Okin is also mistaken if she believes her own view of the matter has been neglected since Rousseau. As we have seen, Karl Nohle views the connection as she does, though he draws other conclusions from it. He, too, thinks as she does that Plato was constrained to concede equality to women, having instituted the other reforms to assure the unity of the state and the moral excellence of the guardians. Because women of excellent quality were needed for breeding, they were placed among the guardians. And once there, women had nothing to do, so they had to be given the same work as men.[61] Thus, he claimed long before Okin that abolition of the family, both logically and psychologically, preceded the proposals for equal role.

The major difficulty of Okin's position is that she never sufficiently clarifies the precise nature of the causal link between the two ideas. Most of the time, she implies that a relation of logical necessity obtains. But she equivocates, and occasionally it seems that she is referring only to some kind of psychological constraint. It is not easy to understand exactly what she intends when she writes, "[I]t was his dismantling of the family which not only enabled Plato to rethink the question of women and their potential abilities but *forced* him to do so" (*my emphasis*).[62]

In response to her earlier article outlining the same position, William Jacobs had pointed out that the connection cannot be a strictly logical one.[63] But her only concession to his decisive objection is a slight change of wording in one instance in her later book. When speaking of one of the other commentators, she changes "entails" to "leads to" and refers to Jacobs.[64] But this is hardly sufficient. She fails to see that what is necessary is a complete rethinking of her position. However, she never clarifies further in what sense family and property abolition "require" equalization of role.

It is obvious, of course, that the proposed plans for superior males still leave open a wide range of logically possible arrangements for women. Male rulers and a colony of female acolytes would suffice. A corps of celibate rulers who adopted the gifted sons of traditional families in order to perpetuate themselves would satisfy the logical requirements. This might even seem far more feasible to the Athenian audience. For Greek heads of households often adopted sons when they were without male heirs. Even in our own time, the American sect of Shakers consisted of celibate men and women who relied on adoption to continue the group.

Perhaps, however, what Okin really intends is "psychological inconceivability" rather than logical entailment. Maybe she means only that he was "forced" in the sense that it would have been very difficult for him to reconsider women's abilities as long as he continued to think in terms of the Greek family. Okin is eloquent in her condemnation of the family arrangements Plato knew best. She stands solidly among those who interpret the available evidence as incontrovertibly indicating that women were thoroughly and indefensibly oppressed in ancient Greece. Her description of what she calls "the Greek family," with its enforced seclusion and rigorous restriction of women to home and child care, is accurate as far as it goes. But she fails to mention that it applies only to the upper classes. She neglects the fact that some citizen women worked in the fields with their husbands and plied retail trades. Below a certain point on the social scale, in families with few or no slaves, it is unlikely that women were segregated. According to Dover, lower-class women would have had to go on errands and sell in the marketplace. He also concludes that attitudes and beliefs about women's moral capacity and responsibility must have varied between social classes.[65]

There is no reason why the visionary Plato could not have

independently conceived of another kind of family. Despite the conventional connection between women and property, and women and inferiority, a man whose genius produced a work that has remained vital for centuries could surely envision a family different from that existing in a city many of whose practices he deplored. If by family we mean only a male, a female and their offspring, forming a social unity (as families are now minimally defined by anthropologists), a great thinker like Plato, even though male, would not necessarily be forced to accept a single kind of family with a fixed set of property relations.

My own view of the proposed reforms is that they are inextricably intertwined. There is a danger that speculation about which of the Two Waves came first will distract from our consideration of the justice of each. For although the co-equal proposals are connected as Plato presents them, the justice of each can be considered separately; and Plato does so. Okin herself seems somewhat uncertain of her ground, despite her twice-published, lengthy argument. For at one point, she writes, "to the extent that a causal relation exists."[66] In ordinary language a causal relationship either exists or it does not, and it is hard to ascertain what she means by degrees of causality. Her statement that once the family is abolished, "there seems to be no alternative" except for Plato to consider women as persons in their own right, would indicate a definite causal link, as does her usage of "entailment" and "forced." But she also states that "if they [women] are to take their place as members of the guardian class," then they must have equal natures.[67] I would agree that the operative word is "if," and that Okin's reasoning is therefore circular and begs the question. The loss of their role as private wives does not require women's elevation to guardianship. And if Plato plans for them to be guardians, then he must have been independently committed to the equality of their natures.[68]

A consequence, as we have seen, of judging the elimination of family and property to be prior, either logically or psychologically (i.e., in Plato's thought processes), is that it fosters the view that the emancipation of qualified women was of relatively little importance to him. Okin seems to be aware of this herself, and thus, like many of the feminists, she fluctuates in her assessment of the degree of credit he deserves. It is always tempting to search, as she does, for unexpressed reasons for a philosopher's theories. Okin is right that Plato's lack of respect for women, as they were in the Athens of his day, is "understandable."[69] Even her allusion to speculation that he had personal psychodynamic reasons for wishing to minimize the anatomical differences between the sexes cannot be rejected. The fact that Plato nowhere shows that he understood the essential inequality of the upper-class Athenian family nor the unfairness of women's position is bound to detract from the enthusiasm a modern feminist can feel for his reforms.

However, in the end all Okin's attempts to show that he himself thought his proposals for women less important than the abolition of the family and property are unsuccessful. She surely overstates her case when she writes that it is *above all* the elimination of the "passion to acquire" which is "the road to virtue."[70] Here, she misunderstands Plato; for it is unity he desires and not an end to acquisitiveness *per se.* Her contention that private interests are to be abolished to eradicate selfishness and divisive interests in the ideal state is not entirely accurate either. They are, after all, only to be abolished for the guardians; we have no reason to believe that the majority would not own property. (We also know nothing about their family relations, nor does Plato tell us how he intends to reconcile identical male and female natures among the third class.)

This retention of property by the bulk of the members of the state makes that frequent usage of the term "communism" for the reforms a misnomer.[71] But even the possession of goods in common by the guardians does not involve the complete renunciation of acquisitive instincts. The entire "military establishment" of the auxiliaries is designed to protect what is theirs against the stranger-barbarian. This contrasts sharply with the Roman Church's requirement of poverty for monastic orders. Okin thinks that to Plato the greatest danger was, in her words, "the fatal preference for material possessions" over the welfare of their souls.[72] But this is to superimpose a Christian view which does not express Plato's intentions. As Okin herself noted at one point, the goal is for all to say "my own" about the same things. Thus, Plato's aim is to redirect the natural desire for ownership so that it can be used for the benefit of the group as a whole.

In sum, Okin is wrong that the threat of acquisitiveness is uppermost among Plato's concerns in the *Republic*. Nor does the reintroduction of the family in the *Laws* have the "direct effect" of putting women firmly back into their traditional place. The standard scholarly opinion for the reversion to convention remains convincing. As Plato grew older and legislated for an actual, rather than an ideal, city, he became more willing to make accommodations to traditional practices.

But what then is it that makes so many commentators sense that Plato's program for sexual equality, even in the *Republic*, is relatively unimportant to him? He is surely less consistent and less eloquent about this reform than about the others. Many commentators must sense that Plato's chief desire is to enlighten his audience about the nature of the true philosopher. He seeks rulers who will know the good, distinguish truth from falsehood, and guide the society wisely. I see his reforms as essentially interrelated. Good guardians come only from good stock and good stock can only be produced from good mothers and fathers. Plato's main concern is to produce guardians who, after emerging from the cave, will see the light and recognize and uphold the principle of unity behind all appearances. In a society in which the utmost unity is possible, able women must do what their nature fits them for. Otherwise, the *kallipolis* will not exemplify perfect justice. But the feeling remains that Plato's dearest aim—the existence of true philosophers—might still be attained without equality of roles. It might still be possible for some men, i.e., males, to escape from the shadows of the cave.

It is then the culmination of the three paradoxical waves which has the effect of overwhelming all of the other reforms and perhaps making gender equality seem less important. By focusing on the final wave, commentators for hundreds of years have succeeded in ignoring the startling wave that precedes it. And it may be this that causes some female commentators to realize that Plato's chief desire is not the one they would make uppermost. This realization, along with the recognition that Plato undeniably had no interest in equality for the sake of what we would call women's individual fulfillment, has perhaps led Okin, as well as many other feminists, to conclude that Plato's commitment to sexual equality was relatively unimportant.

EDUCATION, ENVIRONMENTALISM,
AND THE CONCEPT OF *PHYSIS*

In the understandable objection of many commentators to Plato's lack of concern for what we think of as self-development, they sometimes underestimate the strength of his conviction that doing what one's nature warrants is the source of human happiness. To understand this, one must explore thoroughly the ancient Greek and specifically the Platonic idea of *"physis."* Both Okin and Jane R. Martin, another writer on Plato's theory of education, are aware of the importance of the idea of innate abilities to the Platonic, as well as to the modern discussion of gender equality. I shall deal first with the views of Okin, since here again I believe her interpretation has serious flaws. She is admirably aware that *physis* is a complicated notion, but in my view, her understanding of it involves a misapprehension of Platonic metaphysics which vitiates her analysis of the reforms for women guardians.

Okin speaks of Plato's "environmentalism," a judgment she can make only on the basis of what I consider a faulty understanding of *physis*. Plato, she tells us, believes in education as the *chief* determinant of character. One assumes she classifies him as an environmentalist in the same sense that we would today so describe thinkers who decline to evaluate the potential of individuals unless they have been exposed to the same opportunities. Presumably, environmentalists in this sense believe that early environment, socialization, and education are far more important than genetic considerations in human development. Okin says that Plato places "the greater weight" on education over heredity, but unfortunately falls short of applying his own convictions. In trying to convince his skeptical audience that women should be trained for the same civic functions, he misses out by failing to employ his best weapon. She concludes that Plato "almost entirely fails to apply" his alleged environmentalism.[73]

Here, Okin seems to have succumbed to the temptation, as have many before her, to report not what Plato did say, but rather what he should have said. I am sympathetic with her desire to praise Plato for realizing the importance of education. But she misleads her readers when she writes of the philosopher's belief in the "influence of the environment" over what translators variously render as "inborn dispositions," "innate tendencies," or "natural capacities." In a book on such a topical subject, with an audience unlikely to have much acquaintance with classical literature, her first obligation is undoubtedly to clarify what Plato actually did say in the Greek text.

Okin tries to support her view that, far more than most commentators have acknowledged, Plato "strongly opposed the prevailing emphasis on the immutability of the innate."[74] It would take us too far afield to try to determine what the prevailing emphasis actually was in classical Athens. Suffice it to say that even Euripides, to whom she refers, did not believe that ability and character were completely unchanged by experience. In fact, the view of many Greek writers compares with a prevalent common-sense outlook of today. The assumption is that a person is born with certain capacities which limit how far he or she can develop; but events can and do affect how the innate capacity is expressed. Our modern version of the "immutability of the innate" occurs in current idioms taken from computer technology. People speak of human beings as "programmed" in a given direction. And in explanations of personality style, some say "that's just the way he's wired," unexaminedly referring to presumably fixed neurological patterns which somehow determine temperament and character traits.

The relevant issue here is that Okin misunderstands the Platonic concept when she tries to set up an opposition between the innate and the acquired.[75] She attempts to establish that some elements of "what Plato calls nature are by no means innate, *but* have been developed by training and habit" (*my emphasis*).[76] Such an opposition, however, is Okin's and not Plato's. She is well aware that Plato's distinction between *physis* and *nomos* is complex and difficult, but she makes it even less intelligible by removing it from its metaphysical context. She obscures the fact that for Plato an entity possesses a certain trait which under proper conditions will be exhibited in the course of its natural development.

The example Okin chooses to show that "we must look closely at the environment" to determine the *physis* of a thing illustrates her misunderstanding of the Socratic view. She refers us to the *Phaedrus*, where Socrates is seeking the true nature of the soul.

But she is mistaken in thinking that the interchange between Socrates and Phaedrus supports her view; precisely the opposite is the case. Socrates intends no recognition of the efficacy of the environment when he says they must reflect on how the soul "acts and can act on other things."[77] Socrates is here searching for what is the *same* in all instances of the soul. One discovers this by a dialectical method which disregards superficial appearances and discovers what is identical "behind" the varying actions and interactions.

Socrates' search for the *physis* in this dialogue has no relation at all to environmentalism. No alleged emphasis on the primary importance of training or outside influence appears in this dialogue on the soul. On the contrary, the Socrates-Phaedrus exchange exemplifies rather that search for the invariant which is the key to Platonic metaphysics. The philosopher believed in an *eidos* of individual things as well as of classes. It is precisely this emphasis on immutability which his twentieth-century opponents have deplored as a dangerous essentialism.[78] In the *Phaedrus*, Socrates is interested in how the soul changes *only* as a basis for a logical analysis that will lead to what is identical in all souls. He likewise assumes that all classes possess an identical attribute, that all men, all women, and all sheep dogs possess an identical nature which constitutes them as a class.

Thus, the changing entities of the world have structure. But he also uses *physis* not only for the concrete *eidos*, but also for the tendency and striving which this form *determines* in every actual entity. As John Wild points out, in Plato there is a ubiquitous factor of "unfinished tendency."[79] Many scholars have attempted to clarify this dual usage. But the distinction between the two senses of *physis*, the static and the dynamic, which Okin takes over from Cornford does not help her case. Cornford rightly makes a distinction between 1) the constitution, structure, essence of a thing, and 2) the way a thing grows.[80] But this latter sense of a thing's development is *not* a distinction, as she would have it, between a fixed element and the partly unpredictable effects of what we call environmental influence.

The crucial point is that for Plato a thing's development is part of its nature. Those with musical natures show an early aptitude, and if their ability is developed they play well into old age. Plato says that each of us is naturally not quite like anyone else, but rather differs in his nature and is apt for the accomplishment of different jobs. Okin considers Shorey's translation of *physis* here as "nature from birth," an overinterpretation.[81] But in my view, the scholar-translator, unlike Okin, correctly interprets Plato's intention, as does Cornford himself, who translates "innate capacity."[82] As Jowett stresses, the point is that all do not have the same "natural aptitudes."[83]

The issue here is more than a trivial argument about the proper translation of a single word. It is rather that any attempt to present Plato as having believed that the different natures of people result primarily from their different environments cannot succeed. Such an interpretation, though it may link Plato with current reformers, leads to a misunderstanding of the chief point of the *Republic* and its concept of the just state. We may wish that he did not find the capacity to be a carpenter or a physician a matter of inborn abilities. But if education and rearing were the decisive elements, then why divide people into classes at birth at all? Why not simply select people at random for different kinds of training, assigning Job A to the first thousand born, Job B to the second, etc.? The principle of each one doing what he is fitted for by nature, which is Plato's definition of justice, might then mean each one doing the job for which he was trained. The myth of the silver, bronze, and gold classes would then be unnecessary, and one could always decide that he did not like his present job and would prefer to be trained for another. But Plato's state could allow for no "mid-life career change." His belief is rather that just as silver has a fixed nature and is not suited for cooking pots, the farmer has certain aptitudes and is not suited for learning the art of medicine.

But Okin persists in maintaining that Plato's predominant stress is on nurture, and that the nature of a thing is "unknowable as long as that thing is the recipient of discriminatory training and treatment."[84] This is her view and not Plato's. Okin speaks from the vantage point of a twentieth-century scientific outlook, from a world of controlled studies where "truths" about natures or what we would call capacities, aptitudes, abilities are supported by experiments in which attempts are made to perform identical operations on like materials to secure highly probable conclusions.

But this is not Plato's universe at all. Plato does not say that the nature of our two hands is unknowable in the metaphor Okin cites from the *Laws*, any more than he says that the nature of women is unknowable. Instead, he declares that "our two limbs are by nature balanced." It is by bad habit alone that we create differences between them. In de-emphasizing Plato's misogyny in the *Laws*, Okin omits to note that the source of these bad habits is, like the source of so many other evils, "the folly of nurses and mothers."[85] Plato has deduced by his dialectical method that the left hand is equal in capacity to the right, just as he has deduced that women are by nature twice as bad as men. Given our different methods of establishing truth, we conclude on the basis of neurological research and empirical observations of moral behavior that both of these Platonic deductions are in fact fallacious.

Okin wants to give credit to Plato for his desire to offer women the chance they did not have in Greek society, the chance to see if they would measure up to male achievement. But we must avoid recasting Platonic thought in the terms of our pragmatic, scientific world view. On our terms, it is only after a long trial period that we could know for certain what women can achieve. To Okin, the result of equal treatment is genuinely unknown. With admirable fairmindedness, she insists that if women have not succeeded thus far in certain areas we cannot at this time prove beyond a doubt that the reasons are purely "environmental." Her belief that equal socialization and education will produce equal results is thus only a highly probable hypothesis which awaits future confirmation. To superimpose such a view on his own—even to suggest that on the basis of the very arguments he presents he could have seen the light—is more than anachronistic. It renders his entire opus unintelligible, so that we lose far more than we gain.

It cannot be stressed too often that Plato's method is to decide through reasoning what the nature of a class is and then to proceed from there. His conclusions are never intended as tentative in our post-Renaissance sense. Okin tells us that from the total context of the Platonic dialogues we can see that it is "the rational" *rather than* "the natural" which is their author's central standard. But here again, she is mistaken in setting up such an opposition. For what Plato means by *physis is* ultimately the rational. In a century which takes "an event" as its basic unit, Platonic metaphysics is perhaps difficult for us to grasp. But it is surely still to a large extent built into our language. When we say that a circle *is* round, or that women *are* nurturant, we employ the Greek metaphysic of substance and attribute and of class membership. That is, what characterizes a circle is its roundness, a given woman her ability to nurture.

Admittedly this geometric model has its drawbacks, and it clearly landed Plato in inconsistencies and outright contradictions, particularly in dealing with the human and animal world. But our aim should be to understand the legacy he left us, in connection with thinking about women's nature, as well as in other respects. To understand the advantages and disadvantages of his essentialist metaphysics, we must take all possible steps to guarantee that we do not distort what Plato actually said.

Unlike many recent commentators Okin does make a genuine attempt to deal with the text. But her conscientiousness is undermined by a desire to mitigate the fact that Plato is inconsistent both in the *Republic* and in the *Laws.* No amount of effort—and Okin certainly works very hard at it—can dissolve the inconsistencies. The very example she chooses as the "most significant passage of all . . . relating to the nature of the female sex" demonstrates how ineradicable they are.[86] Once again, I think her example demonstrates the exact opposite of what she attempts to prove.

The passage she refers to concerns the aesthetic education of the two sexes which, as she rightly points out, Plato considered enormously important for the formation of character. In the *Laws,* the Athenian stranger proposes that different words and music should be assigned to boys and girls because of "the natural differences" between the sexes. Okin admits that such a pronouncement certainly "seems at first" to be hard to reconcile with the conclusion of *Republic,* Book V. But she tries to convince us that the statement is in fact *not* a description of the natural differences between the sexes, but rather a *prescription* about what are "to be regarded" as the natural differences between the sexes for the purposes of that society. It is, she tries to convince us, solely a ruling about how the two sexes must come to think about themselves and about each other.[87]

But neither Plato nor the legislator are practicing any deception here. Once again, Okin has superimposed the modern ideas of self-image and sex-stereotyping instituted for a hidden purpose. Plato, however, clearly intends that the legislator prescribes only on the basis of what is natural and rational. He makes no distinction here between the prescriptive and the descriptive. His meaning is exactly as construed by Glen Morrow, whose interpretation of this passage Okin rejects (although in other respects she says she has relied heavily on his analysis). Morrow rightly states that Plato is here referring to "the specific differences between the psychical nature of women and that of men."[88] Taylor's translation captures Plato's unequivocal meaning well: "[W]hat music should be assigned to females is indicated by the actual natural distinction of sex, which should therefore be our basis for discrimination."[89]

Okin gives us no plausible explanation of why the legislator should prescribe on a basis which Plato himself knows to be false—or even questionable. If such were the case, wouldn't Plato reveal that his proposal is actually based on an expedient falsehood? Morrow's interpretation is the correct one, and we have every reason to believe that as Plato wrote those lines he was expressing his belief in a fixed female human nature. It is evidently difficult for Okin to think herself into the position of one who wants the political order to reflect, be based on, be in tune with a "natural" ontological order which exists independently of what anyone legislates. But such was Plato's belief. And what Okin calls "apparently contradictory" conclusions about the nature of women in his two societies are not in fact only apparent. No enthusiasm for Plato or for equality or for her thesis that the reinstatement of private wives necessitates a betrayal of his increasing egalitarianism can reconcile the inconsistencies.

Unfortunately, however, we are not dealing only with outright contradictions such as the opposition between the clearcut statement in *Republic*, Book V that women and men have identical natures and this passage in the *Laws* that there are psychic differences between them. The issue would be clearer if Plato always used the word physis in its strictly metaphysical sense. But we must admit that he sometimes uses it in a less precise vernacular sense, much as we today might talk of someone having, for example, a disagreeable nature, indicating traits or qualities, but making no definite commitment to their permanence. That is, sometimes we cannot ascertain whether Plato means that a trait he describes is, as contemporary sociobiologists might put it, "irremediable." Although more often he uses physis in the technical sense, clearly implying necessity, he sometimes, both in the *Republic* and the *Laws*, falls back on the common sense usage still current today, which blurs the distinction between the habitual and the inevitable.

Because of this variability in usage, translators have found it necessary to vary according to the context the expressions they use to translate "nature" and "natural." Sometimes the personal concerns of the translator affect the choice he makes. Okin cites Bury's omission of "nature" from his translation of "women are twice as bad as men by nature." She admits that Plato's statement "seems grossly inconsistent."[90] I suspect that Bury knew very well that this was a use of physis denoting a fixed attribute. Most likely, he desired to soft-pedal this no longer acceptable idea. Jowett faces the issue head-on and unself-consciously translates "in proportion as women's nature is inferior to that of men in capacity for virtue."[91]

Understandably, Okin would have preferred Plato to state that women's true nature was unknowable. And although he says no such thing here, there are occasions when it is difficult to tell whether a human trait he describes is not only inborn, but immutable. Immediately before his declaration in the *Laws* of women's twofold inferiority, he has stated that women are prone by nature to secrecy and stealth because of their weakness. This weakness is surely intended as biological. Plato's statement then might generously be interpreted to mean that, in this instance at least, women's deprivation causes their depravity. In most places, women cannot endure to have the truth spoken, "but in this state they may," he tells us. As we have seen, a twentieth-century self-styled feminist considers women's secretiveness to be a natural rather than a cultural trait.[92] The elder Plato probably believes that extra-strict legislation would always be necessary to counter this inborn defect, but that perhaps the flaw could be remedied. But however we interpret it, there is no chance that women's moral weakness and tendency to hide "in dark places" is purely environmental.

Nor does the example she adduces from the *Republic* show that Plato ever thought that environment alone could shape a person's nature. Socrates does say that education will produce, engender, create, implant good natures or constitutions, using the word *empoiei*.[93] But even here the analogy is with breeding stock and the assumption is that, although you can improve the breed, you must start out with the best materials. In another example which Okin thinks will illustrate that *physis* indicates abilities which are not innate she also errs. Quoting again from the Bury translation of the *Laws*, she cites the lines suggesting that women may participate in horsemanship although it is not compulsory for them: "But if, as a result of earlier training which has grown into a habit, their nature allows, and does not forbid, girls or maidens to take part, let them do so without blame."[94] In this more acceptable context, Bury does translate *physis* as "nature."

However, no opposition is intended in this example either between a girl's nature and her training. What Plato says is that if a girl has had the earlier training to prepare her, she may take part. That is, a girl may ride if, as Jowett puts it, she is strong enough and desires to do so. It is clear here, as elsewhere, that what Plato intends is that some women may be born with physical ability which can then be sufficiently trained. That is, some women may have enough innate capacity to perform the same tasks as men. But women's native ability is in general always inferior to men's.[95]

So much for the theory that Plato's views have grown increasingly radical! Okin is surely mistaken that in the earlier *Republic* he may have chosen to present "the less radical line of attack" as a sop to the misogyny of his audience. She proposes tentatively that, although Plato himself actually believed that environmental changes alone could show what women were capable of, he purposely advanced a different argument because it was more persuasive. But we cannot possibly ignore the great importance of the actual line of attack that he chose. In demonstrating that there are no differences between men and women relevant to the job of ruling, he establishes the value of the dialectic method over the eristic. Socrates' desire to illustrate the superiority of his analytic method, as has often been noted, is crucial at this point in the dialogue. For in order to reach the highest Good, rulers must be adept at the use of this analytic technique. Would Socrates really choose to show us faulty conclusions resulting from the use of his method, conclusions which Plato himself (and presumably Socrates) knew to be erroneous, but which his misogynous listeners accepted? I can see no value in entertaining the hypothesis that the argument for sexual equality in Book V involves "a convoluted route" which Plato takes "in spite of his own beliefs."[96]

Instead, we must accept at face value that Plato in the *Republic* clearly maintained three connected propositions. 1) The capacity to perform certain tasks is innate and can be detected very early. 2) Such capacities or aptitudes are in general not, as we would now say, "sex-linked." 3) These innate abilities in all areas, even given optimal conditions for development, will always produce lesser results in most women.

Plato then does not consciously use "according to nature" more as a sanction for decisions he has already made than as a standard by which to make decisions. It is true, as Okin says, that the philosopher frequently exposes what is commonly regarded as natural as merely alterable convention.[97] But his own view of the natural is surely meant to approach the eternal truths of an intelligible universe rather than the mere *doxa* of the many. If Plato believed, as she asserts, that what is natural is only what the philosopher-ruler tells his citizens, he would surely say so.

Nor did Plato's view of the natural capacities of women become more egalitarian as he grew older. The traditional explanation of why the reforms are less far-reaching remains more plausible. The society of the *Laws* was designed to be an actual realizable state rather than an ideal city of speech. In both works, Plato expresses some ambivalence about women's abilities. To summarize, the *Republic* contains two kinds of statements. There is: 1) a strong argument that women as a class are equal to men in capacity, although on the whole, weaker in all pursuits; and 2) other overt statements and intimations that women are more cowardly, less trustworthy, innately worse than men. The same

mental split occurs in the *Laws*. There are strong declarations
that women are capable of pursuing the same tasks as men, alongside statements about women's natural moral inferiority and
secretiveness. Even in the strongest statements in both works, the
qualification of complete equality appears. The metaphor of ambi-
dexterity, which alludes to the need to train both sexes, contains
the same reservations about total equality as in the *Republic*. For
the limbs, he says, should be trained equally "as far as possible."[98]
So in both the *Republic* and the *Laws*, as earlier commentators
have gleefully noted, women should do what men do only "so far
as possible."[99]

In conclusion, I believe that Okin is mistaken not only about
the increasing radicalism of the *Laws*, but also about Plato's
alleged "environmentalism." Nonetheless, she has undoubtedly
made a valuable contribution, for she has countered the view that
the *Republic* ignores biological differences. She has shown that
Plato, unlike some of his interpreters and millions of others
throughout history, "very rationally" avoided the mistake of
assuming "that the entire conventional female sex role follows
logically from the single fact that women bear children."[100] Okin
has called attention to the significance of Plato's radical ideas, to
the possibilities for building on these ideas, and to the need to
counter the hostility of earlier commentators. She has placed
Plato solidly at the head of a long line of thinkers whose work
students must assimilate (and on many issues overcome) as
women move into new positions in society and begin to get the
equal education they need, desire, and deserve.

Let us turn now to the opinions of Jane R. Martin, who
addresses the same questions of the importance of education in
Plato and also considers the issue of innate ability. Unlike Okin,
she argues that equal education is not enough. She agrees with
those feminist commentators who praise Plato for favoring equal
opportunity. But, in sharp contrast to Ithurriague, that alleged
feminist of the 1930s who, as we have seen, lauded Plato's
emancipationist views, but feared that in the philosopher's enthusiasm "he went too far," Martin thinks Plato's reforms did not go
far enough to produce the results he desired. She openly admits
to using Plato only as a "point of departure" to help us understand what is required if sex equality is to be achieved in

our own society." Like Crossman, she is writing about Plato today. Thus, she differs from most of the other commentators who, in the guise of clarifying what Plato said, in fact tell us rather what he should have said. Martin, however, informs us at the outset that her objective is less to interpret the *Republic* than to show how assumptions about education have implications for a theory of women's societal role. She concludes that given Plato's assumptions he would have failed to guarantee sex equality. But it is not her aim "to condemn him for doing less than he should have for female guardians."[101] She wants rather to show us how we can learn from the shortcomings of what she calls his "Production Model of Education." This view of education as preparation for pre-assigned functions in society has unfortunately dominated Western thought and still has an unwholesome influence today.

Martin's effort suffers from the drawbacks of all such attempts to juxtapose modern terminology and assumptions on theories formulated in very different historical periods with very different presuppositions. She does not offer an interpretation of Plato's aims nor present the total context of the earlier thought, nor does she give us an explication of her own educational theory. Therefore, readers only superficially acquainted with Plato are likely to come away with serious misunderstandings. Their views of what equality would entail today might be reinforced, but they would not be prompted to examine their own presuppositions. Thus, there is a cost to Martin's failure to clarify the thought of the *Republic* in its own terms. The likelihood is that she ends by preaching solely to the faithful. This, of course, has some merit, but it is not the usual aim of the "modern philosophical discussion" as the volume in which her article appears describes its contents.[102]

Martin believes that Plato would provide equal "role opportunity" for female guardians, but it is her tentative assumption that he *might* not provide what she terms "equal role occupancy." What she means is that there is no guarantee that identical education will yield identical results, though evidently she allows that it *might* do so. The fact that people with "similar talents" often learn in different ways requires different modes of instruction. Unfortunately, Martin never clarifies what she means by "similar talents," giving us no theoretical model or operational definition of them. Plato, of course, had no concept of genes. But anyone speaking today of natural talents presumably refers to genetic inheritance, or to a hypothetical, if still unverifiable, similarity of brain structure or chemistry. Despite these presumed similarities, Martin maintains that some people *start* with handicaps having nothing to do with natural ability. In fact, if the early socialization of females in the ideal state parallels that of girls today, let alone of girls in Plato's Athens, "it is unlikely" that an identical education would produce equal numbers of male and female guardians. The likelihood is, she says, again tentatively, that without special treatment female warriors and rulers would not be able to finish the required curriculum in physical skills and abstract thinking.[103]

She believes that when Socrates proposes that men and women with the same talents should have the same education, he is extending to women a kind of education which has been designed for future male guardians, what she calls education in the male mold. The passage she cites from the text can only be used to support her case if you already believe that educational content and methods are intrinsically sex-linked. In Book V, Glaucon says there will be ruling men who are morally good and noble (*agathon*). And Socrates immediately corrects him: "And ruling women, too, Glaucon, I said. Don't suppose that what I have said applies any more to men than to women, all those who are born among them with adequate natures." But this does not satisfy Martin for "there is no reason at all" to assume that "male-based educational methods" will transform most females who are potential guardians into actual ones.[104]

Like Adela Adam more than sixty years earlier, Martin interprets this passage as showing that women are only an afterthought to Socrates. Martha Nussbaum takes a much more positive view. She considers this statement in which Plato uses *archousas*, the female present participle of the verb "rule," along with the masculine form *archontas*, to be "a very important passage." She describes it as the first known argument for linguistic feminism. In it, she says, Socrates implies that Glaucon's failure to use both forms will obscure from his imagination the genuine possibility that some women will meet the test not only of guardianship, but also of philosopher-rulership.[105]

Martin, however, uses the passage as evidence that Plato and his recent commentators have failed to see that a property or a characteristic which doesn't make a difference to the performance of a role "might in fact" make a difference to the learning of that role. The differential socialization which she evidently thinks would persist in Plato's state "might make a difference" in the ways females learn. There "may" also be physiological differences relevant to how they learn.[106] She does not clarify whether she considers these differences to be solely environmental. She is, of course, eager to avoid "biological determinism."[107] But some, at least, of the sources she cites on sex differences do claim that biologically based differences in learning exist even if they do not completely determine achievement. Martin herself hedges on this question. She prefers to focus on the purported differential socialization in Plato's state, which would affect females' motivation to learn and "readiness" when their formal education for ruling begins. But Martin here underestimates the consequences of significant social change. As the mother of the first female candidate for the vice-presidency of the United States put it, the assumption from birth that every little girl could become president will surely make a difference.[108] Martin underestimates the effect the possibility of being chosen as a guardian would undoubtedly have on female motivation.

In a sense, Martin ends up voicing, almost in spite of herself, the same objections to the Platonic proposals that most of the earlier male commentators had raised. The unavoidable conclusion to her line of thought is that ultimately biological differences *are* relevant to the ability to learn and accede to the guardian class. But she equivocates. Her tentative formulations allow for the possibility that some females will not be impaired by early training or "sex-related physiological and psychological differences."[109] In Plato's scheme that is all that is necessary.

For, as she well knows, Plato's intention differs from her democratic ideal of developing the multiple abilities of every individual to their fullest. Plato wishes to make the earliest possible selection of those who learn most easily. For those of us committed to complete egalitarianism, sympathy with Martin's principles should not obscure the contradictions of recruiting brain surgeons and

Olympic athletes on the basis of democratic rather than Platonic assumptions.

It is clear that Martin does not clearly face the problems raised by the existence of differing innate characteristics. In fact, her chief example, designed to buttress her case against the same education for both sexes, contains a fatal flaw. Her discussion presupposes familiarity with current psychological and educational research. Modern educators have shown that there are varying methods of teaching basic mathematical, verbal, even musical and drawing skills. Such methods will produce a degree of proficiency, despite differing abilities. Martin chooses to discuss proficiency at the game of tennis. But it is not proficiency at which Plato aims, but the highest possible degree of skill. And therein lies the rub.

Martin explains that a tennis instructor will tell students to watch his racquet in order to learn how to serve the ball. But she confesses that since she is not visually oriented, the instructor's method will improve the serve of her colleagues, but will have no effect on her own. It is only when the instructor analyzes the serving motion verbally, introduces a meaningful metaphor or actually takes her arm and puts it through the correct motions, that her game will equal that of the others. She thinks that although some of the "fast learners" have more aptitude for the game, it is not true that all of those whose serve is improved quickly by the visual method actually have more innate aptitude. "Where education is concerned natural talent is only part of the story."[110] But in my view, this is wishful thinking if what you are trying to do is to produce superior tennis players. For the best tennis players must have visual acuity; they must be able to learn orally, kinesthetically, *and* visually. Extra effort and high motivation, as well as varying training methods, may produce the outstanding, superior competitor who has all those benefits *plus* the natural ability to learn easily by any method. Without the natural advantage of the ability to learn visually, I fear Martin will never make the guardian-class tennis players!

Unfortunately, although Martin has told us that she opposes Plato's "Production Model of Education," she has not made clear what she herself considers the purpose of education to be. Nor has she offered any arguments to refute Plato's idea that only the best must rule. We can probably assume, however, that in so far as she is interested in a just state, she would be satisfied with producing "good enough" citizens.[111] If, however, excellence or superiority is what one seeks, the use of tennis as a paradigm carries great dangers for a feminist. The problem is not only one of discrepancies in natural ability which may include learning styles (which, in turn, may or may not be themselves "natural.") Nor is it the handicap Martin mentions of some female players' difficulties in acquiring serving skills because of their inadequate practice in throwing balls. This obstacle has been overcome, and many women now throw balls competently and can beat many men in many sports.[112] But no alterations in educational methods can successfully compensate for the fact that tennis also requires physical strength and upper arm development. And this would seem to be the sticking point.

The evidence that the surge of testosterone at puberty produces the specific male physique with its greater muscle mass and upper arm strength seems incontrovertible. The ideal tennis player then must have overcome any personal obstacles and be visually and kinesthetically acute. And although I am doubtful that Martin can currently assess the presence and precise degree of natural ability in herself and others, let us grant that the best players must have superior aptitude for the game. But part of this aptitude, no matter how you construe it, must include great strength. This is undoubtedly why the top male players repeatedly defeat the top female contenders and few would deny that they will continue to do so.

This is precisely Plato's view of the differences between women and men in all activities. If all functions *were* like the game of tennis, then his view that men are inevitably better at all pursuits, even though some women can do them very well, would indeed hold universally. The point made by some commentators that specific females might still excel even under Plato's class inclusion model, would not even apply. If life *were* like tennis or football, then there very well might not be enough women to go around to comprise the partners for the guardians.

At least Martin bases her account on a sounder interpretation of *physis*. She refers to Socrates' assumption that for all pursuits a person has a natural aptitude which is both "fixed and unchanging" and also capable of being developed (or thwarted) over time. She seems to accept this Platonic view when she asserts that, although she does not learn quickly visually, she nevertheless has as much aptitude for the game as some of the fast learners. I am not myself so sanguine that such convictions can be translated into the language of verification of our modern scientific world view.

One final objection remains to be made to Martin's evaluation of *Republic,* V. In her praiseworthy eagerness to promote an end to sex stereotyping in our own society, she underestimates the revolutionary character of Plato's ideas about what she calls "socialization." Martin is not satisfied that Plato's abolition of the family will eliminate differential socialization. Her disapproval of the "genderization of traits" prevalent today clouds her vision of how different the values of the *Republic* were to those of the Athens of Plato's time.

For the purposes of changing our images of male and female characteristics, Martin believes that Plato's provisions for censorship do not go far enough. She says that aggression in females might still be differentially valued. But the image of Spartan women riding to war was admired by the Platonic circle. Furthermore, gentleness is to be a valued attribute of all guardians, and the very nature of the philosopher is to be a lover of beauty. The description of the true lover of wisdom in the *Symposium* and elsewhere is hardly the macho image of the ruthless businessman or philandering athlete she fears. Plato's choice of desirable human characteristics and his ideal of "manhood," though still more bound up with physical courage and ability in war than we might desire, nevertheless differ markedly from those of the mass of mankind throughout history. They are far from those of the Americans who have provided the data she quotes to show "the genderization of traits."[113]

Because Plato himself is aware that his proposals are shocking, he finds it necessary to convince his audience that recommendations like naked physical exercise for females will at first seem laughable. But they must see beyond the conventional and realize that what promotes society's goals is in the end beneficial. And that is why children in the city will be sent away so that completely new rearing and education, new forms of what we now call socialization can occur. The guardians will then take over: "[T]hey will rear them—far away from those dispositions they now have from their parents—in their own manners and laws. . . ."[114] And we must remember that in striking contrast to current practice, the creators of the manners and the laws will be both males and females working together. Women will be equally responsible for formulating and enforcing the laws and establishing which traits are to be valued.

Martin's thesis, that Plato's educational reforms may not produce the results modern feminists desire and will involve a "masculine mold" of education, has two drawbacks. First, her efforts to update Plato are likely to distract from the value of what the philosopher actually said. And in addressing the modern issue, she may shift the focus from what I believe is the most important aim, that of planning for, as one female primatologist put it, "getting the job done."[115] This was Plato's goal, and I consider it still uppermost. In my view, if the traits required for a desired result happen to be those historically valued as "masculine," it is more important to re-evaluate them as "human" than to try to change or eliminate them. Undoubtedly, some of the traits Plato valued are inappropriate for our democratic society. But even in modern terms, for many reasons, including the importance of cooperativeness, it is inaccurate to describe his philosopher-ruler as cast in a "masculine mold." Plato's primary aim, the loving pursuit of reason, was then, and seems to me still, to be a truly androgynous goal.

DOWN WITH PLATO—DOWN WITH THE LIFE OF REASON: THE FAMILY AND NEW THEORIES OF WOMEN'S SPECIAL VIRTUES

In Jean Elshtain's book on women in social and political thought, she includes a section entitled "Divine Plato, Down to Earth."[116] In it, she denounces Plato with sarcasm and vituperation for his excessive rationalism.[117] Her discussion is lively and provocative, clearly deeply felt rather than an academic exercise. She enters the debate as if she were arguing with a contemporary opponent.

By stating her case forcefully, she reinforces the vital nature of the questions and invites her audience to participate in an ongoing discourse.

Before considering her view of the *Republic* and her suspicion of reason, I wish first to call attention to the pronouncedly a-historical character of her scholarship. Despite her strong protests to the contrary and her avowed aim of judging individuals and issues in their historical context, she often isolates Plato's thought from the philosophical problems of the day. She does not mention the major commentators of the last hundred years, nor give credit to those who have already raised all these issues, which she discusses in a tone of debunking discovery. As I have mentioned previously, many current feminist commentators exhibit this same lack of reference to their fellow workers in the field.

Elshtain also displays a certain hubris. She tells us, for example, that Plato just did not have the "conceptual adequacy" to deal with the concept of human nature.[118] Whereas some writers have declared that it is impossible to determine what is or isn't "natural," others have suggested that Plato had a coherent concept of nature, but nevertheless reached the wrong conclusions about women's nature. Still others have told us what he should have meant by nature on the basis of consistency with his own premises, but Elshtain is the first to suggest that he was simply inadequate to the task.

The a-historicism of her approach is apparent in the fact that, although she quotes or refers to over fifteen secondary sources who have commented on Plato or whose comments can be applied to Plato in her text of over twenty pages, not one of these sources is a classicist, philosopher, political scientist, or other thinker *writing prior to 1967*. That is, in making use of the thought of others, she neglects the vast amount of earlier scholarship that might shed light on the problems she discusses, referring only to that published in the fourteen years prior to her work.[119] There is one exception to what might be considered this short-sightedness. She does mention Freud in a footnote, suggesting that Plato may have been one of those the psychologist had in mind when he observed that philosophy frequently "goes astray in its method by overestimating the epistemological value of our logical operations."[120] This speculation on what Freud might have had in mind is not convincing if we refer to what Freud actually wrote about Plato. The founder of psychoanalysis greatly admired Plato, and, unlike Elshtain, valued him as a forerunner in the recognition of the power of hidden emotions and the presence of psychic conflict.[121]

Elshtain's general tone is of one bent on dethroning a figure too slavishly worshipped, despite the fact that she expects that there will be feminist readers who do not believe that "patriarchal theorists" should be given the sympathetic consideration she presumably intends.[122] But in order to maintain this view of general adulation, she must omit entirely the great disrepute Plato fell into after World War II. She seems unaware of Fite's condemnation of Plato's homosexuality and "the Platonic legend" in general, and does not even mention Popper's notorious attack on him as an enemy of the open society. Almost forty years earlier, in his frequently reprinted *History of Western Philosophy*, Bertrand Russell derided Plato's totalitarianism.[123] Since then, there have been many who have attacked Plato as authoritarian and elitist, as well as many who have come to his defense. Most feminist scholarship is a continuation of this tradition of attack and defense; and even the search for unconscious motives has been present for a long time.[124] The idea that Plato remains on a pedestal simply does not square with the facts.

Elshtain, however, sees herself as setting Plato's "feminist defenders" straight, though she would be hard put to find a single writer of the last ten years who is not well aware of the presence of anti-female sentiments in his work. At least half a dozen writers, as we have seen, make the pointing out of this misogyny their central concern, though Elshtain does not allude to this fact.

Take, for example, the controversy we have discussed over the use of *koinōnia* in Plato's statement that the guardians will have all things in common, including wives. She assumes this to be the quintessence of the Platonic position, without considering the total discussion or the use of the concept in the Athens of the time. Taking the translation as unproblematic, she insists that what Plato really meant, despite any internal evidence to the contrary, was that women were to continue to be the property of men. Neglecting the articles written dealing with the intricacies of Greek usage, she offers the Pomeroy position as if it were original and makes no attempt to explain any apparent contradiction.[125] She fails to put the question in terms of the language and customs of the time. Nor does she give any credit to those who, in far greater depth, have already explored the territory she covers. Much of Elshtain's lack of sympathy comes from her mistrust of reason; she warns against the consequences of overvaluing "rational thought, dear to the heart of Western philosophy."[126] Along with what is by now the standard opposition to Plato's "intellectualism," Elshtain fosters what I consider an even more alarming tendency. There is in some current feminist thought an attempt to polarize male and female ways of being, suggesting that women are primarily concerned with care, responsibility and attention to relationships, while cold, abstract, logical reasoning and concern with universal principles is the male mode.

In Elshtain's case, this de-emphasis of reason is accompanied by a search for emotional, i.e., unconscious in the psychoanalytic sense, motives for Platonic doctrines. Thus, although she professes herself to be against reductionism, her repeated descriptions of politics as a "defense" and of Greek, particularly Platonic misogyny as based on "fear of Mother," are specifically designed to reduce the importance of Plato's conclusions.[127]

Elshtain deplores not only Plato's continued search for the unchanging, but she resents even more his devaluing of everyday affairs, which she sees as directed more against women than men. Her own conclusions on the public and the private, the point toward which all her researches into women in social and political thought have been converging, are diametrically opposed. Her view is what she herself terms "a perverse version of the Platonic epistemology." She describes herself as "calling for the redemption of everyday life."[128] It is not easy to ascertain precisely what she means given the difficulties of her telescoped and imprecise phraseology.[129] But it is clear that she agrees with the view that a major concern of feminists must be "caring about what seems to be of no importance, to be the insignificant, . . . the well-known, the familiar" details that make up human private lives.[130] Evidently these, rather than any abstract principles, nor what current psychologists call peak moments, the trances and visions and mythological meanings that lead Socrates to transcendence, must be the starting point of political theory. In fact, they turn out not only to be the starting point. At base, the individual concrete experiences of women, which she accuses feminists of having heretofore neglected and which must be taken into consideration when deciding as Socrates would say "how we are to live," assume major importance. For Elshtain they become the chief value of her entire world view, or as she puts it "epistemology." Whereas Plato is searching for what she calls "Extralinguistic Truth," she is searching for some infinite variety of meanings that come out of dialogue like that of the psychoanalytic encounter whose truth, she tells us, is "created" in the encounter.[131]

Reason is characterized repeatedly as "cold," exercises in formal logic are contrasted with lived meanings. The purported enemy is always "the absolute, the universal." But Elshtain is not the first thinker to find it difficult to maintain such a position consistently. She recognizes that in writing political theory others will charge her with employing abstractions. Clearly, she herself cannot escape some acceptance of that quest for a "one in many" that Plato taught us to undertake. Nevertheless, Elshtain both rejects the Platonic emphasis on the rational and the conceptual, and deplores the liberal and "liberal feminist" belief in "abstract individuals."[132]

But she is in the trap of the Cretan who protests that all Cretans are liars. A political theorist, anyone who writes books, even, in the last analysis, anyone who uses language, is dependent on reason. Humans, she tells us, are not distinguished by their capacity to reason, but by "their imperative to create and find meaning."[133] Let us leave aside the epistemological distinctions between "creating" and "finding"—that is, between making what has not existed and discovering what is already there—with which she does not deal and which might, if developed further, vitiate her anti-rationalism. Here, the important point is that Elshtain writes as if you could have meaning without truth and a criterion of truth. In another place, she offers, almost parenthetically, a criterion for sound political theory, speaking of internal consistency and coherence. It is as if an adherent to a "Coherence," rather than a "Correspondence Theory of Truth," could eschew the workings of reason. In actuality, any criterion for the truth of theory requires concepts, words that name those concepts that can be used by many to describe what is the same in many instances, many experiences, many private lives.

Thus, Elshtain emphasizes the aspect of Plato she sees as most dangerous, the Plato for whom differences between individuals do not ultimately make a difference. She sets herself in opposition, particularly so, one presumes, from her vantage point as a woman, a mother-scholar, to Plato's eternal forms. She rejects those other aspects of the Platonic corpus, embraced by many who have read and been inspired not only by the reasoning, but by the dramatic and lyrical force of the dialogues. She fails to appreciate Plato's skill in creating concrete characters; the aging Cephalus, the drunken Alkibiades, even the rounded portrait of the snub-nosed, barefoot seeker after Truth, his beloved teacher, Socrates. She finds only that Plato is wrong about the value of the life of the mind. She denounces his call for participation in what is everywhere the same and the source of certainty, that search which has always characterized religious thought.

To this one-sided, incomplete picture of rationalistic abstractions, she opposes an equally one-sided construction of her own. The view presented by Elshtain and others, whom she quotes approvingly, is that it is not reason, but care, concern, connection, embodied private existence that is important and valuable. Furthermore, Elshtain obfuscates the issue by telling us that it is also "interesting." Diversity and conflict are what provide interest. Plato's ideal republic, in eliminating these, will be "joyless and tedious."[134] Although she contradicts herself at various points, there is a sub-theme that because what is different about people—their biological distinctions and personal connections—is what is interesting about them, maintaining these differences is therefore a positive good. Presumably, she would not want to retain class distinctions, divisions between the rich and the poor, because they, too, are interesting. (Tolstoy begins *Anna Karenina* with the idea that all happy families are happy in the same way, and each unhappy family is unhappy in a different way. This makes the latter more interesting, no doubt, but neither she nor Tolstoy would argue for the perpetuation of unhappy families.)

It is interesting diversity, rather than the Platonic emphasis on the examined life, that Elshtain values. She scathingly attacks "liberal dualisms" in this book and elsewhere, rejecting distinctions between mind and body.[135] But nevertheless, though she presumably would deny it, it is a surprisingly "liberal" emergence of diverse opinions in the free marketplace of ideas that turns out to be a major value. In fact, it is the vision of many concrete experiences of individual women in myriad private households that must be the cornerstone of feminist theory. The incorporation of diapers and diversity into a total view of the relationship between the public and the private is the theoretical aim which she opposes to what she sees as Plato's "social engineering."

Another of her chief complaints about Plato enters here. It is not only his emphasis on abstract reason, but his abolition of the family, that she denounces. Here again, she is caught in a dilemma of her own making. Having disavowed abstractions, she is forced to talk about "the family" which has existed transculturally. She writes: "What we call human capacities could not exist outside a familiar mode; for human beings to flourish a particular *ideal* of the family is necessary. . . . [T]he family's status as a moral imperative derives from its *universal,* pan-cultural existence in all known past and present societies" (*my emphasis*).[136] She even quotes Stuart Hampshire's view that "language constitutes the essence of man as a species" and it is the family setting that humanizes him. How surprisingly Platonic to hear her talk of the *ideal* family!

Although she is aware that some will object that what has always been is not necessarily beneficial, she proceeds to build her argument against those who would change family arrangements on the basis of the fact that to be human is to have a family. Theorizing, she thinks, must focus on our current concept of the family as an ideal. Nor should we be swayed by any of the evidence that a large number of Americans, at any rate, no longer live in a nuclear family, evidence which she considers skewed. Families are undeniably preferable to any communal alternatives. This is undoubtedly one of the chief reasons that she is so unwilling to give Plato any credit at all for the suggestions in the *Republic* that others have seen as alarmingly or happily egalitarian.

Plato's abolition of the family is disastrous. She is as sure as

Bloom that the philosopher did not have women's welfare in mind. In fact, she adopts, again without crediting him, though she is clearly familiar with his writing on the subject, the *exact* view of Bloom. Plato only included women among the guardians because he needed them for their reproductive function, not because he genuinely entertained the possibility of their having the same natures as men. She even goes further than Bloom in imagining that the women would soon realize this themselves.[137] For reasons of his own, Plato mistakenly wanted to change basic family patterns. She brings the force of selective psychoanalytic thinking on early childhood attachments to show that we violate at our peril the mother-child bond which is crucial—and presumably always has been crucial—to developing a secure, empathic adult citizen. Children of the American communes of the 1960s make bad citizens presumably because of the inherent impossibility of communal child care. Likewise, children of the kibbutz supply an inordinate number of army officers, which, needless to say, is not seen as an admirable devotion to the general welfare.

Most disturbing of all in this anti-communal diatribe is the fact that even the day care arrangements advocated by the most moderate of feminists turn out to be fraught with menace.

> To advocate and provide full-time public day care for children from the age of two (or younger) would allow some women to stride full-time into the public arena much sooner than if they had to wait until their children reached school age, but the take-over of child-rearing by public institutions would also denude the private sphere of its central raison d'etre and chief source of human emotion and value.[138]

For one who espouses diversity, this is a curious devaluing of the variety of private arrangements that exist and have existed in human lives, including the lives of those who bore no children or whose pre-school age children occupied less than one-tenth of their life spans. Now that human life expectancy is more than seventy years, the idea that *no private life* can meaningfully exist apart from a specific type of early child connection and rearing, seems at best unsubstantiated.

Just as Elshtain sees politics as a "defense" against the lure of the private, those who rail against reason and against Plato's and some recent feminists' undervaluing of the family might be seen psychoanalytically as a defense against the genuine lure of hard thought. One could speak of the temptation to neglect one's family that must be overcome by many modern scholars. Women still teaching in predominantly male establishments often feel the conflict between family and public duties more acutely and might well need to guard ("defend") against a desire to minimize family concerns. All such speculations, however, particularly when unsupported by biographical information and actual associations, shed very little light on the validity of a position.

Part of a defense against the lure of the world of work is a syndrome that might be characterized as "whistling in the dark" or the "Sour Grapes School of Female Differences," which I touched on in my introduction. The position is not unlike the condescending theory of "special excellences," which earlier Plato scholars have used to justify the exclusion of women from politics. It, however, is intended as a feminist argument and proceeds slightly differently. The discussion of Carol Gilligan's version of women's differences will take us somewhat afield from interpretations of the *Republic* and anticipate the conclusions in my final chapter on the continuing vitality of the questions Plato raised. But it is important to discuss her argument here, because it is currently influential in feminist circles and is quoted approvingly by Elshtain.

On the basis of her psychological research, Gilligan describes what she considers the "different voices" of male and female thinking about morality. She attempts to establish that women take the feelings of others into account and act so as to maintain relationships and social networks, whereas men do not. Females, she believes, employ "a moral language profoundly at odds with formal, abstract models of morality defined in terms of absolute principles."[139] To Elshtain's credit, she does see the implications of such a conclusion, rather than remaining with Gilligan's presumed view that these voices are merely "different." Commenting on an earlier article which appeared before Gilligan's book-length study, Elshtain urges, "*if* it is the case that women have a distinct moral language," then we must preserve that private sphere that makes such a morality possible and *"extend its imperatives to men"* (*my emphasis*).[140]

Officially, Gilligan tables the question of the origins of these alleged differences in moral reasoning. She says that she is making no claims about either the origins of the differences nor their distribution in a wider population, across cultures, or through time. She is aware that these differences arise in a social context, "where factors of social status and power combine with reproductive biology to shape the experience of males and females." The origins of the greater sense of connectedness that she finds in her interviews with women discussing both hypothetical moral dilemmas and actual decisions about abortions might then be solely cultural, but she does not stress this. Instead, despite her disclaimer, there is some sense throughout the book that "reproductive biology" may be crucial, that the distinction is so pervasive that more than socialization is surely at work. For example, she believes the fact that the female does not have a primary task of separating herself from her mother since her body and biological role will be identical, plays a decisive role in shaping female morality. The developmental task of separation-individuation that leads men to think in terms of individual achievement is different because of this body-based difference.[141]

Whatever the reasons that women deviate from a standard model of ethical thought founded on abstract justice and rule-following, the feminine mode is different, more empathic, and compassionate. Gilligan finds women's truths "contextual," rather than abstract. What she neglects is the fact that, even if we assume that in making moral decisions many factors in a given context must be considered (factors which are peculiar to each individual situation and include the feelings of the agents), some decisions are *better* than others in that context. And what makes them better is an objective matter. In other words, contextual relativism in ethics must be distinguished from subjective relativism. Gilligan would not wish to advocate that all thinking about morality is equally valid, that "right you are if you think you are," or even, like twentieth-century emotivists, that there can be no genuine moral judgments but merely expressions of preference. She clearly thinks that women do well to consider feelings and the furthering of relationships. If this is the case, then some "abstract" standard of truth is involved. Contextualism in ethics involves logic just as any thinking or "moral reasoning" does. If there is such a thing as "maternal thinking," as Elshtain suggests, then it leads to correct decisions based on factors neglected by non-mothers, but used logically as premises to support a conclusion. Otherwise, it is not thinking.

In my view, Gilligan has in fact set up a "straw person" in her contention that previous ethical thought has been based on a sex-linked concept of right action. Her criticisms may have some validity in connection with the contemporary developmental theory of Erikson and Kohlberg, whom she specifically attacks.[142] But what of the Biblical injunction, also presumably devised by males, to "Love thy neighbor"? The morality of Jesus, which emphasizes care and concern for the least of humans, for the one sinner who strays from the flock and is more important than the entire herd, is also morality devised and promulgated by men. The Roman injunction that *"summa ius, summa inuriam,"* that following the law slavishly can be harmful and morally wrong, is a male position as well. The very phrase Gilligan uses to describe the female as opposed to the male mode of thinking about morality, "justice tempered with mercy," is an ideal invented by men. The *"Eyl maleh rachamim,"* "God filled with compassion," is as powerful an impulse in Judaism as is the rule-following an "eye for an eye"— supposedly "male" thinking, exemplified in other passages on the Biblical Jehovah.

Gilligan also neglects twentieth-century existentialist statements about morality. Although invented by men, it is a morality based strongly on care, on what Heidegger calls *Mit-sein,* or being-with. It involves evaluating each existential situation on its individual merits and is about as "contextualist" an ethic imaginable. In the version of Martin Buber, the I-Thou connection must be the main consideration in all choices. Thus, for atheist existentialists like Sartre, Catholic thinkers like Marcel, and Jewish existentialist moralists, all male, care and concern for others always take precedence over rationality and any abstract sense of justice that supposedly characterizes the male mode.

It is the idea of a hierarchy of moral values that both Gilligan and Elshtain reject. In discussing the responses of eleven-year-old boys and girls to moral questions, Gilligan emphasizes that we should not "scale differences from better to worse."[143] But, although Elshtain, like Gilligan, is in principle against hierarchies, she sees that a value system including considerations of responsibility rather than rights alone must be extended to men, i.e., is preferable.

Thus, in the end value judgments must be made, and some kind of hierarchical order cannot be avoided. It would seem that a morality which includes a synthesis of logic and concern for others' feelings is in some sense "higher." It is not simply a matter of a different voice. If women have fears of achievement because it involves isolation or an unwanted standing out, such fears must be alleviated. Either the society must be changed so that women do not end up any more isolated than men, or women must be ready on occasion to choose isolation or personal loneliness for the sake of realizing their ambitions and developing their gifts to the highest degree possible.

To my mind, no studies to date conclusively prove that women are in fact always more likely to take the feelings of others into consideration when thinking about moral issues. But even if this were to be convincingly demonstrated, the reasons cannot be shown to be biological. Further, I consider thinking in general a human, not a male trait; there is no reason to undervalue it, nor to characterize a particular kind of thinking as "maternal." And if women are or have been less effective at logical reasoning, then it would be better to socialize them so that any such discrepancy was eliminated. It would also be equally crucial to educate males to include emotional factors and the maintenance of human connections in the principles they use in ethical thinking.

To return to Elshtain's interpretation of Plato, I want to say a word here about her use of what she calls "depth psychology" to explain away much of what Plato says, as well as to show the importance of the emotional as against the rational in philosophical thought. Elshtain's approach is to "look for clues" in the writing of all her political theorists that they are fending off some idea, fear, or desire they find incompatible with their self-concept, or their vision for society, or their understanding of the world.[144] Unlike Bennett Simon, Elshtain only hints darkly about what Plato's motives for eliminating private life for the guardians must have been.[145] But evidently, her view is that Freud has taught us to see metaphysical systems as "defenses" against perceived threats and dangers.[146] In my own view, an equally important use of Freud is as a reinforcement of the importance of reason, of the search for a rational method to understand what otherwise appears to be irrational behavior.

Elshtain wants to exonerate the true Freud from those feminists who have vilified him. But just as I have tried to show the many contradictions in Plato so that there can be no "true Plato", so, too, there is no true Freud. However, Elshtain's very undertaking of such an enterprise is further evidence of the power of the Platonic model. Like so many other theorists, she still searches for what a body of work "really means." One can find in Freud numerous statements about the importance of the emotions, the irrational, what has come to be called "being in touch with your feelings." There is no doubt that one can also find a devaluation of the female, despite Elshtain's attempts to ignore this aspect.

There is clearly a strain in Freud that advocates what Gilligan describes as a male model of morality. Elshtain does not mention the Freud who considers genuine conscience and the ability to make just and impartial decisions as having their roots in castration fear. Since women, for him, are in a sense already castrated, they do not have this need to internalize authority. Freud therefore believes, unlike Plato, that women's relation to justice will inevitably be different.[147] Although the Freudian theories that Elshtain values are those that emphasize the importance of bodily difference, presumably she does not champion this particular instance of that emphasis.

Surprisingly, however, she does quote approvingly the fact that, although Freud knew the truth about the symptoms of one of his female patients, he decided it would be unwise to enlighten her. She was married to an unsympathetic husband and burdened with marital and parental responsibilities. Since Freud believed the woman to be objectively constrained by her economic and emotional dependency on her husband, he "found it better to allow the woman her 'escape into illness' than to confront her with the self-serving nature of her periodic incapacity."[148]

Elshtain finds this a model worthy of emulation. Freud's example is one we should follow in listening to the voices of women today, in treading carefully before we attempt to rid them of their illusions, even illusions fostered by commerical interests encouraging them to spend time and money to increase their seductiveness.[149] No doubt Elshtain's motives for not wanting to disturb the lives of the mass of women, who she thinks are unlikely to attain most of the goals fostered by the women's movement, are sincere. Her aim is the genuine one of avoiding the inflicting of unnecessary pain. But in my own view, fostering such "paternalism," or perhaps in this case, "maternalism," rather than taking on the Socratic task of shaking people from their complacency, is more harmful in the long run.

What makes her advocacy of protecting women's illusions particularly surprising is that she condemns Plato most strongly of all for a similar belief. In the *Republic,* Plato tells us that the mass of mankind need their illusions and therefore the guardians must invent stories that will keep them from knowing the truth. Her vociferous condemnation of Plato does not acknowledge the fact that the matter of when to reveal and when to conceal the truth is not always such an easy decision to make. My own view is that in the long run, truth-telling—seeing the good, formulating it rationally, and relating what one believes—will bring more value into the world.

This presumes the environmentalism and some version of that ultilitarianism she deplores, a utilitarianism characteristic of the currently out-of-favor liberal view. It assumes that, even if individuals are not blank tablets (as Elshtain wishes to convince us), they can nevertheless be taught to recognize the truth, as Socrates believed they could. For Freud to decide beforehand to deny his patient the possibility of seeing the meaning of her illness and perhaps finding an alternative, despite her limited options, does not seem praiseworthy. At the very least, it would seem Freud might have offered his patient the opportunity to refuse to accept his truth with all the force of that human capacity for denial that Freud himself made us aware of. Neither the Plato of the Noble Lie, nor Freud, nor Elshtain have sufficient faith perhaps in that poster slogan, "The truth shall make you free although first it will make you miserable."

Thus, one can stress many different aspects of Freud. But there is certainly a dominant strain which advocates reason-infused-with-feeling as the best basis of human choice. Plato, too, is an advocate of what Georges Grube calls "intellect . . . vivified by a stream of deep emotion." I agree that the third and fourth books of the *Republic* present us with a picture of human functioning such that "the accusation of anti-emotionalism, or at least of cold intellectualism so often levelled against Plato no longer holds."[150] In discussing Plato's theories on the nature of the soul, Grube concludes, "[W]e have here a carefully propounded psychological theory which combines the uncompromising intellectualism of the *Phaedo* with the magnificent defense of emotion which is the *Symposium.*"[151]

A proper understanding of Plato, as has often been pointed out, includes the realization that his belief that "knowledge is virtue" is not the naive intellectualism of one who blindly assumed that abstract knowledge of morality would automatically produce moral behavior. Freud admired Plato precisely because the Greek philosopher was aware of the subterranean force of feelings and because his concept of knowledge involved what today would be called authentic "insight." It is only when we genuinely understand what is right, what is the best life we can live, what is in fact in our self-interest in the long run—only when we know it with the combined force of thought and feeling, that we will behave morally. Isn't this the therapeutic goal of that psychoanalytic encounter Elshtain values? The aim of psychoanalytic practice can be seen as the attainment of insight, the fusion of knowing and feeling, that enables us to behave as our best selves. And this was also Plato's goal. To see him as a thoroughgoing rationalist committed only to abstract principle, is to misconstrue his purpose and undervalue his contribution.

HOW IMPORTANT IS THE BODY?
HOMOEROTICISM, HUMAN NATURE, AND ANDROGYNY

Many feminist commentators deplore the atmosphere of Plato's famous and eloquent dialogue on the nature of love, the *Symposium*. Elshtain takes the extreme position that this dialogue shows that Platonic metaphysics *in its very nature* excludes women.[152] The passage advocating equality in the *Republic* cannot possibly be taken seriously because the ambience in which Platonic theory was developed was one in which women did not, or even could not, participate. Even though *hetarai* did on occasion participate in male conversation in classical Athens, and although a few women probably attended Plato's Academy, Elshtain is clearly correct that there are no women present at the symposia or other events described in the dialogues. The atmosphere was indeed generally uncongenial to women.

There is no doubt that one of the ways Plato uses to show the path to his eternal Forms is through the use of that erotic feeling that his male listeners felt for the beauty of other males. But Elshtain misunderstands both Plato and K. J. Dover, whom she quotes in this context. In my view, she is mistaken in her belief that homoeroticism is the only, or the chief, or in any sense, an essential element in the doctrine itself.

She writes:

> The good man . . . comes into being through a process of private speech from which women . . . are excluded. . . . His debarment of women from the search for wisdom can be explained both by the social milieu within which the search occurred, including its sanctioned homoerotic attachments between older and younger men, as well as the particular *nature* of the truth at which Plato aimed. That is, a particular homosexual ethos . . . fused with what we call the Platonic metaphysic.[153]

Elshtain actually goes so far as to say that the *process* of reaching the Forms, as she puts it, "infected" the substantive conclusions.[154] But surely generations of neo-Platonists, modern Platonists, and advocates of various aspects of Plato's metaphysics, epistemology, and ethics have seen themselves as followers of a doctrine essentially separable from the "infection" of Athenian homosexual practice.

It is not my intention to underplay, as other commentators frequently have, Plato's use of homoerotic attraction as a method of making the search for ideal prototypes of earthly particulars intelligible. But Dover describes the situation accurately and incisively when he says that Plato *exploited* the homosexual ethos for his own purposes. Contrary to Elshtain's interpretation, Dover concludes that, although the sexual behavior of fifth-century Athenians influenced the *form* in which Socratic philosophy was realized, it did not influence its basic assumptions.[155] In other words, the existence of a world of Being, the accessibility of that world to reason, and its dependence upon Good are *not* dependent on the homosexual ethos.

It is true that in the Socratic ambience, intense eros was experienced more often in homosexual than in heterosexual relationships. Such attractions also made more sense as instances of the desirability of restraint from bodily gratification. Dover reminds us with that combination of scholarly mastery and common-sensical detachment that is characteristic of his work, that "it was after all the prescribed role of women to be inseminated," whereas popular sentiment romanticized and applauded the chastity of an *erōmenos* and the devotedly unselfish *erastēs*.[156] Plato's main point is that true eros is not a desire for bodily contact, but rather "a love of moral and intellectual excellence."[157] If there is in fact a special applicability of the analogy between a man's love of one *like him*, but more beautiful, to the idea of the attraction of beauty in its purest state, Elshtain's conclusions still do not necessarily follow. For one could then effectively substitute the unconsummated attraction of a woman for another woman to approximate his meaning. This was evidently done by literary women in the eighteenth century, who based their theories of friendship for each other on what they considered the Platonic ideal. And, of course, heterosexual eros has often been seen as a stage on the path to higher beauty. As Erich Segal reminds us, there is a distinct parallel in Dante's love for Beatrice, a love which inspires his ascent from worldly error to the pure light of Paradise.[158]

Surely anyone, regardless of gender, can understand the erotic attraction of ideas. Bertolt Brecht has his Galileo say he loves "old wine and new ideas," reminding us of the sensual excitement of intellectual activity. But here again, Elshtain does not attempt to understand Plato, but rather to discredit him, to disenthrall Plato's feminist defenders.

To accomplish this end, she uses any ammunition she can muster, and even makes an error in her reference to one passage in the *Symposium* to demonstrate Plato's incorrigible misogyny.

Her accusation is that Plato speaks of the heavenly Aphrodite, inspirer of sacred love, as having no female strain in her; practitioners of such love value the male sex as stronger and more intelligent.[159] But this is not Plato (or his spokesman, Socrates) talking at all. The mythic description is offered by the notorious homosexual Pausanius from whom one would expect exactly such a speech. One of the major points of the *Symposium* is that the speakers preceding Socrates do not have the true picture of love. Even if we assume that Socrates does not see his own speech as directly contradicting each of the others, but grant that there is meant to be some validity in each of the preceding versions, it is still a distortion to assume that every voice in a dramatic dialogue represents the author.[160] In her eagerness to show Plato guilty of even more than the ordinary Greek misogyny, she distorts what Plato actually said so as to invalidate the passage on equality in Book V. Although we need not be enthralled by his granting the best women a place along with the best men, one must take greater care in any attempt not only to knock Plato from his pedestal, but to grind him to the ground.

As we have noted, Elshtain is not alone in objecting to the homoerotic atmosphere of the dialogues, and it is important to understand the anger generated in many contemporary feminists by their feeling of being excluded. Wender's objectivity toward the fact that Plato did not like women although he favored their emancipation is unusual. In my view, further analysis of the precise connections between homoeroticism and misogyny are more useful at this point than outrage.

These connections are not clear-cut. Through the centuries, some homosexual males, but surely not all, have combined their sexual preferences with a distaste for women and a general disparaging of their capacities. The question of whether homosexual males are more guilty of anti-female attitudes and exclusionary practices than heterosexuals is an empirical one that we do not have the data necessary to answer. From my study of Plato commentary, it should be clear at least that scholarly husbands have displayed a goodly share of misogyny, while Plato himself, though partial to young boys and wifeless, did suggest females rule equally. Plato puts the egalitarian proposals in the mouth of Socrates who, in Plato's portrayal, was constantly attracted to young boys. But the historical Socrates was also twice married and later tradition even describes him as "actively involved with women."[161] Thus, in the long run, it is not only possible, but advisable, to consider Plato's theories independent of his or Socrates' sexual preference.

It is worth pointing out that scholars particularly enthusiastic about the ideas in the *Symposium* (where being "pregnant in body only" is disparaged) have been guilty of particularly flagrant male chauvinism. I shall digress briefly from Elshtain's views to show how disparaging attitudes persist today in those inspired by Plato. For example, the classicist Thomas Gould who, in his book *Platonic Love*, makes a case for its superiority to Christian and modern Romantic Love, also makes a case for the general inferiority of women. Gould found the world in the 1960s just as much a man's world as it was in Plato's time. Artistic, scientific, and civilizing activities he judged still to be carried on, on the highest level, almost entirely by men. "In all this time there has still not appeared a great woman philosopher, mathematician, painter, composer, tragedian, or physicist—and poets, novelists, and scholars only of the second order. Nor can muscular inferiority or time lost in pregnancy and suckling really explain this fact in modern times." He tells us that we must probably assume that there is some additional difference between men and women. Although he grants that there is no evidence for a difference in intellectual ability, he is certain that "there must be something" which causes men to develop a more compelling sense than women of what he calls an "urgency in abstract standards."[162] This urgency (which he covers himself by saying, at one point, "usually" is not developed by women) is what causes personal feeling to fade by comparison and is at the root of all the major accomplishments of Western civilization.

He expects his readers to agree that "the most splendid achievements are realized in masculine society."[163] He respectfully considers Freud's theory on the anatomical explanation for women's lack of reason for internalizing authority and abstract standards, the famous castration anxiety explanation of male achievement. He believes that women are less subject to ideas of justice and patriotism and assumes that only a genetic or biological explanation will suffice. He ignores the fact that despite differential socialization throughout history, many women have professed and acted on abstract loyalties. Queen Elizabeth I was as loyal and effective a ruler as any that England has had. She clearly displayed the capacity, in Plato's terms, for "the most efficient possible pursuit of what is most worth having" for her subjects. In the twentieth century, many political opponents would insist that Indira Gandhi, Golda Meir, and Margaret Thatcher somehow seem to have internalized all too well that "threatening authority" whose wrath, according to Freud's anatomically-based theory, only men fear. Whatever the reasons, these women have been as uncompromising on abstract concepts such as national sovereignty, the imprisonment of political opponents and the undesirability of compromise with opposition parties as any men.

Furthermore, many would disagree that the highest level of accomplishment has been carried on throughout history only by men. Gould classifies George Santayana as a first-rate philosopher. But presumably George Eliot (Marian Evans) must by his standards be considered only a "second-order" novelist. The most generous conclusion to be drawn is that Gould has not made his standards clear, nor would his judgments be widely accepted. For he even seems to believe that the production of only second-rate, rather than first-rate, *scholars* is somehow genetic. Gould might convince some that poetic, painting, and musical geniuses are born, not made, and that outstanding artistic ability is carried through sex-linked genes, or is an inevitable result of physiology. But few, I think, would accept that the differences between a first-rate scholar and a lesser one can really be anatomical. Nor is his rewriting of history to show that in fact wives have not inspired men to great deeds convincing. "The will to write great novels or symphonies would have had to have been there before marriage and might just as well have been realized in celibacy," he writes.[164] Women have thus neither written great books nor been responsible for them vicariously. With such attitudes still abroad in classical studies among Plato enthusiasts, it is no wonder that Okin and Elshtain connect love in the *Symposium* with the belittling of women.

It is troubling to Gould that the view that immortality is better achieved through the production of great works than through human offspring is offered by the female Diotima. Those annoyed with Plato's homoeroticism do not even mention this fact. It is indeed hard to give a satisfactory reason for the fact that a speech on the central concept of Platonic metaphysics is pronounced by a woman, albeit a foreign and unusal one. Can it be that not only in the *Republic,* Book V, but even in the *Symposium,* Plato was not as convinced as this contemporary twentieth-century professor that women are incapable of making first-rate speeches and articulating important ideas?

Gould thinks one cannot simply substitute boy-girl or conjugal love for the erotic attraction between older male lover-and-mentor and beautiful young man. He is right about this if we consider the *Symposium* solely as literature. For to make such a substitution is to detract from the particularity of a special ethos and moment in time. But as philosophy, the appreciation of the beauty of, and passionate desire for union with, another human being can and has been used making just such a substitution. Logically speaking, erotic attraction can provide a "way in" to the Realm of Forms for all true philosophers, including the female guardians of the *Republic.*

In my view then, Elshtain is mistaken that the use of homosexual eros is a fatal infection. It is, in fact, only one device among many. It is surely of no more importance than the Allegory of the Cave which, unlike the exposition of eros, appears in the very work which claims female equality. In that allegory, both men and women are chained and both must find their way into the light of true Being.

The analogy of homosexual attraction to the relation between particulars and universals has a metaphorical function similar to the device that Wittgenstein uses to make his opposing position about the existence of universals clear. Wittgenstein uses the notion of "family resemblance" as a way of clarifying the connections between members of a class designated by the same word. He believes, contrary to Plato, that such particulars do not have a common element uniting them, do not participate in or serve as examples of any real form, but are merely a "network of overlapping relations."[165] These relations he likens to the family resemblances we observe in related individuals. This theory based on his analogy has captured philosophical imaginations as has Plato's analogy of the ascent of eros. But in the end the espousal of Wittgenstein's non-essentialist position does not depend on whether one accepts this particular analogy or not, on whether one notes that members of a family *do* have a common element, though it is not an observable feature. The theoretical position is distinguishable from the analogy used, one might say exploited, to clarify it. In the same way, Plato's metaphysic is distinguishable from the analogy used to help his listeners understand it.

The theory of ideas in fact appears in many other dialogues where it is not explicitly connected with homoeroticism. It seems wrong to say that because these other dialogues also describe an all-male atmosphere that the conclusions reached cannot be shared by women, or do not apply to, or automatically "disbar," women. If this were true, then all metaphysical or epistomological positions expounded by any philosopher in a work describing an atmosphere *sans* women would be equally suspect. Hume's skepticism and Berkeley's idealism might be seen as equally infected in substance, since their dramatic dialogues also occur in all-male atmospheres. In general, such a species of the genetic fallacy might ultimately lead us to reject all views formulated in or addressed to groups that excluded women. This would of course involve the rejection of most previous philosophical and scientific truth.

The surprising fact is that far from discrediting Plato for all time, Elshtain must rely on the very Platonic doctrines she deplores in her own ethical stance. The feminist theory she propounds in her final chapters, long after she has brought the divine Plato down to earth, involves a rejection of current ethical subjectivism. She denounces the twentieth-century separation of fact from value, basing her own "moral imperatives" solidly on her assessment of truths about human nature. Thus, without acknowledgement, she returns to the presuppositions of Plato who was perhaps the first philosopher to maintain that human beings are possessed of a fixed nature, and that it is only on the basis of this nature that we can decide how we ought to live. As we have seen, Elshtain stresses that the family is a universal element of our humanity. She finds evidence of this in reports that prehistoric man was found buried with flowers. She assumes these tributes were obviously left by family members.[166] It seems feasible to me that these tokens of the value of human life and its aesthetic significance might have been left by companions in the hunt rather than blood relatives. But the point here is that she adopts the basic premise that humans have certain *universal needs* that unite them as a species. Although, unlike Plato, this leads her to emphasize the importance of the private sphere, the relevant issue is that in this assumption of common human characteristics, she follows the lead taken by Plato.

In the context of her condemnation of him as the villain who is responsible for the Western undervaluing of our animal nature, she quotes the English philosopher Mary Midgley. Midgley, in her book *Beast and Man,* also urges an appreciation of tendencies, feelings, and behavior that we share as a common biological heritage. She advocates the rethinking of concepts used by ethologists to describe animal species, so that they can be employed for understanding human nature. But Midgley, even if she rejects Socrates' facts, sees merit in his approach. She is in general less disparaging of Plato, less eager to save us from what Elshtain calls our filiopiety. Unlike Elshtain, Midgley credits Plato with basing his morality on his idea of human nature, which is the method she also thinks we ought to follow.[167]

Midgley seems to accept that there are "natural differences of emotions" between the sexes, though she also maintains that sex-linked moralities cannot really be of much use. It is not only that their potential efficiency would be halved by the fact that fifty percent of people belong to each sex. She writes: "More important still, we all have the emotions of both sexes within us—not enough to realize them fully, but enough to need more, enough to make a single sex world a poor one for anybody."[168] She apparently finds some validity in Plato's description, taken over by many others, notably Spinoza, that pity is "womanish," whereas courage is manly. But her contention here, like my quarrel with Gilligan, is that "splitting the human race like that is not rational at all" and should not be fostered. A man without pity, she tells us, is a monster, as is a woman without courage. If there is something specifically wrong with the kind of pity normally felt by women, then it can be stated, and ought to be, in other ways than just by mentioning the sex involved.[169]

In my view, this is precisely the meaning of the passage in the

Republic on women's nature. But Midgley, despite her appreciation of Plato for wisely giving the central role in his philosophy
to the concept of the Good, objects strenuously to his arrangements for women in Book V. And it is this aspect that Elshtain
quotes approvingly. Midgley, like so many commentators before
her, finds the family arrangements proposed for the guardians
hopelessly unnatural. Although writing in the late 1970s and
clearly conversant with Freud, she does not, however, look for
unconscious motives for Plato's distortions.

She accepts that Plato hoped to get rid of private property,
"most of all in what he rightly saw as its central case," attachment to one's own family. Midgley's concern is that, although
man is indeed a political animal, he cannot possibly become
merely that. She finds that there is a natural balance of private
and public which defies distortions as extreme as Plato's. She
admits that sacrifices of the private can be made, as in religious
communities and kibbutz life. But, like the sociologists I discuss
in my final chapter, she, too, stresses that these sacrifices have
inevitable costs. Although the price can be paid, provided that
the goods secured really seem worth it to all concerned, it will be
paid with effort. The bargain, she says will need constant attention and there will be special dangers of emotional stunting and
self-deception. She believes that "natural feelings like our strong
and special affection for our children" could only be replaced with
something that would be worse.[170]

Plato, of course, was aware of the fact that sacrifices would be
involved for his rulers and knew that most people would see such
sacrifices as unbearable. His aim was to convince his listeners that
specific rewards of status and added pleasures, and ultimately the
intrinsic rewards of the philosophical life, would compensate for
the sacrifices. Midgley points out with a generosity that Elshtain
cannot muster that the experience of religious and other special-
ized communities should by now have shown us "what Plato,
when he wrote the *Republic*, could not know."[171] She believes
that the experiences of the intervening centuries have shown the
difficulties of a way of life which overrides the natural balance of
human feelings.

The violation of that balance she finds most apparent in two
features of the Platonic proposals, at which she tells us even the

most drastic reformers quail. Actually, although Bloom objects to expecting a man to feel fatherly emotions for the child he did not "engender," Midgley is unique in objecting to the provision that mothers be expected "to suckle, indiscriminately and without continuity, any baby that on any given occasion is handed to them."[172] Unlike the commentators of the previous hundred years, Midgley's vantage point as a mother may well make her particularly sensitive to this point.

Midgley shares with many other writers, as we have seen, her objections to the state's requiring citizens "to be ready to leap into sexual activity each time that the state confronts them with a breeding partner, but to be abstinent all the rest of their lives."[173] It is not clear exactly what she intends by this latter phrase, but she would surely seem to be mistaken if she forgets that Plato is providing only for what might be considered a short period of adult sexual life. It is important to recall that not only adolescents, but also older men, as well as women over forty, are free to follow their inclinations. In the end, Midgley thinks that tackling the quite tough problems of women's lives with the concept of equality is like trying to dig a garden with a brush and comb. She wishes to reconcile the idea of our having a specific nature, a capacity to do "what each of us has it in him to do," with the possibility of freedom and ameliorative social change.[174] Thus, she does not object to the use of the word "unnatural" to describe treating men and women altogether in the same way. Nor does she mind anyone saying that Plato's idea of abolishing marriage and "the family" is unnatural. She differs from those of us who find the concept of "the natural" vacuous; she finds it useful in so far as we make clear its double sense. Things, she says, can be natural in the minimal sense—widely practiced, emotionally seductive, hard to eradicate—and yet do not have to be so in the strong sense in which we are called to approve them. But will people be willing to give up the advantage of the positive connotations of calling something natural, of the emotive force of such a usage? In our modern secular society, few would be inclined to say "that practice is natural but very bad." The danger is far greater that thinkers will continue to capitalize on what Lovejoy termed "the metaphysical pathos" of words like "natural," just as Elshtain calls Plato's reforms "social engineering," but would never describe the radical changes she might propose in such terms.

Because Midgley desires a better world for all, she declares it "hard to take much interest" in the question of whether the few at the top are male or female. Understandably, she is more worried about the majority of men and women left in what they regard as outer darkness, even if all sex barriers were removed. Elshtain, on the other hand, is concerned with gender equality, but asks what woman would accept parity on Plato's terms? She believes that the vast majority of individuals, both in Plato's time and today, would prefer to remain in their unjust societies.[175] I myself am not so sure that the circumcised wife in modern Sudan or even the elderly impoverished American widow whose family lives thousands of miles away might not well prefer the life of one of Plato's female guardians to their own existence. This is not to deny the extreme nature of Plato's reforms, but only to reiterate that the family arrangements that have existed and persist in many parts of the world have surely not been any more consistent with that human flourishing that Elshtain desires. There is a certain lack of sympathy for this fact in her vituperative attack on Plato's attempt to find a more just ordering of society.

Elshtain's diatribe against Plato also includes a rejection of the mind-body split underlying his metaphysics and of his consequent devaluing of the body. In rejecting the idea that men and women do not differ in their fundamental nature, she tells us that her being a woman is the "essential and interesting bedrock" of her identity. (Presumably, a commensurate formulation is true of men, too.) She speaks of the "bio-social" and "psycho-social and sexual identity" of women that is "stripped away" in Plato's scheme.[176] Doubtless, our physiology is a component of our identity; nevertheless, at the risk of feminist and modernist heresy, I would still suggest that de-emphasizing the body has some value. One need not commit oneself to oldtime religion or repressive psychological theories to advocate less preoccupation with the body. Women have suffered for a long time from the persistent emphasis of the world's thinkers on the anatomical differences between the two sexes. The great paintings of the Renaissance show graphically the belief that the evil temptations of women's anatomy keep humankind (or men at any rate) from entering the

Kingdom of Heaven. Plato at least saw that deeply felt moral knowledge and scientific excellence were attainable regardless of one's sexual anatomy. Women have suffered greatly from being taught to focus on their bodies, enhance their physical charms, minimize their so-called anatomical imperfections, and use their bodies to barter for advantage. Even today, among the best educated women, there is alarming evidence that females continue to be more preoccupied with their bodies than males. Researchers and clinicians find female college students troubled by body-related concerns. These show up in obsessional concern with clothing, constant dieting patterns, and acute disturbances in eating behaviors. College counselors describe women as caught up in an unending struggle to reshape their bodies, change their faces, and clothe themselves in expensive and often uncomfortable clothing. One researcher notes, "This consistent societal emphasis on a woman's body leads women to use their bodies as a primary source of validation."[177]

Such negative results of emphasis on the importance of the body do not decisively prove that Plato was right to de-emphasize anatomical differences. But it does suggest that there may be some merit to Socrates' minimizing of the importance of female anatomy for his guardians. Numerous studies have concluded that, although more than half the undergraduate students in the United States today are female, women's growth in general competence and knowledge in college does not match that of men. Research shows that this is attributable at least in part to women's continued obsessions with their bodies.

Nor does Plato de-emphasize the body in the way that some feminist scholars would have us believe. Bodily excellence is a great value to Plato; it is only anatomical differences that he wishes to minimize. His program of rigorous physical activity is crucial to the development of male and female guardians alike. In contrast, today the competitive sports that colleges support to foster individual achievement and collaborative effort among men are, in the words of one educator, "only grudgingly being opened to women." An American judge, in ruling on a case of sexual discrimination in education, stated that athletic competition builds character in our boys, echoing the ancient Platonic view.

But, he adds, "We do not need that kind of character in our girls, the women of tomorrow."[178]

In my view then, Elshtain is wrong in condemning Plato so vociferously for minimizing bodily differences between individuals. Her own accentuation of diversity, spontaneity, plurality, the concrete uniqueness of the way each individual as Heidegger puts it, "stands in" the world, has merit. Nevertheless, for the task of shaping political theory, the ability to reason clearly, and use language precisely is crucial. And if we are committed to discourse, we must employ the laws of logic, laws to which one's "psychosexual identity" is ultimately irrelevant. Even for those of us who prefer the twentieth-century view shared by existential-phenomenologists and British linguistic philosophers, that we are not separable bodies and minds, but beings who as Sartre phrased it, "exist" our bodies, aspects of the Platonic view remain useful. There is still a sense in which, for the purposes of thinking, femaleness or maleness remains as she puts it contemptuously, merely "contingent."[179] Even if it could be shown that my experience of the public and private sphere will always differ from male experience, regardless of how egalitarian societies become, the fact remains that in order to understand any descriptions there must be intended meanings whose referents are the same for both sexes. Otherwise, Elshtain writes only for women, or for those who have had similar, or even somehow identical, experiences to hers.

Elshtain's attack on androgyny also seems to me mistaken. She rejects this movement toward identifying traits which have been socially stereotyped for one sex and fostering their development in the other sex. Elshtain says that although equality can be used as a political rallying cry, androgyny cannot.[180] But in fact many have already put their energies into such a movement, and we have already seen the resulting changes in social behavior even at the elementary school level in the United States, changes for which we can and must continue to agitate. Plato, as we have seen, was aware that his guardians must combine the traits of gentleness and spiritedness. Elshtain finds little value in this call for an amalgamation of traits made twenty-four hundred years ago. In my view, however, such wisdom is one of the many reasons why the text of the *Republic* has had such enduring vitality and will continue to merit admiration despite her attempts to disenthrall us.

THE PERSISTENCE OF SEXISM IN RECENT COMMENTARY

Most of the writers in the 1970s have chosen to examine the Platonic proposals primarily because they are themselves interested in the achievement of gender equality. Allan Bloom is a notable exception among them, and I shall therefore conclude my analysis of recent commentary with a discussion of his views. As a well-known classicist and translator, his chief interest is in explicating the text; and his sympathies do not lie in the direction of changing the traditional relation between the sexes or equalizing opportunity. His earlier remarks in his "Interpretive Essay" have been widely attacked. In the 1970s and 1980s, he has chosen to defend his position and even to expand and reinforce those assertions which have caused him to be repeatedly termed "sexist."

He is not only courageous in maintaining his unpopular position, but adamant in his interpretations of the text. He maintains that the consequences of Plato's assumption of the inferiority of women as a class would inevitably mean that the best women are always inferior in capacity to the best men. Recent commentators challenge this interpretation, demonstrating that Bloom's logic is fallacious. All that is implied is that on average women are less capable than men. Logically speaking, the most outstanding *individuals* could still turn out to be female.[181]

As an example to dramatize this point, I offer the biological fact that in living mammals, the class of males is on the whole larger than the class of females. However, many species do exist in which females are larger than males. Relevant to a refutation of Bloom is the fact that females are the larger sex in the blue whale, the largest species which has ever lived on earth. The biologist Katherine Ralls points out that, therefore, the largest *individual* animal was or is undoubtedly a female.[182]

Thus, the most competent individual in the *kallipolis* might well have been a female and among the best (as among the biggest) there might well be a great number of females. We have no way of knowing whether Plato thought out these implications. But at the very least there seems no reason to believe with Bloom that there wouldn't be enough females to go around if education and earliest training were identical, just as today at elite traditionally male universities we have reason to believe that if only test scores indicating scholastic ability were considered, entering classes would be at least half female. As we have seen, Bloom contends that females are needed only for their difference, for their ability to reproduce the guardian class. But this rejection of the idea that their nature warrants their participation remains unsupported.

The argument of Bloom's which receives most attention in the new commentary is his repeated insistence that the proposals are offered in jest.[183] Several writers attack this claim that in Book V, Plato is trying to outdo Aristophanes at his own game. Dale Hall attempts to prove that Bloom is wrong about the seriousness of Plato's intent, and thus about the desirability of equality for women as well as the possibility of the combination of philosophy and ruling. He charges Strauss and Bloom with pursuing an approach which is "anachronistic and unhistorical."[184] Like the other critics of Bloom, he suggests that nudity in the gymnasium is not such an absurd impossibility. Even if there is a connection between *Ecclesiazusae* and Book V, Hall finds no convincing reason to accept Bloom's speculation on a comedic rivalry. Barker's view that Plato was seeking to meet the current satire or Adam's conclusion that Plato is taking seriously Aristophanes' parody of views with which Plato himself sympathized, is every bit as plausible.[185]

An extended discussion of the probable relation between Aristophanes' *Assembly of Women* (*Ecclesiazusae*) and the implications of that connection is necessary, and I shall consider the matter shortly. First, however, it is important to refute the view of the *Republic* as irony on general grounds. I wish to cast doubt on Bloom's total account of human sexuality and its relevance to gender equality. Hall's charge that Bloom's views of gender are "anachronistic" is probably mistaken. For the proposals would undoubtedly seem as strange to fourth-century Athenians as to even the most biased of modern professors. As Bloom himself says, Socrates was well aware that he was wounding the "dearest sensibilities of masculine pride."[186] In general, however, Hall's attack is well aimed and his objection that Plato gives us no evidence that Socrates' intentions are ironic as he does in the other dialogues, is cogent.

To this, I would add other crucial objections. Bloom accuses his opponents of not paying attention to the text.[187] But if we pay close attention to the text, we must find a convincing interpretation for the oft-quoted statement that the useful is beautiful and the useless ugly. Even if we read Plato as Bloom would have us do, as primarily a dramatist in the *Republic*, rather than a metaphysician offering serious arguments, we still have only two possibilities for giving the statement meaning. Either Plato is totally ironic here and does not mean that only what is useful is beautiful, or he in general believes this, but in this particular case, thinks it doesn't apply. If Plato is being ironic about the value of the useful, then his banishing of the poets because of their detrimental effect on the state is based on some kind of satirical falsehood. This would be true of many other of the major tenets of the work, making the whole enterprise a kind of doublespeak, a conclusion it is not clear whether Bloom himself is willing to support.

The other possibility is that Plato usually believes this, but is showing us how such "utilitarianism" doesn't always apply. Plato would then be taking seriously the opinion of the masses that women exercising naked alongside men is laughable and, though useful, nevertheless absurd. His argument (which we have no reason to doubt) that non-Greeks originally laughed at that Athenian practice which his audience accepts as useful, would be invalid, somehow underscoring the alleged comedy. Our knowledge of the text of the *Crito*, where Socrates explicitly demonstrates that it is not the opinion of the many which is to be considered, must also be ignored. Here, the opinion of the many is correct and Socrates is suggesting an absurdity.

Either possibility does not seem satisfactory. We can concur with Bloom that "senses of humor... do differ."[188] Nevertheless, he has not succeeded in proving his case, neither in his original essay nor in his rejoinders to his feminist opponents. He has not demonstrated that Plato only jested about equal training for women, nor has he shown that the proposal is, was, and always will be, laughable.

I do not wish to belabor further the point about the hilarity of female nudity, for the focus should be on equality of training, rather than on the clothing worn (or nor worn). But it is worth pointing out how very idiosyncratic Bloom's sense of humor is. He writes that imagination suggests that "the external signs" of erotic attractions on the playing fields "might provide some inspiration for tasteless wits." And, when reminded about Athenian homosexuality in connection with the need to control eros, he states that homosexual intercourse can be consistently forbidden, but not heterosexual intercourse.[189] But wouldn't the tasteless wits have had just as much of a field day watching men attracted to men, if there were no way of controlling the physical signs of attraction? Socrates is clear about such physical signs as in the passage from Kharmides (155c–e), when the philosopher is inflamed by the sight of the sexually aggressive Kharmides' provocatively open cloak.[190] Of course, when men are concentrating on another important activity, the erections to which I assume Bloom is referring can presumably be controlled. On Bloom's own terms, such control would have had to be exercised in the Greek gymnasia in order to avoid constant comic outbursts.[191]

The issue is only important because it helps show that Bloom's entire view of sexuality is askew. He says we need freedom from a moralism which forbids us to see what in nature defies convention in order to read a Platonic dialogue. But Bloom fails to appreciate that human sexuality is a much more complicated phenomenon than his assumption of a fixed natural condition allows. Plato did not believe that *desire* for same-sex intercourse was unnatural. The Catholic Church does not find total sexual abstinence "unnatural," but rather both possible and admirable for its elite. Masturbation, on the other hand, it does judge "unnatural." Regulation of sexual expression has always existed; and if gender equality really entailed the elimination of that shame which he considers natural, then it seems to me that revisions of what we consider shameful both can and ought to be undertaken. The burden of proof remains on Bloom to demonstrate that the connection between shame and eros is unalterable.

To Bloom it is completely absurd for Socrates to found his argument on the assertion that the difference between male and female is no more to be taken into account than the one between bald men and men with hair. The proper question here is: taken into account *for what?* My answer is to support a functional view of human beings. Such role-oriented arguments are still tenable despite the opposition of many feminists who would like to abandon a functional approach because it has worked against females in the past. It is true that male philosophers have traditionally asked "What are women useful for?" and come up with only one answer. But the question itself does not entail that women are solely for childbearing any more than men are solely for inseminating. But if the aim is to increase the size of a family or a total population, then the sex of the two people engaged in the activity is relevant, whereas their baldness is not.

Thus, certain qualities are relevant to certain tasks as Plato clearly pointed out, and it does not make sense to say that these qualities are never sex-linked. For the task of incubating a human infant, as opposed to a bird embryo, having female reproductive organs is relevant. For the task of nurturing children—which I assume to include unselfish and affectionate concern for the infant's welfare, investment of time and energy teaching the child skills and guiding the child's values, as well as provision for the material well-being of the child—I cannot see that the nature of the reproductive structure or function is any more relevant than the amount of hair. If this point of view is absurd, then it is an absurdity being maintained by an increasing number of otherwise intelligent people. At the very least, the absurdity is not self-evident. The question of what women are for is not different from the question of what men are for. To be human is to be capable of choosing certain goals, and it is always relevant to ask which capacity and which action, whether by female or male, can best realize a particular desired goal.

The accusation that feminists make against political thinkers that they ask "what is man's nature?", but "what are women for?" cannot be legitimately leveled against Plato. Instead, he asks in general "what are men and women for"? He believes that some men and presumably some women (although he does not so specify) are equipped for carpentering—as we would say, have the genetic talent for it. Some men and some women, on the other hand, are suited for doctoring, an activity he does mention for women, although we have no other account of the existence of any female physicians in ancient Greece. He believes education can foster excellence in medical practice, but basically one either possesses the ability to learn that function more easily and therefore ultimately better than another, or one doesn't. Each person thus has a natural function suiting him or her to a particular task. And Plato's whole concept of justice is based, not in jest, but seriously, on the idea of each one "doing what comes naturally."

Bloom's judgment of his own belief in the vast importance of the differences between the sexes is probably correct. He judges that his view is "not due solely to his ethnocentrism." Unless ethnocentrism has become a code word for male chauvinism, the charge against him must be broadened. His sexism no longer pervades our entire culture. For today, in electing a leader in some countries, as well as in the selection of a professor of Greek or philosophy by some of those academics whose pedantry he derides, reference to gender has indeed become as irrelevant as Plato suggested it might be. This is not to claim that any modern culture has achieved the total disregard of gender. Some argue that the choice of a female prime minister in England was made because she was the best qualified individual; whereas, in the United States the appointment of a female to the Supreme Court, as well as the selection of a female vice presidential candidate, was based precisely on the candidates' femaleness. Such strategic necessity has arguably influenced the appointment of female professors. But the point behind such choices is that it has now become wise strategy for justice to be seen to be done. And the answer to Bloom is that when female appointments are made, his "masculine pride" must cope with the fact that the gender of the candidate will eventually turn out to be no more relevant than the baldness of the cobbler is to his performance of his trade.

This brings us at last to that connection which Bloom has persisted over the years in maintaining is absolutely crucial to a correct reading of the *Republic*. The fact that Socrates refers to the *Ecclesiazusae* he considers "too evident to need discussion."[192] It will be remembered that the great German classicist Wilamowitz, author of numerous books on Plato and on ancient literature, asserted precisely the opposite, in the same impatient tone.[193] But Bloom summarily dismisses all those, and the number is great, who have denied any connection between the bawdy comedy—in which women dress up in men's clothing, take over the assembly and impose their will on their husbands—and the proposals in Book V.[194] The most recent editor of the Greek text, R. G. Ussher, points out that chronology can support either the view that Aristophanes guys the views of Plato, or that Plato builds (with *"reproaches for his levity"*) on the principles put forward by the playwright. Neither dating nor similarities of language and expression prove that Plato is referring to the play. Ussher leans toward the view that the model for Plato's political views is "some now unknown thinker, prominent at the period . . . of the play, but later ignored by Aristotle. That Plato copies Aristophanes is very unlikely, whereas the possibility that both rely on an earlier philosophy is not only likely but attractive."[195]

Ussher points out that as early as 1811, Book V had already been seen as an answer to Aristophanes' travesty of Plato's already known views. I assume Bloom would consider Ussher's position merely another in a long line of inventors of "schools of thought the existence of which has no basis in historical fact."[196] But, of course, his own interpretation also has no basis in historical fact, but must rely largely on his idiosyncratic reading of both texts.

Ussher is clearly correct that any statements about the relation of the two texts *must be tentative,* given our current state of knowledge. Is Bloom's absolute certainty then based on some ulterior motive? Ussher's argument that the play itself does not even prove that Aristophanes himself is rejecting either the rule of women or communism in the last scenes, but rather "playing for laughs," is convincing. The last scenes are not chapters in a textbook as they have sometimes been misread to be. I think, although I am not certain, that Bloom's view of their vying for comic effect also involves that both Aristophanes and Plato actually rejected the idea of equality for women. Bloom hints on several occasions that his view of the *Republic* would all come clear if we understood the Platonic view of the relation between poetry and philosophy. But while we await his promised clarification of the subject, it is hard to ignore the fact that Aristophanes was clearly writing the former.

Even if we grant that Praxagora's speech about the lot of women and the fact that parents would not know their own children bear pronounced resemblances in content (and perhaps in style, although this is less certain) to passages in Book V, this hardly proves that Plato, too, is playing for laughs. Praxagora is married to an offensive old man who, it is hinted, has difficulty satisfying her sexual needs. A consequence of the reform she demands involves a beautiful young man being forced into intercourse with an ugly old woman. Bloom describes this as an instance of what is "most private and most unequal by nature" being subject to the public sector. It shows "the absurdity of trying to make politics total, of trying to make an equal distribution of all that is rare, special and splendid. . . . It reveals the tension between *physis* and *nomos*, nature and civil society."[197]

But what of the unnaturalness of Praxagora's union, or of any beautiful young woman, like the fourteen-year-old described in Xenophon's *Oeconomicus*, forced to take over the running of the household and the duties of the marriage bed of a man twice her age? Are we to assume that this is merely one of the natural inequalities which Bloom considers "necessary concomitants of any political order"? If erotic choice is rare, special, and splendid, surely it is so as much for a beautiful young woman as for Bloom's beautiful young man. Aristophanes himself perhaps has some idea of the purely conventional nature of such arrangements.

At any rate, to take Plato comically assumes that he knew only too well that all the equality of training which he proposes could never make women men's equals. Bloom believes the "actualizable regime" of the *Laws*, where "women are educated differently and lead very different lives," is the political result of the inquiry of the *Republic*. But even in the *Laws*, Plato proposes an education far more similar than that current in Athens. Why does he bother, if the pronounced inequalities noted in *Ecclesiazusae* are simply natural and necessary? Why propose women magistrates who make important decisions if a state in which even the best females have no voice in the assembly is somehow natural?

I shall not dwell here on the rest of Bloom's idiosyncratic interpretation of the relation between philosopher and city in the *Republic*, for he says himself that he is only offering a series of hints about the permanent human problems involved in Socrates' "playful competition with Aristophanes." I applaud this rare expression of the seriousness of the issues of erotic choice and gender equality. The reader must decide, however, whether Bloom is convincing when he asserts that the focus of the issue of political reform for both Praxagora and Socrates is sexual affairs, and the reason that philosophers must rule is also chiefly a matter of sexual activities. For according to Bloom, the philosopher-guardians are "primarily matchmakers or eugenicists who have to spend a great deal of time and subtlety . . . to get the right people to have sexual intercourse with each other."[198]

At the risk of laying myself open again to that charge of the "stiff pedantry" of academics which Bloom deplores, I would suggest that sexuality as a means to other ends is Plato's intention in Book V, as it is in the *Symposium*. There is no way to know for certain whether Plato, if he in fact knew the *Ecclesiazusae*, would have shared the Athenian acceptance of Praxagora's copulation with the flatulent Blepyrus as natural, whereas a young man copulating with an old woman would be judged unnatural. We know only that in his ideal city, he found no reason to advocate such a reversal. The unions proposed were not laughable in the Aristophanean sense. The best were to be mated with the best, presumably the young and the fair with the young and the fair. (Among the guardians, theoretically, a fifty-five-year-old man could mate with a twenty-year-old woman, and a forty-year-old woman with a twenty-five-year-old man.) I cannot see that such arrangements would seem outrageously comic even on the basis of the Athenian categories of "the natural" versus "the conventional." How much less so to those of us who find such categories ultimately unworkable. In this case, I do not even think senses of humor differ all that much. In this, as in most of the other issues, we have reason to believe that Bloom's certainty about the permanent inequality of the sexes is gradually becoming a minority opinion.

3

The Continuing Importance of Plato's Questions

Enthusiasts and disciples of Plato have repeatedly claimed that he had already raised in the 5th century B.C. all the fundamental questions of philosophy, that subsequent discussions, as Whitehead remarked, have all been merely "footnotes."[1] In respect to what used to be called The Woman Question, that claim is no exaggeration. For all the major contemporary issues of sexual equality are touched on in the arguments of *Republic*, Book V. And even the order in which Plato raised the questions still remains cogent. For decisions about the roles desirable for males and females today still must be based on a general theory of what kind of society we want. That is, some answer to the question of what society best promotes the welfare of all underlies all current demands for change in the position of women. We cannot ask what is best for women without inquiring, with equal urgency, what is best for men.

Further, in this process of deciding what makes a society desirable for all, we still need to ask if there are any innate biological differences between the sexes that must be considered. The search for "natural differences" now leads us to research in genetics, biochemistry, and neurology. But there is also still an interest in ethology, in observations and theories about the behavior of animals and its relevance to the roles the sexes ought to assume in human society. Plato referred his listeners to the behavior of guard dogs. Contemporary sociobiologists point instead to the apes and other primates, terming them "our closest relatives," and referring to their "fixed action patterns" in discussing possibilities and norms for human behavior. So, too, Plato's discussion continues on whether current sex roles are conventional, that is, primarily (or entirely) the result of culture. Reformers and anthropologists are interested in what the evidence of other societies can teach us. Just as Plato pointed to Sparta and to practices in legendary societies, modern anthropologists make statements about the feasibility of change or the "stubborn resistance" to change in sex roles on the basis of cross-cultural studies.

The connection between the family, private property, and women's role is also as vital an issue today as it was when Plato proposed the abolition of private families for his philosopher-rulers. Plans to liberate women, or to keep them in their traditional place at the hearth, still depend on choices between the creation of new family patterns or the retention of the old husband-as-breadwinner-and-protector of his own family unit. Radical feminists charge that capitalism and female obedience with its stultification of women's possibilities are intertwined. And advocates of women's primary role as helpmate and mother wish to retain the economic *status quo* with fixed family and property relations. Those who do not want to throw out the baby with the bathwater and who hope to retain romantic love, companionate marriage, and the exclusive affectional bonds of nuclear families still must consider the question in Plato's terms. They still have not solved the question of how these values can be maintained if women are to have exactly the same opportunities and responsibilities as men.

While we are in the process of deciding what the just society ought really to include, and to what extent the roles of the sexes should be identical, we continue to face decisions on educational policy. Once again, the progression is the same as it appears in Book V. Given our aims, what kind of education can best produce the results we seek? If equality of role is best, then should the education of the sexes be identical? If women have always been at a disadvantage, should current educational practices be designed to compensate for this fact? What if the "slight disadvantage" is biologically based, as Plato himself believed and some contemporary scientists also conclude? In other words, current thinkers, in asking whether the discrepancies in attainment are merely the result of age-old differential socialization, are asking the same questions Plato raised. Plato thought in very broad terms about what we now call the "socialization" process. He wanted to control the music and dance his *kallipolites* learned, and to censor the stories they heard. So, too, today's reformers see the need to change media images of the two sexes. They wish to alter the forms of address and restrict publication of sexist language.

Even the final question that Plato asks and never really answers decisively continues to plague us. Is a society ruled by reason and committed to gender equality genuinely possible? Can androgynous lovers of wisdom really accede to leadership in a modern state? Some thinkers describe democracy as threatened constantly by the discrepancy between the myth that all men are created equal and the reality that biology produces unequal and irreversible distribution of crucial abilities.[2] For the same reason, some classicists believe that the basic innate inequality between the sexes makes Plato's egalitarian proposal an unrealizable goal. A current educational strategy of using different methods for different "learning styles" presupposes some possibility of roughly equal attainment. Plato, of course, entertained no such democratic notions and the success of such contemporary efforts to equalize results is still questionable. We cannot prove that a just society which provided equal opportunity not only for its rulers, but for all its citizens, would result in the virtuous happiness of all. This irremediable inequality is what the distinguished scientist E. O. Wilson considers the basis of "the tragic contradictions of human existence."[3] As a sociobiologist, he deals with the same questions that Plato raised; but he answers with certainty that, given our biological heritage, the ideal society of the philosophers could not come into being.

I shall deal at some length with Wilson's views and those of other sociobiologists. For although they are researchers trained in scientific disciplines, they are also the thinkers in contemporary society who, like Plato, have combined their empirical observations with speculation about human social organization in an effort to explain why human societies are as they are. Many of them consciously intend to supplant the philosophers and prescribe, as Plato did, how society *ought* to be, given its biological basis. It is true that some of them equivocate on whether their findings have implications for social policy. As we shall see shortly, one researcher, who insists that there is a distinctive male human nature and a pronouncedly different female human nature—thus contradicting the Platonic view—nevertheless, argues that his conclusions have no policy implications whatsoever.[4] Such an assumption is naive, "wildly unrealistic," as one critic put it.[5] Undoubtedly, all those commentators we have discussed who, through the centuries, have assumed without evidence that there are profound biological differences which invalidate the Platonic reforms, would have welcomed such "scientific" conclusions. They would surely have considered such sociobiological theories about the radical differences between the sexes as decisive support for their own views.

In fact, many of the practitioners of this new scientific discipline, which attempts to build evolutionary theory by showing the interaction between genes and culture, explicitly ask both of the Platonic questions in regard to sexual equality. Leading proponents have addressed both issues: 1) what is the best arrangement for human welfare; and 2) what is biologically possible. And they have assumed these questions to be related in exactly the way Plato did. We must think through what is just, but the possibilities are limited by what ethology and empirical observations about actual practices teach us.

Writers often try to divide those theorizing about the best society into opposing camps, positing a Nature Versus Nurture debate. David Barash, a leading sociobiologist, thinks that Plato, unlike Aristotle, maintained that human beings were "the products of society."[6] Such an interpretation has two flaws. A persistent complaint against the *Republic* is that it would result in a class society in which those who were biologically superior would always remain on top. Whatever else can be said in Plato's defense by egalitarian thinkers who would stress his emphasis on the importance of education, there can be no doubt that his commonwealth is based on a belief in innate merit. In fact, as we have seen, his ideas about the breeding of human beings in the manner of race horses would place him more likely in the camp of the "naturists," were such clear-cut divisions ever workable. The truth, however, is that few have ever seriously argued for the existence of such mutually exclusive alternatives. As Stephen Jay Gould, one of the most vocal and most convincing of the scientific opponents of sociobiology, puts it: "Every scientist, indeed, every intelligent person, knows that human social behavior is a complex and indivisible mix of biological and social issues. The issue is not *whether* nature or nurture determines human behavior, for they are truly inextricable, but the *degree, intensity, and nature of the constraint* [my emphasis] exerted by biology upon the possible forms of social organization."[7]

Indeed, the question now, as it was in Plato's time, is precisely whether there are any "constraints" limiting the possibilities of women's participation in society. Wilson, the founder of sociobiology, informs us that ethical questions (and presumably, by extension, questions of the best organization of society) should be removed from the hands of the philosophers since they have insufficient knowledge of biology and evolutionary theory.[8] Let us turn then to the pronouncements of several sociobiologists, ethologists, and primatologists who have used their superior biological knowledge to supplant the philosophers. In my view, they shed less light on the relation of biology and society than did Plato more than twenty-three hundred years ago.

Wilson's own view of sex differences is that the current role distinctions have only "a slight biological component." At birth, he tells us, "the twig is already bent a little bit."[9] A feminist disciple of his defends his use of this metaphor, judging that it indicates only a slight deviation from the desired norm, a minor constraint that need concern us little in deciding what women's role ought to be.[10] In my view, the formulation is neither helpful nor quite so innocuous. It carries the overtones of deformity which have historically appeared over and over from Aristotle to Freud in discussions of women's sexual differences. Furthermore, the implications of Wilson's image are ambiguous. For with careful treatment, bent twigs can be straightened; and for some construction at least, bent twigs might be as good as, or better than straight ones. The real question is what the implications for human societies are of Wilson's "modest predisposition" toward the sex-role inequities which are an "inconvenient and senseless residue" of our biological legacy.[11]

The problem is that the oft-used metaphor of a biological "inheritance" does not help us in assessing the *degree* of constraint. For we can always renounce a legacy, give up an inheritance. And if we attend only to the literal meaning of Wilson's pronouncements, ignoring their tone and the uses some of his followers have made of his views, this biologist is no more anti-egalitarian than Plato himself was. Wilson concludes that biological evidence alone cannot prescribe an ideal course of action, but only help us to define the options and assess the price.

He sees the options concerning sex roles as limited to three possibilities. We can 1) condition members so as to exaggerate sex differences, as is done in most societies; 2) train members so as to eliminate all sex differences; or 3) provide equal access to opportunities, but take no further action. This last option he dubiously calls a *laissez faire* course of making *no choice* at all. This last possibility he finds internally inconsistent and unworkable; in his view, this has been demonstrated in the Israeli kibbutz.[12]

Plato's proposed state is closest to the second alternative. The philosopher assumed his proposals to be based on exactly the sound biological knowledge Wilson accuses philosophers of neglecting. He deemed further action necessary to eliminate sex differences, but such action was designed only to re-educate the upper echelons and change the previous sexual divisions which were based solely on convention. Although he judged men to be biologically more competent as a class in all activities, he did not think any extraordinary methods were necessary to correct women's slight disadvantage.

For Wilson, however, although women's disadvantage is also considered only slight, more strenuous measures will be required. For it is not a matter of degree of competence alone. There are what we would have to call biological differences *in kind*. The discrepancies Wilson finds will require quotas to correct the socially induced disadvantages, but also will require what he calls "sex-biased education" to compensate for biological differences. If we institute both measures, it will then be "possible to create a society in which men and women as groups share equally in all professions, cultural activities and even athletic competition." Although such a society would require the blunting of early predispositions, "the biological predispositions are not so large as to make the undertaking impossible."[13] Both the modern biologist and the ancient philosopher agree that such control over society would result in a much more productive and harmonious society.

Wilson, however, notes the cost of such regulations. Personal freedoms would be jeopardized and some individuals would not be allowed to reach their full potential, he warns. Most commentators in the last hundred years have expressed concern over the first cost, the loss of personal freedom. But since Plato did not call for compensatory measures, none of his interpreters have needed to worry about what we have come to call "reverse discrimination." So whereas they have been outraged at the human cost of solidifying a class system, no commentator has consciously noted that if you promote female guardians, some capable men might be prevented from entering the guardian class.

Commentators have noticed a possible loss of human potential in the Platonic state. They have worried that women's potential for fulfillment through nursing their children and bonding with them would be lost; and some have even remarked about the loss of family affections for men. Although Wilson does not address the question directly, we can assume that his judgment on a state in which neither men nor women are involved in the care of their own children would be that it hinders that "complete emotional development" he desires for both sexes. For Plato, freedom from child care is entirely positive. Wilson, however, states only that abstention from participation in child rearing "might" stunt men's emotional growth. (Presumably, then it would also stunt woman's growth, as so many commentators have noted. Wilson perhaps thinks this so obvious as to be unnecessary to mention as he considers possible alternative societies.)

In Wilson's third possible society, where no action is taken to offset the differences of the bent twig, the provision of equal opportunities and access, he says, will not suffice. If identical education is provided, but no heroic measures are taken, men will continue to hold a disproportionate representation in political life, business, and science.[14] Evidently, he assumes a separable phenomenon called "identical education" could occur. Men have often taken this view, as if equal exposure to the same subject matter were all that was involved in education. But surely all aspects of the educational process cannot be identical unless there are concomitant changes in the roles of the adults that students see in the world around them. Without changes in the subtle gender expectations of teachers, there is no way that education can be truly identical. It is a curiously abstract notion of education that allows Wilson to assume that we could provide truly equal access to all professions and yet make no choices about sex differences. Plato knew better and realized that even the music and body motion of very young children presupposes a theory about their future roles.

Wilson sees the Israeli kibbutz as an example of the workings of an egalitarian ideology without the necessary strenuous compensatory measures. The desired equity has not occurred. His attitude toward the current regression toward traditional roles in the kibbutz is ambiguous. On the one hand, he thinks that "inadequate regulation" has kept gifted women from developing their potential for commercial and political leadership and has also denied men the emotional rewards of involvement with children. On the other hand, he emphasizes much more forcefully that, "despite being trained from birth in the new culture," Israeli women have opted for the development of their emotional potential.[15] He does not stress that they have thereby given up the emotional satisfactions of guardianship. Instead, we are back into a framework where women's "nature" leads them to fulfillment through family rather than leadership.

The Israeli kibbutz *is* the community that most comes to mind when we seek modern examples of Plato's planned society. Like Plato, the original founders of the kibbutz movement sought to eliminate sex differences, traditional family arrangements and property ownership for the good of the community as a whole. The ideology of the original pioneers was designed to establish a special subgroup which, although not composed of philosopher-rulers, was intended to provide an inspirational example for the larger society. Melford Spiro, one of the foremost authorities on gender in today's kibbutz, has come to believe that the lack of sexual equality in today's kibbutz is the result of certain "pre-cultural" factors. Chief among these are sex-based differences, what he calls "motivational dispositions," which he has clearly come to consider as, in some sense, biologically innate. He writes that "even if it were the case that the only natural difference between males and females is one of sexual anatomy, this one difference apparently is not as trivial as had been assumed."[16]

Spiro tries to show that all the provisions he once believed would make for complete gender equality in the kibbutz have failed largely because for the female "the parenting need was the most powerful of all their needs."[17] He tries to show, too, that the free associations of male kibbutz toddlers proves that the degree of aggression they exhibit is biologically programmed, despite efforts of caretakers to treat male and female children equally. Furthermore, even the nudity encouraged between youngsters of the kibbutz (reminiscent of the nude exercises Plato prescribed for both sexes) has not had the desired effect. At puberty, adolescent girls experience shame despite the official views.

Like his fellow anthropologists, Fox and Tiger, he finds support in the reversion to more traditional roles for the view that we must seek equivalent, but not necessarily identical, roles for both sexes in a society. He sees the enhancing of female charm, or as he puts it, "femininity" in beauty parlors, a new development in the kibbutz, as a positive value.[18] However, in my view, the new arrangements have clearly not produced gender equality either in the identity or the equivalence sense. Spiro admits that women no longer hold leadership roles and that many of those involved in early child care are dissatisfied. He even puts it (somewhat grudgingly) that these female caretakers "claim" they don't have the temperament for it. The important issue is that a society in which women choose not to take leadership roles and yet are strongly affected by decisions made by all-male governing boards cannot be a society fostering separate but equal roles.

The key question is why women no longer choose to rule jointly, but have returned to the laundry and the nursery. Plato was well aware that it would not be an easy task to motivate unpaid rulers. And Spiro points out that men, too, are not enthusiastic about taking on the committee work involved in kibbutz management. Presumably, women prefer having the time for their children and grandchildren. But is it really for biological reasons that men do not express the desire to take time for their children, rather than for onerous committees? Can Spiro really show by means of psychological testing of three-year-olds that men have no "internal" interest in the early care of their offspring?

Feminists and others have sought alternative answers for why the original egalitarian kibbutz ideology failed.[19] Surely the fact that early caretakers of Israeli children have always been female suggests the possibility of differential treatment of infants even in the critical pre-verbal years. Nursery workers would be likely to handle (literally and figuratively) little future soldiers differently. From the beginning, Israel was a society geared to military preparedness which—despite female conscription and a nominal role for women in the army—always needed and lauded male warriors. Such a society can hardly be expected to have fostered completely equal leadership roles.[20]

Wilson himself worries that there may be a genetic link between valued qualities like cooperativeness toward groupmates and obsolete, destructive ones like aggressivity toward strangers.[21] Plato, without the benefit of any theories about pleiotropism, the control of more than one phenotypic character by the same set of genes, clearly also thought such a combination natural. Wilson fears that in the planned society, whose creation "seems inevitable" in the coming century, the valuable cooperativeness might be lost if we try to steer people away from the aggressiveness which once provided our "Darwinian edge." Such inevitable social control, he says, would rob man of his humanity in the ultimate genetic sense. In other words, to tamper with the linked phenotypes of cooperation-aggression is absolutely crucial for survival, and yet the results of doing so would be completely disastrous. Evidently, in order to flourish cooperatively, we cannot give up our aggressive traits. But if we continue to act aggressively toward enemies a nuclear war may result. The dilemma is unresolvable, and Wilson thus ends his book with great foreboding. Plato, of course, did not have to deal with our current mutual capacity for total annihilation, and so could allow his guardians to be gentle with each other and fierce toward the barbarian.

Wilson is well aware that cultures can be designed rationally. Like Plato, he believes we can teach and reward and coerce. But like many of the anthropologists who note current changes in the kibbutz and almost all sociobiologists, he stresses the costs rather than the benefits of trying to straighten the twig of sexual inequality. His sympathy is for those whose natural bent has been violated. Thus, he expresses great concern for the cost in personal suffering that homosexuals are paying in a society that does not realize the value of their innate dispositions and mistakenly judges heterosexuality alone to be "natural." But in his role as wiser-than-philosopher biologist and ethicist, he expresses no compassion whatsoever for the thousands of years of oppression and stultification of the possibilities of women which, unlike the persecution of homosexuals, has characterized every known society. Nowhere does he lament the cost paid by women in ancient Greece and China, nor the fate of female infants in modern Asia. He does not consider the widows encouraged to immolate themselves on their husband's funeral pyres well into the twentieth century as worthy of mention alongside his justified horror at Hitler's treatment of homosexuals. Like so many of the earlier Plato commentators, the force of Wilson's social theory, despite his protestations, remains that society as a whole will probably benefit and women themselves be happier if they surrender to their biological constraints.

Even among sociobiologists there are disagreements about exactly what women's innate dispositions are. Melvin Konner accepts the current evidence, rudimentary as it is, that there are marked biological differences between the sexes and judges that these differences will inevitably affect their functioning. He does admit that there is still too little information to make responsible inferences about human behavior. But he clearly finds most telling the fact that there are differences in the male and female rat brain visible to the naked eye and that data on eighteen individuals with a defective gene demonstrate that androgens, and not solely environmental or sociocultural factors, contribute to gender identity.[22] However, the problem for Konner in drawing implications for social policy on the basis of biological research is the reverse of that of Plato. Plato's audience was likely to find the possibility of equal participation of women laughable and highly improbable. Examples of women engaged in desirable occupations were completely non-existent. Proving that a woman ruler was not impossible was the very difficult task that Plato faced. In many intellectual circles today, proving that women are constrained by their biology from performing important societal roles has become the more difficult task. Since females are increasingly moving into leadership roles, it is harder to support the view that traditional sex-role differentiation is inevitable, or even desirable. Sociobiologists find themselves on the defensive. So while Konner, as a biologist, is absolutely convinced that the genetic differences between the sexes result in behavioral differences in degrees of aggression and nurturance, he is eager to assure his audience that discrimination in societal role is not warranted.

Once again, however, although the avowed position is an egalitarian one, hidden biases, conclusions not warranted on the available evidence, emerge in Konner's popular book, *The Tangled Wing.* He expresses sympathy for the women scientists whom he describes as having found gender differences to be "in part biological" and as "uncovering and reporting" that the "sexes are irremediably different."[23] He sees their position as one of "complexity, even anguish." At this stage of research, it is surely impossible for any scientist to "uncover" the *immutability* of gender differences; how could a biologist ever state definitively that a "remedy" for differences could never be found?

Most important, however, is Konner's automatic assumption that the female scientists that he praises for their intellectual courage in facing unpalatable facts, have "sacrificed more than the average brilliant man" to get into problems that trouble them intellectually.[24] Men often worry about the sacrifices women will have to make to pursue a career. Konner is admirably aware of the "oppression . . . bulwarked and bastioned by theories of 'natural' gender differences" that women have suffered. But in speaking of women's sacrifices, he merely assumes, like the male Plato scholars and his fellow sociobiologists, that female researchers have had to sacrifice their emotional potential, presumably the loss of the joys of family life, of carefree leisure and male protection.

But almost all the distinguished women scientists he mentions, ranging from those born early in this century to this current generation, were married and most have children. Their sacrifice is undocumented. When he describes Margaret Mead as "enduring hardships rare for a woman in any era," his description is surely a-historical and ethnocentric. For millions of women have, and still do, endure far greater hardships in daily toil, forced infanticide, clitoridectomy, psychological abuse—no matter what the loneliness and intellectual courage of a scientific trailblazer. The truth is that the life of a twentieth-century woman scientist, as the lives of women go, is probably among the most satisfactory. In fact, a recent study has shown that far from being victims of great sacrifice, married women in the United States with high status jobs consider themselves and can be objectively rated as having the highest sense of well-being.[25] Since most of his scientists have experienced the satisfactions of rewarding work as well as some of the satisfactions of family life, it is certainly unwarranted to assume that they have sacrificed more than men, and doubtful indeed that they have sacrificed more than the average non-brilliant woman.

Plato, as we have seen, has been accused of making female guardians sacrifice their greatest joys in addition to the general sacrifices that the "average brilliant" male guardians would have to make of family and material goods. In stressing genetic differences, this contemporary biologist might seem to be giving additional support to this view.

He himself is eager to make clear that he does not want to be allied with traditional arguments restricting women to particular societal roles. In discussing gender differences, he calls attention to the finding that women's mood cycles can be predicted from the menstrual cycle, but that men also have the same number of days per month of physical discomfort. Therefore, he assures us that anyone who believes that menstrual distress disqualifies women from such positions as airline pilot and president must consider whether they would want their plane—or their country—piloted by someone who has a few days a month of distress that are completely predictable, or someone who has the same number of uncomfortable days arriving randomly.

Arguments about the negative effects of women's physiology are still with us in public life. In 1982, the United Nations representative from Argentina, when faced with Prime Minister Margaret Thatcher's aggressive stance over his country's invasion of the British-owned Falkland Islands, publicly referred to the "fact" that women were subject to the whims of their hormones. Suffice it to say that the influence of hormones in post-menopausal women has not been adequately studied and that the Argentinian's infuriating comments were based no more on empirical evidence and no less on prejudice than those of his Athenian counterparts. Aristotle, for example, considered the very state of femaleness to be a deformity, since women were unable to concoct or cook their menstrual blood to the final stages of refinement, the fertile stage reached only by male semen.[26]

In fact, Aristotle's belief that there is more difference between women and men than between females and males of other species would undercut Plato's argument from analogy with other animals for opening all societal activities to women as well as men. Most direct evidence of hormonal effects on social behavior have at this point been demonstrated only on animals, rats and songbirds. Even the studies of the effects of the menstrual cycle, which Konner uses to support his view that women should not be limited in their jobs, involve the subjective reports of women describing how they feel rather than direct neurological data.

Subjective factors are, of course, impossible to eliminate in the reporting of all information about sex differences. Konner himself, under the guise of presenting biological information, is guilty of introducing highly speculative theories based as much on wishful thinking as on solid evidence. For he offers us his own version of the Special Excellences argument raised by Plato and rejected by him. As we have seen, many of our commentators believe Plato to have been mistaken; and claim, though without advancing any empirical evidence, that women do have special characteristics that make them ideally suited to certain roles, though not the public high status roles. Konner, however, on the basis of what he considers a growing body of empirical evidence, concludes that women are specially qualified *to govern* at this moment in history. It is his "guess" that in the very near future, objective observers will agree that women differ in the degree of violent behavior for reasons that are in part physiological. And this part is sufficiently important to justify the policy implication that serious disarmament may ultimately necessitate an increase in the proportion of women in government.

Konner discounts the record of past female rulers because such women have invariably been embedded in and bound by an almost totally masculine power structure, and have achieved their positions by being "unrepresentative of their gender."[27] He does admit that some women are as violent as almost any man, but does not note that as cultural roles change, there has been a steady rise in the number of violent crimes committed by women. It is perhaps one of the shortcomings of sociobiological explanations that we cannot be certain that women of the future will not be selected for the presence of aggressive behavior tendencies, causing a more violent female to evolve.

The view of Konner's is currently fashionable and sometimes advanced—equally without definitive evidence—by feminists who point to the so-called gender gap in American politics and to the strength of women's participation in nuclear disarmament movements. Unfortunately, women's tendency to vote for less militaristic candidates, in so far as such a tendency can be substantiated, may as well be the result of women's current role as primary caretaker of sons and her powerlessness, as of any genetic predisposition to pacificism.

Konner nevertheless believes that, since what is required at this historical moment is a tendency to non-violence, given the statistical tendencies of women, "we would all be safer if the world's weapon systems were controlled by average women instead of by average men."[28] Eager as I am both to foster disarmament and to increase the number of women in government, Konner's argument remains more worrisome than convincing. I can see no reason to believe that men advocating disarmament do so because they have a biologically less violent nature. There is no evidence that political peacemakers, past or present, differ in brain structure, have a lower than average level of testosterone, nor even initiated fewer violent interactions in their everyday functioning. There is no guarantee that a political dove would necessarily be less aggressive in his private interactions. The average female that Konner's fellow sociobiologist, Sarah B. Hrdy, describes as highly competitive might well be just as inclined to follow what she saw as her self-interest as the average male. I cannot see that biological factors would guarantee any clear-eyed and possibly unpopular assessment of the need for disarmament. Observation of women in competitive sports who are bound, not by a "masculine power structure," but rather by the desire to win the game in question, use their intelligence and skill with a high degree of aggression, which should not be underestimated. The rulers we need are not those dependent on biological priming, but those capable of overcoming biological constraints, heritages, legacies, etc., in favor of making rational choices. We need representatives of both sexes who are able to reason clearly about alternatives and feel acutely the horrors of war, regardless of their biological predispositions. The presence or absence of hormones, like the reproductive differences Plato discounted, are today just as they were then, irrelevant to suitability for guiding and guarding the flock.

Plato's example of the equality of role in sheep dogs was chosen selectively to buttress his argument. But contemporary sociobiologists, despite their vastly increased knowledge of animal diversity, continue to use their information selectively. Thus, a leading female primatologist and sociobiologist has produced much data that contraverts Konner's optimistic belief in the pacifist nature of females. Sarah B. Hrdy points out, for example, that among all marmoset monkeys studied, fights between females are more frequent and fiercer than those between males. Wild dog and chimpanzee females murder the offspring of subordinate females.[29] She aims to demonstrate that, in general, the prevalent view of the greater competitive potential of males is incorrect. Her years of observation of primate societies convince her that the previous emphasis on the importance of males in structuring the society and the apparent inability of females to maintain stable social structures is inaccurate.

Instead, Hrdy offers a picture of assertive, dominance-oriented females. The primates she has studied exhibit, beside their commitment to reproduction, an equally powerful and universal commitment to compete, and in particular, to quest for high status. She concludes in fact that the central organizing principle of primate social life is competition between females. Although such a picture of the potential of women would have satisfied Plato as equipping them well for their task of guardianship, it does not jibe with Konner's wishful assumption that biology shows that women should rule because they will make better peacemakers.

Over and over again, we see researchers and the social scientists who rely on their work using selected observations primarily to support views they undoubtedly hold for other reasons. Hrdy speaks of the androcentric fantasy of certain primatologists. The physical anthropologist, Donald Symons, whose work has been with Rhesus monkeys, exemplifies the extreme when he assures us that there is a separate male and female human nature based on their vastly different, genetically determined sexual feelings. Symons' position is based on much dubious pre-1960 primate data and highly selective anthropological research as well as impressions gathered from fiction and accounts of female acquaintances. Although it would take us too far afield to attempt a refutation of the many questionable statements Symons makes on the "profound differences in psyche" between the sexes, it is worth discussing one of his contentions which is relevant to the Platonic arrangements.[30]

According to Symons, the male sex drive is critical in human evolution, whereas sexual desire in the female is merely vestigial, a by-product of the masculine phenomenon. Most sociobiologists are inclined to believe that men are always more likely than women to desire sex with more than one partner. Hrdy, on the contrary, questions the pair-bonding hypothesis, which Symons offers, as an explanation of the inevitable differences between the sexes. According to her, recent observation of monkeys and apes make it highly unlikely that the human female's concealed ovulation, non-reproductive sexual activity, and female orgasms are unique. In many primate species, females exhibit aggressive sexuality with numerous mates. Hrdy herself, though she admits that more evidence is needed, believes that there is a selective importance to females of an active, promiscuous sexuality, and that enjoyment of sex could also serve the female's interest at the expense of the male's. She speculates that Western scholars, reluctant to de-emphasize the values of monogamy, may well have overrated its biological importance to the human female. This may explain why, like the Victorians, male biologists assume a lack of sexual feelings in women.

The Greeks did not hold this view at all. In fact, far more prevalent throughout history than the Symons view of the maladaptiveness of promiscuity for women has been the widespread belief in and fear of female sexuality. As Hrdy points out, the majority of the world's cultures have made some efforts to control it. Many deplorable practices, including the surgical alteration of twenty million women today to ensure their faithfulness and the legitimacy of offspring are based on a belief that women are "naturally" every bit as likely to be promiscuous as men. Neither Socrates nor his listeners seemed to have worried about women's unwillingness to engage in sex with multiple partners, though some of his nineteenth- and twentieth-century commentators have been concerned about it. In eliminating monogamy, Plato did not see himself as violating any biological predisposition for either sex. Given recent data on the sexual fantasies and practices of women in the 1970s and 1980s in countries where their activities are relatively less regulated, there seems to me to be less and less support for a belief in the wide discrepancy between males and females in sexual desire.

What is far more convincing is Hrdy's concern that the absence of cooperative effort, the inability to work for the advantage of the entire group rather than that of the individual, may be the biological dispositions that must be overcome by both females and males. Plato's view of the cooperative behavior necessary for successful guardians conforms far more closely to what another primatologist describes as the female "communal" rather than the male "agentic" pattern of social interaction. In discussing sex differences, this researcher points out that "the evolution of self-awareness and language makes much of what we have learned about our primate heritage somewhat trivial."[31] She also points out that females are taught to define their well-being in terms of relationships rather than in terms of self-concern. Presumably, this results from the fact that men, who in every society have more power than women, have succeeded in institutionalizing what is to their advantage, despite any contrary biological disposition of females. But Plato quite correctly realized that both male and female guardians will have to learn to put the welfare of the whole before their own selfish interests.

The question that Plato faced remains as cogent as ever—how what these biologists call "altruism" is to be promoted in a society, since it is crucial not only for survival, but for the maximization of the welfare of all. The philosopher Midgley suggests that as an intellectual position, egoism is perhaps a male "sex-linked doctrine."[32] But few sociobiologists would accept the possibility that women are not only less aggressive, but also more altruistic. Wilson describes only homosexuals as true altruists. While believing women less competitive and less promiscuous, Wilson has founded the entire discipline on the principle that underlying both men and women's social behavior is their "selfish" need to maximize the chances of their genes appearing in the next generation.

Some feminist psychologists, as we have discussed, have sought to demonstrate that women speak in a "different voice," that is, are more concerned with the feelings of others. They do not always declare themselves on whether this is solely culturally induced. Generally, however, they imply that change of social role or education might not eradicate women's greater concern with relationships, since the tendency is in some way tied to their reproductive function. In my view, such speculation on who is programmed to be altruistic has not progressed at all beyond Plato's description of how we can decide what nature an individual has. In the *Republic*, Socrates says that if one learns something faster, then he has a natural bent for the activity. If women can be taught to consider others "more easily" or seem to do it more often without being taught any differently than men, then they're "naturally" less egoistic. But women aren't socialized in the same way as men—we know that—and they never have been. No contemporary social science research can possibly demonstrate that were the identical moral values and emphasis on personal relationships inculcated in both sexes, heterosexual men would nevertheless remain less altruistic. Nor am I sure that Wilson's view of the altruism of homosexuals in the evolutionary sense has much to do with our ordinary usage. The speculation that homosexual males have been selected for helping others rather than competing to get their own genes into the next generation deviates from our usual sense of altruism which includes placing the general welfare of society above one's own immediate self-gratification.

Plato clearly did not believe that women or the avowed homosexuals in his circle were constitutionally more pacifistic or altruistic. Aristophanes can be seen as believing women less ready to support war, but only because it was not in their self-interest to do so. But there seems no empirical evidence nor need for the assumption that one sex is "primed" to be less egoistic. If altruism is a value, we dare not take it for granted that one sex needs less reinforcement to practice it. The task exactly as Plato saw it is still to determine how a society can best promote this quality in all its citizens.

Even among sociobiologists there is a range of opinion about the relations between biology and values. Socrates wanted to demonstrate that the values he sought were at the very least in no way "contrary to nature." If Symons talks as if the fact that "the double standard" in sexual behavior has a biological function, makes it not only understandable, but inevitable and perhaps not undesirable, others are more careful. David Barash wishes to defend his scientific discipline against charges of sexism. Thus, he writes that, although there is a "potential biological basis for the double standard," he is not suggesting that what is biological must also be ethically right or unavoidable. He grants that with the current changes in social tradition and the perfection of birth control, there are sure to be "dramatic changes." He says, however, that we can afford equality of sexual behavior only when the biological consequences of such behavior are equal. And "so long as women, not men, get pregnant, some differences can be predicted."[33]

Presumably, women will always be better at getting pregnant than men, but it is not clear to what extent this makes the "double standard" of male promiscuity and female fidelity inevitable. Plato himself attempted to make allowances for the fact of women's pregnancy, ascertaining that the cost of pregnancy and early child care would be as minimal as possible for his Philosopher-Queens. He evidently saw no particular difficulty that might arise in motivating females to participate in multiple matings. In fact, he assumed that guardian women over forty should be free to handle their sexuality exactly as they pleased so long as no children resulted. Kinsey's statement, that "among all people everywhere in the world, the male is more likely than the female to desire sex with a variety of partners," is often quoted by sociobiologists.[34] But Plato seems to have believed, as did most Greeks, that females were every bit as interested in sex as men. Dover believes that except for the Victorians, it has been widely assumed that women were highly desirous of coitus, presumably not only with one partner, though Dover doesn't explicitly specify.[35] In teaching a wide range of female students from eighteen to seventy-five, my own informal research would suggest that female *desires* are no more monogamous than males. The Hite Report and the Cosmopolitan survey would seem to confirm this. At the very least, sociobiological accounts of female desires surely suffer from lack of adequate evidence.

What needs to be considered is that among all people every-where, the male has on average been better able to express his desires and choose his encounters, so we really don't know what the female desired or desires. Plato himself stressed the diversity of behavior in different cultures, believed Spartan women to behave in all ways more like men, and no doubt was reinforced in his conviction that women would consent to his mating arrange-ments by the stories of the promiscuous sexual behavior of Greek goddesses.

It is hard to believe that promiscuity for men and fidelity for women must persist as long as women bear the children. Barash himself states that "humans have achieved liberation from repro-duction's tyranny over sex."[36] He does maintain that there is a biological basis for the alleged fact that female politicians have almost invariably been "desexed," that is, less physically attrac-tive than male politicians have been allowed to be. But if this was previously so, it is no longer true in the mid-1980s. Barash would then have to attribute previous choices of unattractive females to the surmountable "influence" of biology rather than to any inescapable constraint.

Barash sees this influence operating in the fact that men are less disposed than women toward "investing heavily in the well-being of their children."[37] Because males of all species must have less confidence in their paternity, "women can be counted on to take care of the kids." That is, the differing reproductive strate-gies account for why women have almost universally found themselves relegated to the nursery, while men derive their great-est satisfaction from their jobs. Can we expect then that since conclusive proof of paternity will soon be possible, that this age-old unwillingness to participate in child-rearing will disappear? The women's movement of the 1980s has come to realize how crucial it is both to the development of the child and to the very possibility of equality that males be ready, willing, and able to care for children from infancy on.

For Plato, both male and female guardians were to be free of the details of early child care, but both were to participate equally in the later education and rearing. Of course, only genetic relat-edness within the group mattered in Plato's society; all children born at the same time were to be considered siblings. Sociobiologists might still not consider this maladaptive, since only a small subgroup would be involved. And for both Barash and Wilson, kin selection—and we would eventually be dealing with an interrelated group—is connected to altruism. And it is exactly such altruism that Plato wished to promote.

Barash not only allows for the possibility that changes may occur in what is adaptive sexual behavior. He even softens the determinist element in sociobiology by attempting to allow for the possibility of free will: "Evolutionary biology is not deterministic. . . . Free will may actually be greatest when everyone is able to behave in accordance with his or her inclinations."[38] Thus what amounts to the determinist view of the majority of the commentators on the Woman Question in the *Republic* might not be warranted on the basis of his answer to the Free Will Question. Presumably, gifted women could freely choose to renounce the influence of their genes and accept their place among the rulers.

This question of whether anatomy is destiny remains as alive today as it was twenty-four hundred years ago. In an item in a respected popular scientific journal reporting on recent discoveries of certain tissue differences in the male and female brain, the writer concluded that this "may be the first indication that anatomy, after all, *is* destiny." These first indications of an anatomical difference between the brains of men and women, they speculate, "may" be linked to the controversial finding that men outdo women at visual-spatial disciplines, such as architecture and geometry. The research by two physical anthropologists who dissected the normal brains of nine men and five women—that is, a total sample of fourteen—found the splenium (the rear portion of the corpus callosum) of the female brain to be larger and more bulbous than in the male brain. This, they suggested, might give women richer communication of visual-spatial information between the two hemispheres and somehow—though they admit it is still a mystery—have the paradoxical effect of limiting women's visual-spatial abilities.[39] But why should such research be seen as an early indication of women's *destiny*, or even as an inevitable limitation on their ability to be outstanding architects or geometricians?

The only answer is that one already presupposes biological

determinism and the inevitability of women's inferiority. Plato, of course, had no knowledge of modern scientific method, no means whatsoever of investigating hormonal and brain chemistry. It is clear that he chose to minimize any possible biological differences other than reproductive ones for his own purposes. But so, too, has the research of the last century and a half into "sex differences" often reflected the unconscious purposes and prejudices of the researchers.

It is now well-known that Victorian scientists argued that if women used their brains excessively, they would impair their fertility by draining off blood cells needed to support the menstrual cycle. (Given the acute need to restrict the birth rate, it is perhaps unfortunate that this "finding" could not be substantiated. Colonies of women working at Greek and algebra might have helped us attain zero population growth throughout the world!) Nineteenth-century scientists stated that it was the smaller brain size that made women less intelligent than men. Then, when craniologists thought intellect to be located in the frontal lobes, autopsy reports showed frontal lobes in females to be smaller. And when researchers decided the parietal lobes were the source of intellect, they found millimeter differences in cadavers whose sex they already knew.[40]

Social scientists, too, have "discovered" sex differences which have not held up upon further investigation. The conclusions of the psychoanalyst Eric Erikson in the 1950s were influential for decades, but have turned out to be highly questionable. He tested eleven- to thirteen-year-old children and concluded that their ways of building and thus of thinking were determined as his mentor Freud had theorized, by their genital anatomy. He found that boys' spatial constructions were dominated by thrusting height and downfall, girls' by static enclosure.[41] Such purported differences in perception and presentation of inner and outer space conformed to early psychoanalytic views of the role which, in Plato's terms, "according to nature" each sex must play. The sanction for Erikson was not the good of society, but rather the psychological aim of avoiding psychic pathology in women. Erikson's conclusions have now been shown to have been based on a very loose interpretation of his own data. And when younger children were tested, thus reducing the effects of socialization, no differences were found in the number, size, or type of towers (the supposedly male construction) built by boys and girls.[42]

Research into sex differences continues today and it is popularly believed that significant differences are emerging through more careful, unbiased investigations. But even those who expect that striking innate differences will eventually be discovered have to admit that so far no important structural differences have been observed between the brains of males and females. And none would deny that differences between men and women have been narrowing over evolutionary time and that this process has recently been accelerated. Furthermore, scientists, social scientists, and philosophers on both sides of the controversy on the existence and relevance of biological differences other than reproductive between men and women all accept one fact. That is that differences among members of the same sex are far greater than average differences between the sexes in all those features that Plato considered relevant to the guidance of an ideal society.

The real danger, then, is not the one so often expressed; the problem is not that we ignore biology at our peril. Instead, what we must guard against is the tendency to accept too quickly whatever the current scientific view of the "natural," the biologically inescapable, happens to be. Even if early cross-cultural research, showing that boys in all societies run in packs, whereas girls do not, has not held up, this does not mean that we should abandon attempts to discover if there are any biological sex-linked behavioral dispositions. Nor should we abandon the attempts of ethology to counteract the ignorance of the ancients of sexual differences in animal behavior. We must by all means continue to investigate hormonal differences and the relations between social events and hormone level.[43] Investigations into differences in brain structure or organization, along with research on how such differences affect learning ability, must continue. The feminists who condemn such studies are shortsighted indeed.[44] If, in fact, as the classicist Thomas Gould insists, there are forces in a democracy which prevent unpopular research into the inferiority of women (an inferiority which he posits on faith) these forces must be combated.[45]

Even militant feminists might find some sociobiological

research useful. They could, for example, exploit the conclusions reached by Hrdy on the competitiveness of female primates. But many feminists are satisfied with "first order" explanations of sex differences, convinced that social and cultural explanations are sufficient to explain differences we observe. The adequacy of cultural explanations, however, should not lead us to foreclose the attainment of power through new biological knowledge. Such power may well help us to accomplish our egalitarian aims more effectively.

Nevertheless, it is true that attempts to base our vision of desirable human behavior largely on biological norms are mistaken. Nor can the sociobiologists' attempts to explain past norms succeed. For it is not only efforts like those which try to show that variations in women's skirt lengths can be explained and assigned numerical significance on the basis of biological predispositions that are fallacious.[46] All biological explanations of culture suffer from the impossibility of reducing an independently valid domain with valid explanatory principles of its own to what are considered more basic principles. But just as it does not make much sense to "explain" that the table represented in Cézanne's painting "The Card Players," is "really" only a system of electrically charged particles in motion, it does not make sense to assert that women do not paint great pictures for biological reasons.

Richard Lewontin, who opposes the sociobiologists' tendency to explain away discrimination against women on the basis of new scientific research, states the objections to such reductionism forcefully. Although earlier "quaint justifications for sexism have lost their force," he warns us against the view that "genes make hormones and hormones influence neural development and neural development makes professors." These new views that chemistry, rather than anatomy, are destiny he finds "equally baseless."[47]

In a sense, Plato himself shared some of the crucial assumptions of sociobiology. And it is partly perhaps for this reason that Lewontin, as we have seen, finds Plato an enemy of current affirmative action programs. For Plato does base his proposals for women on selective biological arguments. Nature, rather than convention, makes women weaker at all pursuits, and ethology helps convince us that women can guide the flock along with men. In Socrates' dialectical process it becomes clear that *if* biological divergence relevant to guardianship, that is, differences other than the reproductive, could be shown to exist, then, no matter what might seem fair, the society must be organized without equality of role. This sociobiological strain underlies his entire concept of justice. For establishing justice involves each one doing what he or she is biologically best suited to do.

All those commentators of the last hundred years who have rejected Plato's proposals did so not because Plato ignored the constraints of biology, for only one with little acquaintance with Plato could believe that. Their objections over and over again were rather that the philosopher was ignorant of or mistaken about the true biological nature of women.

Another frequent objection has been that Plato's society is totalitarian. Women, they insist, must always have the choice of pursuing a career or devoting themselves to their husbands and children. Even among committed feminists, few are willing to declare themselves as "anti-choice." But the crux of the problem lies in the fact that human choices are never made in a vacuum. An infant can perhaps "decide" whether to sleep on her stomach or her side, but even a four-year-old cannot decide which toys to play with in any given society without her choices being shaped, though not entirely determined, by the expectations of the culture. Plato realized that if one refuses to rule, one is doomed to being ruled by "inferiors." So, too, if we refuse to guide choices rationally, our options will be controlled by hidden factors. And these will reflect the desires of the current power structure. Women's choices will, in fact, represent the interests of the Thrasymachuses among us—that is, the interests of the physically dominant group.

But am I really suggesting that women who wish to stay home and bear, nurture, and raise children, cook and clean their houses, as Plato would say "sew and spin," should really be prevented or at the very least discouraged from doing so? Isn't there as much satisfaction in facilitating the development of others, in "ruling one's own roost" in the words of Wilamowitz, as in being a doctor, lawyer, merchant chief ? Or if we discard Plato's three-tier society in favor of a democratic ideal, isn't it all the more likely that the satisfactions of homemaking will often be even greater than those of the non-creative, menial jobs that most men have always done and will inevitably continue to have to do? Surely many would say there can be a division of labor which provides equal status for men and women without thrusting them into identical roles. Even if one takes the extreme Platonic position that sexual differences are in fact as minor as the differences between the bald and the curly-headed, shouldn't women be allowed to maximize or increase those differences if they so choose?

Heretical as it may seem, the answer to these questions must be that in the long run, both society as a whole and women in particular will benefit from the conscious abandonment of the idea of separate but equal roles. If the rewards of nest-building and child-rearing are great—as I believe they can be—then, in the interests of fairness, men must be allowed to participate in these satisfactions. If there is no way to eliminate dull, potentially alienating jobs in modern industrial societies, then women must do their share. In short, we must devise a mode of life and job sharing which satisfies the needs of all, and we must keep these needs from being artificially or "naturally" divided on the basis of sex.

One can always play the "animal game" to support one's own opinions. Instead of looking to sheep dogs or chimpanzees, we could as well find the natural in the arrangements of most birds. We can choose a species in which there is heavy male investment in the incubating and rearing of offspring. Our model might well be male and female birds in which there is lifelong pairing and also polyandry. The point is that present family arrangements are neither desirable nor inevitable. To continue to tell women that they can "choose" to be housewives when their lifespan will soon be more than eighty years, of which only twenty or so can possibly be taken up with childbirth and rearing, is cruel to women and wasteful to society.

The *Republic* proposes a society which succeeds in fulfilling the natures of all. But it is a class society based on a very dubious idea that some people's biological nature fits them *only* to serve others through manual labor. Plato firmly believed that very early we could decide what each citizen could do best, and that by each one pursuing his natural bent, the welfare of all would automatically be fostered. His *polis* would be led by those who are genetically bred for all-round superiority and who have gained true knowledge and great love for the best and the most beautiful. Among the best he proposes absolute equality with the lighter tasks assigned to the females. He assumes that males *as a class* do everything better, an assumption which belies an undeniable unconscious prejudice against women. Nevertheless, he also assumes that this slight class superiority of men will not affect the process of finding women to make up their share of the guardian group. Given the cultural context, his assurance of complete equality in kind, no matter what its motivation, stands out as a unique declaration. It adds to the importance of the *Republic*, contributes to its continued vitality, and explains some of the renewed interest in it today.

For Plato, the only innate differences are the reproductive ones. We still do not have a clear picture of what the precise biological differences between the sexes are. In general, we are far from discovering the genetic encoding, neurochemical processes, or brain structures that produce specific abilities or make it easier for us to acquire specific psychological traits. The Athenian clearly believed that there were no inborn barriers to women's participation in the highest positions. Plato thought mastery of mathematical principles necessary for his philosopher-rulers. And recently, there have been controversial studies showing that mathematical giftedness appears less often in adolescent females than in males.[48] But no reputable scientist has yet come forward with evidence that women cannot excel in the characteristics Plato considered essential to ruling his city-state. Although some classicists still believe that women are not capable of the greatest achievements, not even the most extreme of the biologists would claim to have any evidence to support such a prejudice.

In arguing for equality of role, Plato looked not only to biology, but also to the myths about and the actual practices in Sparta to show that societal arrangements varied and were therefore to some extent as we should put it, the products of culture. The choice of whether to use biological or environmental arguments to support his point depended for Plato, as it does for the commentators we have discussed, on the preconceived opinion he wished to buttress!

Plato proposed that private property and the family could both be abolished. We do not know any better today than he did then whether the cost of eliminating these is inevitably greater than the benefit sought. Surely we now have an anthropological record of more *kinds* of families than he might have imagined. If Spiro is right that the family is in some sense universal, new issues of what constitute a family—surrogate mothers, known and unknown sperm donor, Anna Freud's concept of "psychological parenting" taking the place of biological units—all challenge not only the conventional Greek family Plato wanted eliminated, but our own norms of the nuclear family. Clearly, no one form of human communal life is instinctive, that is, biologically necessary.[49] But we do know that the institution of family as practiced, in which women have almost always been considered as property, has caused great suffering.[50]

On the other hand, we have, as Plato did not, examples of the actual costs that have resulted from twentieth century totalitarian efforts to abolish private property. Contemporary examples of such abolition, whatever benefits they have produced, have not succeeded in establishing societies consistent with Plato's vision of the well-being of all. This hardly proves, as interpreters have claimed, that Plato himself knew very well what the effects of equalization would produce and therefore knew his *Republic* to be an "impossible dream." Nor can we be sure that collective ownership and new forms of families are doomed to failure.

Plato considered his proposals for equal education for female and male guardians would be sufficient to guarantee the development of a superior group composed of both sexes. He wanted their training to begin in earliest childhood. So far as we can establish, he wanted gifted children socialized by officers of both sexes who would guide them to assume identical positions in society. Such a city would point the way to true justice. And there is no convincing textual evidence that he considered the equality he proposed laughable or unattainable.

Regardless of recent feminist objections to the word and the concept, the androgyny Plato advocated remains an achievable and desirable goal. The old cry of *"vive la différence"* has a hollow ring when one considers the devastating effects such assumptions have had on the potentialities of women. Modern science cannot show any inevitable relation between anatomical differences and the expression of personality traits. Plato's goal of guardians that are both spirited and gentle remains a worthy aim. If Freud and Plato were right that death can only be outwitted by the production of new life or great works, both of these possibilities ought to be available to both sexes. If child care and the nurturing and teaching of the young is a valuable activity, then it is valuable for both sexes. If mechanical labor is alienating, then it is alienating for all. If many of the jobs that must be performed in an industrialized society are better performed by machines, then men and women should benefit equally from the freedom technological progress ought to provide.

There is no value in seeking to label standards of excellence as "masculine" and therefore to be abandoned. If the ability to compete is necessary in modern society, then it must be encouraged for both sexes. If a measure of altruism and cooperation is crucial for human survival, then we must facilitate the development of these traits in men and women. If gentleness and compassion are useful, then they are useful to male and female surgeons as well as to male and female grandparents. If creating a comfortable and aesthetically pleasing setting for human pursuits is valuable, then the ability to choose and decorate a human "nest" should be fostered in both men and women. Excellence in needlepoint is excellence whether performed by a football player or by Homer's Penelope. In their eagerness to upgrade traditionally feminine jobs, some feminists fall into the trap of assigning different scales of evaluation. But this is doomed to failure. The fastest marathon racer can be judged in only one way. And if the strength of the male and the percentage of muscle to body fat will always make it the case that the best male will beat the best female, then it is gross self-deception to act as if the race is not really, not actually, not, when all is said and done, to the swiftest. In today's world, there are few activities where brute strength is important. With the exception of athletic contests, none of the activities Plato valued, including excellence in warfare, depend today on muscle power. To refuse to recognize that women in fact *did not* contribute to such great cultural achievements as the Italian Renaissance and suggest that they did make an important contribution so long as we desert the "masculine definition" of importance is ultimately self-defeating. One ought to assume only that sociological

reasons can adequately account for why there has not thus far
been a female Michelangelo. We have every reason to believe
that there will be great women sculptors. Nor must one change
the standards of excellence to say that Sappho and George Eliot
and Emily Dickinson made outstanding literary contributions.
The call of some feminists for different standards of excellence is
indeed misguided.

In fact, what we need today, are clear standards of excellence,
and perhaps more than ever, leaders who possess a *combination* of
the traits that have in the past been identified as exclusively
either masculine or feminine. And above all, we must be passionately committed to the uses of reason. We must cultivate the
ability to think clearly not only in a superior elite, but in all citizens. Any scientific research that will help us achieve these goals
must be fostered. It is important not to discourage biological
investigations into sex differences, but we must be ever vigilant to
reveal hidden agendas and unconscious assumptions.

We must now undertake measures that Plato did not know
would be necessary to counteract the damage done through centuries of exaggerating gender differences. We know far better than
he the enormous cost of clinging to the view that there is a separate male and female human nature. We know both the
intrapsychic costs, and the cost to society in general. We have
seen the damage done to women raised to think of themselves as
second class and second-rate, to men forced to suppress their feelings and conform to a pattern of self-serving aggressiveness.

Before this species goes the way of the other 85 percent now
extinct, we must change the current relations between the sexes.
We can no longer afford to waste the abilities of more than half
of our population. This is even more true now than when Plato
proclaimed it in the *Laws*. Just as in Plato's day, proposals for a
better society must include radical changes in economic relations.
Economic life must be organized so that men and their offspring
are not denied the benefits and satisfactions of involvement in
child-rearing. All the commentators we have discussed, chauvinists and feminists alike, have asserted that Plato was overzealous
in eliminating families entirely. If in fact he was mistaken, and
pair bonds are necessary for rearing of the young, ideas of what
constitute a family nevertheless require thorough restructuring.

Certainly, if marriages are to involve more permanence than Plato desired they must become, as they have never yet been, partnerships between equals.

Our review of the recent history of Plato's egalitarian proposals leads us to a final paradoxical conclusion. Just as the world will know no surcease from ills until philosophers become kings, so, too, philosophy will know no end to prejudice until women become philosophers. But doesn't this contradict my entire thesis? If men and women have the same capacities, and reason with identical skill, then surely there can be no special reason why female philosophers are needed. Men can point out inequities and suggest reforms as effectively as women. But the truth is that for generations to come women will have a unique connection with all females before them who were condemned because of their physiology. Women philosophers will have a "special relation" to those who were once thought, in Aristotle's words, to provide only the "matter" for the offspring for whom men provide the *psyche*. For there is no philosophy performed by disembodied souls, and all thought arises out of a particular situation. As we have attempted to show, philosophy is not only abstract reasoning, but also social expression. Women are needed to recite as the Jews do each year at the Passover, "We were slaves unto Pharoah in Egypt." It is we who were confined to household chores, whose sex life was regulated and whose mental capacities were denigrated. This was done to us, to us throughout the centuries. We who reason, think, imagine alternatives, weigh the just with the unjust, must keep alive the memory of those inequities. We must see that full equality is reached and maintained, not only in the ideal city, in the city of speech, but here in the real world where philosophers, though not kings, are a small voice for sanity and the life of the mind.

Notes

INTRODUCTION

1. Leonardo Bruni, *Epistolae*, lx, 4. "Multa sunt in iis libris abhorrentia a moribus nostris, quae pro honore Platonis tacere satius est, quam proferre." Quoted in G. Holmes, *The Florentine Enlightenment: 1400–1450* (New York: Pegasus, 1969), p. 114. Three centuries later, H. Spens in the first translation of the *Republic* into English in 1763 exhibits the same attitude. R. Gannett remarks in his preface to the reissued edition that in Spen's analysis, "the delicate question of the community of women is evaded." H. Spens, *Republic of Plato* (London: Dent, 1906), p. xi.

2. For an account of Greek misogyny see, e.g., Sarah Pomeroy, *Goddesses, Whores, Wives, and Slaves: Women in Classical Antiquity* (New York: Schocken, 1975). M. R. Lefkowitz and M. B. Fant present excellent documentary evidence of Greek attitudes. They provide numerous examples including an excerpt from Aristotle's will (taken from Diogenes Laertius) to show that "restrictions of women's rights to own property and to determine the course of their own lives" illustrate the Athenian male's low estimation of females' capabilities and general value. *Women in Greece and Rome* (Toronto: Samuel Stephens, 1977), p. 19. See also K. J. Dover's section on "the unusual extent to which the Athenians had come to regard women as objects," in *Greek Popular Morality in the Time of Plato and Aristotle* (Berkeley: University of California Press, 1974), pp. 95–102.

3. Leonardo Da Vinci describes experiment (guided by reason) as "the one true mistress." *The Literary Works of Leonardo Da Vinci* (London: 1880), #12, quoted in Anthony Blunt, *Artistic Theory in Italy 1450–1600* (New York: Oxford University Press, 1956), p. 26. And Peirce writes in "The Fixation of Belief," that man's logical method should be loved and reverenced as his bride whom he has rightly chosen; he will work and fight for her and will "strive to be the worthy knight and champion of her from the blaze of whose splendors he draws his inspiration and courage," 5.387 p. 247, in *Collected Papers of Charles S. Peirce*, vols. V & VI, ed. C. Hartshorne and Paul Weiss (Cambridge, Mass.: Harvard University Press, 1965). Such figures of speech cannot easily be translated for the use of female readers and tend to add to women's sense of exclusion.

4. *The Collected Dialogues of Plato,* ed. Edith Hamilton and Huntington Cairns (Princeton: Princeton University Press, 1963), p. vi.

5. A. E. Taylor, *Plato: The Man and His Work* (New York: Meridian, 1956), p. viii.

6. This was a pervasive theme in George Boas' work. He wrote that when the "so-called immortal masterpieces" are admired it has been for shifting reasons; "men can read with the mind of an Athenian only by a definite act of will and even then one forgets that a real Athenian did not have to make the effort." From "A Sermon for Humanists," in *The Johns Hopkins Magazine,* October 1984, p. 16.

7. Joachim Bannes, *Hitlers Kampf und Platons Staat* (Berlin: W. de Gruyter, 1933). See below, p. 53.

8. Information about women in Plato's Academy comes from Diogenes Laertius. He mentions two women disciples, Lastheneia of Mantinea and Axiothea of Phlius, and says of the latter that she "is reported by Dicaearchus to have worn men's clothes." Diogenes Laertius, *Lives of Eminent Philosophers,* Book III. 46 with English trans. R. D. Hicks (Cambridge, Mass: Harvard University Press, 1966), vol. 1, p. 317. Although Diogenes is not always reliable, G. C. Field accepts the information and says that Dicaearchus, a pupil of Aristotle, "was probably well informed." *Plato and his Contemporaries* (London: Methuen, 1967), p. 118.

As for women's participation in modern academies, studies done in the 1980s show that inequality of treatment persists. C. G. Krupnick found that when men are in the majority in a classroom and the instructor is also male, women are called on and speak up less often. B. R. Sandler and R. M. Hall reported that instructors inadvertently practice discrimination by such behavior as coaching men more when they do not know an answer and asking men "higher order" questions, involving more theory and analysis. For a summary of these studies, see A. M. Heim, "Harvard Study Reveals Gender Inequality in the Classroom," *Second Century: Radcliffe News,* April 1986, p. 2. I would not claim that such studies are decisive. Nor can statistical information or even personal reports conclusively prove my claim of women's continued exclusion. Nevertheless, one measure of the degree of their acceptance would undoubtedly be the number of females in the top ranks of university faculties today. In the United States the statistics remain discouraging. Of slightly more than 115,000 full professors, 103,380 are male, 11,830 female. That is, there are about nine times as many males as females at the highest levels. For the latest available figures see W. V. Grant and Thomas D. Snyder, *Digest of Education Statistics: 1985–1986* (Washington, D.C.: U.S. Government Printing Office, 1986), p. 113.

9. Thomas Gould, *Platonic Love* (New York: Free Press, 1963), p. 54.

10. Jean B. Elshtain, *Public Man, Private Woman* (Princeton: Princeton University Press, 1981), p. xv.

11. The assessment is Karl Popper's and is particularly striking because

Popper devoted a lengthy work to demonstrating Plato's "reactionary" and totalitarian tendencies. *The Open Society and Its Enemies* (London: Routledge & Kegan Paul, 1945).

12. I have attempted to paraphrase at this point only as literally and straightforwardly as possible to prepare for the discussion of varying interpretations that follow. All quotations are from the translation of Allan Bloom, *The Republic of Plato, with Interpretive Essay* (New York: Basic Books, 1968), except where indicated otherwise.

13. Plato, *Republic*, 454e.

14. Ibid., 455e.

15. Ibid., 473d.

16. Gilbert Ryle, "Plato: Moral and Political Theory," in *Encyclopedia of Philosophy*, ed. Paul Edwards (New York: Macmillan, 1967), Vol. VI, p. 331.

17. Plato, *Timaeus*, 90e. In *The Dialogues of Plato*, trans. Benjamin Jowett (New York: Random House, 1937), vol. II.

18. For a summary of attitudes of the early church and a bibliography on the subject, see Marie Augusta Neal, "Women in Religious Symbolism and Organization" in *Religious Change and Continuity*, ed. H. M. Johnson (San Francisco: Jossey-Bass, 1979).

19. See al-Fārābī, *De Platonis Philosophia*, ed. F. Rosenthal and R. Walzer (London: Warburg Institute, 1943).

20. It would take us too far afield to enter the controversy over whether Islam is essentially anti-feminist. However, even the political leader Benazir Bhutto who sees the Qur'an itself as basically egalitarian admits that "a reactionary interpretation" by men has resulted in women's inferior status in Muslim countries. Thus, although she sees Islam as less sexist than Christianity, she admits that a discriminatory patriarchal society reemerged after the death of the Prophet Muhammed. See the account of her Rama Mehta Lecture at Radcliffe College, in *Second Century: Radcliffe News*, June 1985, pp. 1, 3.

21. William James, *Some Problems of Philosophy* (New York: Longmans, Green & Co., 1948), p. 7.

22. *Averroës' Commentary on Plato's Republic*, ed. E. I. J. Rosenthal (Cambridge: Cambridge University Press, 1966). Rosenthal here stresses Averroës' regret that no proper use is made of women in the service of the community. See also his "The Place of Politics in the Philosophy of Ibn Rushd," in *Bulletin of the London School of African Studies*, xv, 2, p. 252. In my view the fact that Averroës in his explication of Plato introduces such ideas as "melodies are perfect if men invent them and women perform them" (454) suggests that his egalitarianism, though remarkable, is not as total as Rosenthal maintains. For no matter how important and necessary performance is, invention—the male activity—is surely superior.

23. Rosenthal, *Averroës*, 456, 9, p. 166.

24. Ibid., 454, 3, p. 164.
25. Martha Nussbaum,"Women's Lot," *The New York Review of Books,* January 30, 1986, p. 7.

1: THE PREVALENCE OF ANTI-FEMALE BIAS IN PLATO SCHOLARSHIP, 1870-1970. SEVEN TYPES OF HOSTILITY.

1. I have concentrated in this section mainly on those books which have had an influence on students and fellow scholars, which have been frequently reprinted, quoted, and cited. When I have deviated from this policy—e.g., used a work addressed to students in China, and a little known commentary by a woman—I have explained my reasons for doing so in the text. Although I have aimed at including as many major works as possible, my survey is by no means exhaustive.

2. This is B. Bosanquet's view. In *The Education of the Young in The Republic of Plato* (Cambridge: Cambridge Press, 1900), p. 11, he speaks of "the violence of the revolution" which Plato advocated.

3. V. F. Asmus, ed., *Platon: Sochinenia v Trekh Tomakh,* vol. 3, no. 1, (Moscow, 1971), p. 606.

4. Z. Diesendruck, *The Republic: Translated into Hebrew with Introduction and Notes* (Tel Aviv: Newman, 1953), p. 3 (Gimel).

5. K. Popper, *The Open Society and Its Enemies* (London: Routledge & Kegan Paul, 1945), p. 307.

6. Nicholas White, *A Companion to Plato's Republic* (Oxford: Blackwell, 1979).

7. Ernest Barker, *Greek Political Theory: Plato and His Predecessors* (London: Methuen, 1947), p. vi. He refers to the 1914–1917 world war which was taking place as he wrote.

8. Ibid., p. 261. In the same vein he wrote that the fact of a woman's sex colors her whole being; "it makes her able indeed to inspire noble enthusiasms, but not to direct a policy or drill a regiment as Plato would require his woman-ruler or woman soldier to do." Ernest Barker, *The Political Thought of Plato and Aristotle* (New York: Dover, 1959), p. 148. Werner Jaeger has a similar view and notes that Plato "does not expect as we should do" that women "will make their creative contribution to the community through family life." *Paideia* (London: Oxford University Press, 1943), Vol. II, p. 244.

9. Barker, *Political Thought of Plato and Aristotle,* p. 244. This is an earlier, longer version of *Greek Political Theory.*

10. See, e.g., Aristotle, trans. Benjamin Jowett, in *The Basic Works of Aristotle* (New York: Random House, 1941). *Politics,* 1254b. "The male is by nature superior, and the female inferior, and the one rules, and the other is ruled. This principle, of necessity, extends to all mankind." See also 1259b, 1260a.

11. The explanatory comment on *Republic,* 452c appears in the anno-

tated edition begun in the 1860s that Jowett did not live to complete. It was published after his death as B. Jowett and L. Campbell, *Plato's Republic: The Greek Text*, ed., with notes and essays (Oxford: Clarendon Press, 1894).

    12. Ibid., vol. III, pp. 215–16.

    13. Ibid., p. 216. His wording here is ambiguous and I am not certain I have correctly interpreted his statement that Plato did not consider "the other differences to which the difference of sex gives rise in mind and feeling." He may be referring only to the fact that biological differences cause men to *think* and *feel* differently about each sex. On this alternative interpretation women's differences would not be innate but rather universally acquired.

    14. Ibid., p. 216. Jowett identifies Plato's view with the line "woman is the lesser man" which he quotes merely from "the poet." The unidentified line is no doubt from Tennyson's "Locksley Hall"; but, considering the context, the British poet's view is actually more reminiscent of the misogyny of Socrates' audience. For in the lines immediately preceding Jowett's quote, Tennyson describes women thus: "Nature made them blinder motions/bounded in a shallower brain." *The Poetical Works of Alfred Lord Tennyson* (Boston: Houghton Mifflin, n.d.), p. 60.

    15. *Republic*, Introduction and Analysis, in *The Dialogues of Plato*, trans. by Benjamin Jowett, 3rd ed. (Oxford: Clarendon Press, 1892), p. lxxxix. He does comment in *Greek Text*, p. 234, on the singular nature of "the infrequency of the opportunity for nuptial intercourse."

    16. F. J. Dover, *Greek Homosexuality* (New York: Random House, 1978), p. 154.

    17. Walter Pater, *Plato and Platonism* (London: Macmillan, 1910), pp. 257, 258.

    18. Ibid. He does not deny that the proposals are consistent with animal "nature"; in fact, he sees the family arrangements as "a movement backwards, to a barbarous or merely animal grade of existence" (p. 257). And he says of women guardians that if we see them as a reinstatement of the Amazon we must condemn them as "a survival from a half-animal world," which adult reason has long since overcome (p. 259).

    19. Bosanquet, *Education in the Republic*, p. 11.

    20. Bernard Bosanquet, *A Companion to Plato's Republic* (London: Rivingtons, 1925), p. 182.

    21. Taylor, *Plato: The Man and His Work* (New York: Meridian, 1956), p. 278.

    22. Demosthenes, lix122. Dover insists we cannot consider this *the* decisive fourth-century view. See *Greek Popular Morality in the Time of Plato and Aristotle* (Berkeley: University of California Press, 1974), p. 14.

    23. Taylor, *Plato: Man and Work*, p. 278.

    24. Dover, *Greek Homosexuality*, p. vii.

    25. This was the view of John Stuart Mill writing in the 1860s. He denied that "anyone knows, or can know, the nature of the two sexes, as

long as they have only been seen in their present relation to one another." We cannot possibly know the capabilities of women, he says, because "most of them have never been called out." His discussion at this point is still stirring and applicable today. See "The Subjection of Women," in *The Feminist Papers*, ed. Alice S. Rossi (New York: Bantam, 1974), pp. 203, 204. Richard Jenkyns thinks Plato's "striking feminism" must have encouraged Mill and perhaps guided him, but provides no evidence for this speculation. *The Victorians and Ancient Greece* (Cambridge, Mass.: Harvard University Press, 1980), p. 230.

26. Since my aim in this study is to focus on the statements of complete identity of nature and education (and the interpreters' rejection of these), I have restricted my analysis as far as possible to *Republic*, Book V. Although the *Laws* contains many interesting and provocative points, I have in general avoided any extended treatment of the altered provisions for women in that work.

27. In R. C. Lodge, *Plato's Theory of Education*, with an appendix on the education of women according to Plato, by Rabbi Solomon Frank (London: K. Paul, Trench, Trubner, 1947).

28. Ibid., p. 307.

29. Plato, *Republic*, Bloom trans., 466d, p. 146.

30. R. C. Crossman, *Plato Today* (New York: Oxford University Press, 1939), p. 202.

31. Leo Strauss, *The City and the Man* (Chicago: Rand McNally, 1964), p. 127.

32. Bloom, *Republic, Interpretive Essay*, p. 382.

33. Ibid., p. 385.

34. See below, p. 191.

35. N. E. Fehl, *A Guide to the Study of Plato's Republic* (Hong Kong: Chung Chi College, 1961), p. 1.

36. Ibid., p. 50.

37. Ibid., p. 53.

38. Plato, *The Republic*, trans. with introduction by Desmond Lee (London: Penguin, 1974), p. 47.

39. Richard Nettleship, *Lectures on The Republic of Plato* (New York: Macmillan, 1967), p. 173.

40. This is the view of W. K. Lacey, *The Family in Classical Greece* (Ithaca: Cornell University Press, 1968), p. 174. He stresses that Greek women had greater economic security than married women today, including protection from the "wayward husband" of the modern divorce courts who could support his family but refuses to do so. He considers Plato's state not so vast an intellectual jump from the society in which he lived "as it is sometimes thought to have been" (p. 176). On the other hand he defends the fact that women didn't go out to eat with their husbands or dine with them at home when there were other nonrelated males present. Giving the same reason offered for asking women to

leave when the port was served at modern British upper-class dinner parties, Lacey suggests that women are thus protected from quarreling and drunkenness. Susan G. Bell, editor of *Women from the Greeks to the French Revolution* (Stanford: Stanford University Press, 1980), objects that "it is debatable whether women wanted to be protected from raucous male society" (p. 122). Lacey seems to have no awareness at all of what a missed opportunity it was for women to be excluded from banquets like that described in the *Symposium*.

41. Nettleship, *Lectures*, p. 173.

42. Ibid., p. 174.

43. U. v. Wilamowitz-Moellendorff, *Platon: Beilagen und Textkritik* (Berlin: Weidmannsche Buchhandlung, 1919), Vol. II. In another work in which he worries that Plato is trying to turn women into incomplete men, he says that we are setting the cause of equality back by making a political issue out of it. Plato, he says, is not in the spirit of modern female emancipationists whose attempts when healthy are based on the *differences* between the sexes. *Die Griechische und der Platonische Staatsgedanke* (Berlin: Weidmannsche Buchhandlung, 1919), pp. 18, 19.

44. George Grote, *Plato and the Other Companions of Socrates*, Vol. IV (London: John Murray, 1888), p. 171, says there is no point on which he speaks in terms of more decided conviction than that women are fit for the same duties as men.

45. Constantin Ritter, *The Essence of Plato's Philosophy* (New York: Russell & Russell, 1933), p. 332.

46. Karl Nohle, *Die Statslehre Platos* (Leipsig, 1880), pp. 136, 137.

47. Adela M. Adam, *Plato: Moral and Political Ideals* (Cambridge, 1913), p. 131.

48. Wilamowitz, *Platon*, p. 199.

49. Ibid.

50. Ibid., p. 200.

51. I. M. Crombie, *An Examination of Plato's Doctrine*, Vol. 1 (London: Routledge & Kegan Paul, 1962), pp. 100–101.

52. Paul Friedlander, *Plato: The Dialogues*, 2nd and 3rd Periods (Princeton: Princeton University Press, 1969), p. 103.

53. He writes, "let us not take away his [that is, Friedlander's] joy in this discovery" that Plato's purpose was to shock the bourgeois. I have assumed from his tone that he does not agree with Friedlander's assessment. See H. Gauss, *Philosophischer Handkommentar zu den Dialogen Platos* (Bern, 1958), p. 159.

54. Jean Ithurriague, *Les idées de Platon sur la condition de la femme* (Paris: Librairie Universitaire, 1931), p. 136. This self-proclaimed egalitarian believes that the, as he puts it, "near nudity" is the *cause* of the *perversions de l'amour* in ancient Greece.

55. W. K. Lacey, *Family in Greece*, p. 25.

56. For a reproduction of a detail of the Roman mosaic at Piazza

Armerina of Roman women in scanty bathing suits and modern hair-dos, see the photo of "La sportive romaine" in Guy Fau, *L'émancipation féminin dans la Rome antique* (Paris, 1978).

57. Strauss, *The City and the Man*, (Chicago, 1964) p. 61.

58. Bloom, *Republic, Interpretive Essay*, p. 381; my emphasis. See below, pp. 205ff, for all those learned scholars who disagree. This would mean that not only Wilamowitz but most of the commentators from Aristotle on have failed in their understanding.

59. See Praxagora's speech before the assembly in Aristophanes, *Ecclesiazusae*, trans. B. B. Rogers, Vol. III (Cambridge, Mass.: Harvard University Press, 1924). For a lively modern version, see Douglass Parker's *Aristophanes, The Congresswomen* (Ann Arbor: University of Michigan Press, 1967), pp. 2, 21f.

60. See Sarah B. Hrdy, *The Woman That Never Evolved* (Cambridge, Mass.: Harvard University Press, 1981), pp. 10, 11.

61. Bloom, *Republic, Interpretive Essay*, p. 382. All references in the following section are taken from Bloom's discussion, pp. 383–89.

62. Ibid., p. 383. This becomes a major issue in later feminist commentary.

63. Bennett Simon, *Mind and Madness in Ancient Greece* (Ithaca: Cornell University Press, 1978), pp. 176, 177, 179.

64. See, e.g., Sigmund Freud, *Analysis Terminable and Interminable*, Standard Edition (London: Hogarth Press, 1964), Section VIII, pp. 250–53.

65. Plato, *Republic*, 465.

66. Simon, *Mind and Madness*, p. 241.

67. Dover, *Greek Popular Morality, in the Time of Plato and Aristotle* (Berkeley: University of California Press, 1977), p. 101.

68. Taylor, *Plato: The Man and Work*, p. 278.

69. For a view contrary to Taylor's, see Winspear and Silverberg, *Who Was Socrates?* (New York: Russell & Russell, 1960). In questioning the veracity of Plato's account of Socrates' death they nevertheless claim that the dramatic picture is accurate in showing Socrates' anti-female, pro-homosexual "disregard for ordinary human ties" (p. 40).

70. Maurice Croiset, *La République de Platon* (Paris, Editions Mellottée, 1946), p. 191.

71. Joachim Bannes, *Hitlers Kampf und Platons Staat* (Berlin: W. de Gruyter, 1933).

72. Adolf Hitler, *Mein Kampf* (Berlin: F. Eher, 1932), pp. 459–60.

73. Xenophon, *Memorabilia*, 2.7.1–12.

74. For an interesting, if highly speculative, account of Hitler's pathological attitudes toward women, see W. C. Langer, *The Mind of Adolf Hitler* (London: Secker & Warburg, 1973). In this study prepared for the U.S. government in 1944, Langer writes that many had commented on Hitler's "feminine characteristics," including what Langer enigmatically calls "his ways of thinking" (p. 172). Langer interprets much of Hitler's

205 Notes to Pages 54-58

neurosis as a reaction against hatred and fears of his own "femininity" (p. 194).

75. C. H. Hoole, *An Analytical Paraphrase of the Republic of Plato* (Oxford: J. Vincent, 1875), p. 27.

76. Jowett, *Greek Text*, p. 218.

77. Jowett, *Dialogues*, 1875 Edition, Vol. III, p. 62.

78. See Jenkyns, *The Victorians*, on Jowett's other attempts to "give the reader license to discount whatever he finds uncongenial" (p. 245).

79. W. Fite, *The Platonic Legend* (New York: Charles Scribner's Sons, 1934), pp. 157–58.

80. This is the phrase of R. Garnett, commenting on H. Spens' "long disquisition on Plato" in which the "delicate question" is evaded. (Spens published the first translation of the *Republic* into English in 1763.) R. Garnett in H. Spens, *Republic of Plato* (London: Dent, 1906), p. xi.

81. Jowett, *Dialogues*, 1875, p. 61.

82. James Adam, *The Republic, ed. with Critical Notes, Commentary, and Appendix* (Cambridge, 1905). Note to V, 457, p. 291.

83. T. H. Warren, *The Republic* (London: Macmillan, 1888). Note to V, 457; also discussed in ibid., p. 291.

84. Some feminists would deny this since rewards of more frequent intercourse are mentioned only for male guardians.

85. *The Republic of Plato*, trans. F. M. Cornford (London: Oxford University Press, 1941), p. 154.

86. Ibid., p. 160. Compare Grote, *Plato and Other Companions*, who forthrightly speaks of "a larger license of copulation with different women" (p. 43).

87. Alexandre Koyre, *Discovering Plato*, trans. L. C. Rosenfield (New York: Columbia University Press, 1945), p. 85, n. 24.

88. *Republic*, Cornford, p. 160.

89. Charles M. Bakewell, *Plato, The Republic with Introduction* (New York: Charles Scribners, 1928), p. 53.

90. Ibid. The consequences of such usage are with us still. In the 1980s in searching for a new member of the philosophy department at a major institution, a tenured female was struck by the continued use of the phrase "the man we need" at meetings, despite the fact that the gender of the candidate was ostensibly irrelevant. The use of such language, betraying unconscious assumptions, even when females participate in the deliberations, no doubt contributes to the continued disparity in the numbers of women faculty. Gerda Lerner reports that as late as 1972 even in women's colleges the majority of teaching and administrative jobs were held by men, while in the administration of coeducational colleges women remain a minority. *The Female Experience* (Indianapolis: Bobbs-Merrill, 1977). For information about tenured women in the 1980s, see above, note 8 to the introduction.

91. Bernard Bosanquet, *The Education of the Young in The Republic of Plato* (Cambridge: Cambridge University Press, 1900), p. 15.

92. Jean Ithurriage, *Les idées de Platon sur la condition de la femme*, pp. 124, 145, 150.
93. Ibid., pp. 151ff.
94. Ibid., p. 142.
95. Ibid., p. 154.
96. Ibid.
97. F. A. Wright, *Feminism in Greek Literature: From Homer to Aristotle* (Port Washington: Kennikat Press, 1969), p. 169.
98. Ibid., p. 176.
99. Ibid., p. 177.
100. Ibid., p. 182.
101. Ibid.
102. Grote (1794–1871) was seventy-one when the first edition appeared. Karl Popper describes him as "that great democrat"; his wife was active with Harriet Taylor in the nineteenth-century British feminist movement.
103. Grote, *Plato and Other Companions*, Vol. IV, p. 204.
104. Ibid., p. 189.
105. These singularly non-sexist usages appear respectively in ibid., pp. 170, 171, 195, 206.
106. Ibid., p. 172.
107. Ibid., p. 196.
108. Ibid., p. 197. It is interesting to note that although women remain less adept than men at many sports they still excel in archery.
109. We know that representations in sculpture of mythical and biblical women who exhibited great physical prowess and performed aggressive acts have historically been seen as dangerous examples of female power. Donatello's statue of "Judith and Holofernes" was banished from the Piazza Signoria (City Hall) in the early sixteenth century partly because the rulers thought it was a bad example "to have a woman kill a man." Previously it had been a symbol of Florentine liberty, and of pride vanquished by humility, "of incontinence crushed by chastity." Eva Borsook, *The Companion Guide to Florence* (London: Collins, 1973), p. 47.
110. Grote, *Plato and Other Companions*, p. 177.
111. Ibid., pp. 189–90.
112. Thus, although I find Martha Nussbaum's analysis of Plato's egalitarian views exemplary, I disagree with her about the means through which change will come. She holds out hope that women will get the jobs they deserve through "consideration one by one on an equal basis." She says that "a willingness on the part of each member of the educational community to look searchingly into his or her own heart" is preferable to affirmative action. The latter, she writes, will have a disastrous effect on women's self-esteem. If more women do not publicly describe or legally protest sexism in hiring it is sometimes because they have "made the difficult choice to get on with their work." "Letters:

Plato and Affirmative Action: Nussbaum-Lewontin Exchange," *New York Review of Books*, January 31, 1985. Here I agree with Grote that the problem is the impetus for reforms. Richard Lewontin answers her appropriately; the problem he says for women in academia and in society at large "is not a lack of merit, but a lack of power." Ibid. I believe that in the best of all possible worlds a small component of women's self-respect might come from the method of selection for a particular job. In the present climate, however, self-esteem can, and does, come from their own and others' judgment of the quality of their teaching and scholarship, once they are given a chance. Before organized pressure the very possibility of getting on with scholarly work was foreclosed for most women. See discussion of Nussbaum and Lewontin's disagreement about Plato below, pp. 91ff.

113. Theodor Gomperz, *Greek Thinkers* (London, 1905), Vol. III, p. 110.

114. Gomperz refers to an experimental community founded by Noyes in 1811 on the Platonic model called "Perfectionists," ibid., p. 123.

115. Ibid., p. 109.

116. Ibid., p. 115.

117. J. Adam uses this phrase and speaks of Plato's "customary disregard of the limitations of ordinary human nature." *The Republic*, ed. *with Critical Notes*, pp. 291–92.

118. Gomperz, *Greek Thinkers*, p. 124.

119. Ibid. Given the strength of Gomperz's statements it is difficult to see why Adela Adam considers that Gomperz is "not willing to go so far as Plato in admitting women to political life." *Plato: Moral and Political Ideals*, p. 131.

120. In the 1960s, Thomas Gould is still maintaining that women have not produced *any* works of the first order. *Platonic Love*, pp. 53ff. Clearly, he would not accept Gomperz's assessment of the contribution of nineteenth-century women to literature. See below, pp. 144–45.

121. Gomperz, *Greek Thinkers*, p. 124.

122. Ibid., p. 126.

123. Ibid.

124. Mill defends the sexual division of duties within the family, assuming that the husband will earn the family income while the wife does the housework, terming this "the most suitable division of labour between the two persons." Susan Moller Okin astutely points this out, referring to Mill's *On the Subjection of Women*, pp. 473, 474, 483. See *Women in Western Political Thought* (Princeton: Princeton University Press, 1979), p. 334, n. 92.

125. Adela M. Adam, *Plato: Moral and Political Ideals* (Cambridge: Cambridge University Press, 1913). See chap. XIII.

126. Ibid., p. 124.

127. Ibid., pp. 126, 129.

128. Ibid., p. 126. For my disagreement with this criticism of Plato, see the discussion of the views of J. Martin, who also interprets *Republic*, 540c, in this way, below, pp. 119ff.

129. A woman can easily see herself as a ruler, guardian, or guard, but never as a king!

130. Even Grote and Gomperz in my view are more genuine feminists. A. Adam seems to see herself as going further in admitting women to political life than Gomperz, but I think she is mistaken. See above, n. 119.

131. Adam, *Plato: Moral and Political Ideals*, pp. 132, 131.

2: THE RESURGENCE OF INTEREST IN PHILOSOPHER-QUEENS

1. See Rosamond Sprague, *Plato's Philosopher-King: A Study of the Theoretical Background* (Columbia, S.C., 1976). Another example is Louise Loomis, who, in her introduction to the *Republic*, has little to say about gender equality in Book V.

2. Such aspirations are now shared by women in other developed countries, too, although significant differences remain in women's expectations from country to country. In some countries there are still servants to support the work of the middle-class scholar, as subordinates were intended to perform the manual labor for Plato's guardians. In the United States, United Kingdom, and some European countries, day care facilities have to a certain extent replaced the extended family and servant class. Thus in an outstanding book to which I refer in my final chapter the young scientist specifically expresses gratitude to her child's day care provider for making her work possible. She is well aware that "such centers are . . . gardens of privilege for a privileged species in a privileged portion of the globe. . . . " Sarah B. Hrdy, *Woman That Never Evolved*, p. ix.

3. In introducing his chapter on women and the state in the ancient world, H. M. Currie describes the current situation well. Although I reject his implication that feminists have confused equality and similarity, I agree with his assessment that "the modern emancipation of women has meant that whilst they have gained many new functions they have lost few of the old ones." *The Individual and the State* (London: Dent, 1973), p. 122.

4. Christine Pierce, "Equality: *Republic* V," *The Monist*, 57, 1 (Jan. 1973), p. 3.

5. Ibid., p. 10.

6. Ibid., pp. 10–11.

7. As Grote correctly suggests, for Plato the first best city, better than that of the society proposed in the *Republic*, would require "a communion that should pervade all persons and all acts and sentiments, effacing alto-

gether the separate self." *Laws* V, 739D. See Grote, *Plato and Other Companions*, p. 179.

8. H. D. Rankin, *Plato and the Individual* (London: Methuen, 1964), p. 98.

9. Ibid., p. 100.

10. This professor says that one way of dealing with the disparities between the athletic promise and achievement of men and women is to view the latter as truncated males. Unlike Plato, he would therefore permit them to engage in men's sports, but in "foreshortened versions." In his chapter on women athletes Weiss also writes: "A woman is less abstract than a man because her mind is persistently ordered toward bodily problems." Paul Weiss, *Sport: A Philosophical Inquiry* (Carbondale: Southern Illinois University Press, 1969), pp. 215, 217.

11. Abigail Rosenthal, "Feminism Without Contradictions", *The Monist*, 57, 1 (Jan. 1973), p. 29.

12. Martha Lee Osborne, "Plato's Unchanging View of Woman: A Denial That Anatomy Spells Destiny," *The Philosophical Forum*, Summer 1975, p. 447.

13. See Anne Dickason, "Anatomy and Destiny: The Role of Biology in Plato's Views of Women," *The Philosophical Forum*, V (Fall-Winter 1973–1974), pp. 45–53.

14. Christine G. Allen, "Plato on Women," *Feminist Studies*, 2, 2–3 (1975), p. 132. Allen herself is aware that the actual role women play in the dialogues complicates the issue of equality. She quotes from the historian Mary Beard that Diotima, the wise priestess of the *Symposium*, may have been based on an actual living woman philosopher. But there is in fact no evidence for this, and Beard is not a reliable source of information on philosophers in the ancient world. Beard cites a discussion by A. W. Benn where the influence of ancient women philosophers is "made important." Mary Beard, *Women as a Force in History* (New York: Colliers, 1971), p. 349. But in *Greek Philosophers* (New York: Dutton, 1974), Benn makes only two brief references to women and philosophy and does not claim any importance at all for the few who may have existed. Beard's enthusiasm provides us with an added example of how eager women writers have been to show that females did make a public contribution even when the evidence is to the contrary. Most of the information we have about the existence of women philosophers comes from Diogenes Laertius, who is himself a not entirely reliable source. Besides Plato's two women disciples that I have previously mentioned, Diogenes describes Hipparchia of Maroneia, a fourth to third century B.C. female philosopher who married the philosopher Crates and chose education "instead of wasting further time upon the loom." *Lives of Eminent Philosophers*, VI, 96–98, vol. 2, p. 101. It is important to remember, however, that we do not have a single word written by a female philosopher in the ancient world.

Allen makes another error in accepting a quote from Simone de Beauvoir to show Plato's mysogyny. De Beauvoir wrote: "The first among the blessings for which Plato thanked the gods was that he had been created free, not enslaved, the second, a man, not a woman." *The Second Sex* (New York: Bantam Books, 1968), p. xxi. But in fact there is no source for this in Plato. Even the oft-expressed claim that it was Socrates who thanked God (as Orthodox Jews actually have for centuries) that he was not made a woman cannot be substantiated.

15. C. G. Allen, "Plato on Women," pp. 133, 134. This is not the place to consider the general role of Plato's myth in his total philosophy. For an excellent discussion, see Ludwig Edelstein, "The Function of the Myth in Plato's Philosophy," *Journal of the History of Ideas*, vol. 10, October 1949, pp. 463–481. For our purposes, there is an important question of whether ideas put forth by characters in a dialogue (even by a Platonic adversary) in some sense nevertheless represent unconscious attitudes of Plato. An extreme psychoanalytic position taken by Hans Kelson is that since they arose from Plato's imagination they have great relevance. Kelson assumes that the myths reveal, "although Plato does not expressly say this . . . that he recognizes in the masculine principle the good, and in the feminine the evil." Hans Kelson, "Platonic Love," *American Imago*, 3(1–2) (April 1942), p. 14.

16. Dorothea Wender, "Plato: Misogynist, Paeodophile and Feminist," *Arethusa*, VI(1) (Spring 1973), p. 76.

17. James E. White summarizes Jaggar's five types from her "Political Philosophies of Women's Liberation" in *Feminism and Philosophy* (Totowa, N.J.: Littlefield, Adams 1977) ed. M. Vettling-Braggin, F. A. Elliston, and J. English. "Liberal feminists believe that changing discriminatory laws and practices can be accomplished without changing either capitalism or the technology of reproduction. They emphasize equal opportunity for individuals within the existing system. Radical feminists think that the source of women's oppression is fundamentally biological. In order to achieve equality . . . women must be relieved of the burden of childbearing; this could be done by technological means. They also endorse the end of exclusively heterosexual relationships. Classical Marxist feminists see capitalism as the primary cause of women's oppression, and hold that women's liberation requires the dissolution of the capitalist society. Lesbian separatists believe that women should refrain from heterosexual relationships. Some see this as a temporary necessity, while others want permanent lesbianism. Socialist feminism . . . agrees with the Marxist contention that socialism is the main precondition for women's liberation. But. . . . other changes in the production of goods, reproduction, sexuality, and socialization are required, too." I agree with White's statement of the necessary condition for calling a person a feminist. He/she must believe, he writes, "that sexism is unacceptable, . . . that women should no longer accept unjust treatment . . . that justice requires equality

for women." *Contemporary Moral Problems* (St. Paul: West, 1985),
pp. 211–12.

18. Wender, "Plato: Misogynist . . . ," p. 75.

19. Ibid., p. 76.

20. W. W. Fortenbaugh, "On Plato's Feminism in *Republic* V," *Apeiron*, IX, 2 (1975), p. 1.

21. Brian Calvert, "Plato and the Equality of Women," *Phoenix*, 29, 3
(1975), pp. 242, 243.

22. Joseph Ghougassian, *Toward Women* (San Diego: Lukas, 1977), p.
41.

23. Other inaccuracies include a confusion between the *Laws* and the
Republic, p. 41, and a misleading reference to Aristophanes, suggesting
communism before Plato, p. 43. Clearly female advocates of gender
equality have no monopoly on excesses.

24. Mary Cohart, ed., *Unsung Champions of Women* (Albuquerque:
University of New Mexico Press, 1975), pt. 4.

25. Elizabeth G. Davis even makes the patently false statement that "in
Plato's time and for long before in enlightened Greece, boys and girls
received identical educations and prepared for identical lives of the
mind." *The First Sex* (New York: Putnam, 1971), p. 331.

26. Richard C. Lewontin, "A Simple Problem Science Can't Solve,"
New York Review of Books, April 12, 1984, p. 21.

27. Richard C. Lewontin, "Plato's Women," Letters to the Editors,
New York Review of Books, Oct. 25, 1984. This is part of his answer to
R. J. Nelson's rebuttal of his original review. Nelson maintains that
"contrary to Lewontin and his wayward exegesis, Plato might well be set
as a standard for women's rightful status in all intellectual and cultural
pursuits including business, the professions, and science." This places the
philosopher Nelson squarely among those who consider Plato unequivocally a great champion of women's rights.

28. Ibid.

29. Martha Nussbaum, "Plato and Affirmative Action: Nussbaum-
Lewontin Exchange," *New York Review of Books*, Jan. 30, 1985.

30. Ibid.

31. Elizabeth Janeway, *Powers of the Weak* (New York: Knopf, 1980),
p. 82.

32. Sarah Pomeroy, "Feminism in Book V of Plato's *Republic*," *Apeiron*,
VIII, 1 (1974), p. 33.

33. E.g., he clearly had mixed feelings about the arts. While writing
powerful literary pieces himself, he banned poets from the state. The aesthetic philosopher-psychologist Rudolf Arnheim discusses another
Platonic ambivalence, the "ambiguous attitude" Plato takes toward
knowing objective existence. Arnheim sees a contradiction difficult to
eliminate in Plato's belief on the one hand that we know through logical
operations and on the other that we grasp reality through "direct vision."

See "Plato of Two Minds," in *Visual Thinking* (Berkeley: University of California Press, 1971), pp. 6–8.

34. Pomeroy, "Feminism in Book V," p. 33.

35. That is, "shared by all." Dover discusses this dual sense of *ktema.* He notes "the use of the verb *ktasthai,* 'obtain,' 'acquire' in a very wide sense," in discussing the fact that the "acquisition" of a sympathetic wife recommended by Euripides does not support the idea of women solely as property. *Greek Popular Morality,* p. 96, n.2.

36. Fortenbaugh, "On Plato's Feminism," p. 1.

37. For an excellent summary of Aristotle's use of *koinōnia, see* Martin Ostwald's glossary in his translation of the *Nichomachean Ethics* (New York: Bobbs-Merril, 1962), pp. 309–10. Ostwald translates "community, society, human relations, social organism," and also "partnership" depending on the context. He points out that the term refers to any kind of group whose members are held together by something they have "in common" with each other; a club, a village, a family are spoken of as different kinds of *koinōnia.*

38. Marylin B. Arthur in *Becoming Visible: Women in European History* ed. R. Bridenthal and C. Koonz (Boston: Houghton Mifflin, 1977), pp. 72, 73.

39. M. I. Finley, *The World of Odysseus,* rev. ed. (New York: Viking Press, 1978), pp. 127–28.

40. Julia Annas, "Plato's *Republic* and Feminism," *Philosophy,* 51 (1976), p. 309.

41. Ibid.

42. Ibid., p. 311.

43. Annas points to the irony that even the utilitarian Mill starts his essay on the subjection of women with the idea that the subordination of women is wrong *in itself,* though she admits that he also offers utilitarian reasons. The question is how Mill would define "in itself" in this context; and I think we have reason to believe that just as he offers his own interpretation of "good" he might well offer a reinterpretation of "wrong in itself" which referred to consequences.

44. Annas, *"Republic* and Feminism," p. 314.

45. Ibid., p. 315.

46. Lynda Lange, "The Function of Equal Education" in Lorenne M. G. Clark and L. Lange, *The Sexism of Social and Political Theory* (Toronto, 1979), pp. 3, 4.

47. Ibid., p. 9.

48. Arlene Saxenhouse, "The Philosopher and the Female in the Political Thought of Plato," *Political Theory,* 4 (May 1976), p. 203.

49. Ibid., p. 199. Two Italian feminist classicists make a similar point. They object to the fact that because "complete uniformity within the body politic" is required "the natural role of the mother" is cancelled. Silvia Campese and Silvia Gastaldi, *La donna e i filosofi: archeologia di un'immagine culturale* (Bologna: Zanichelli, 1977), p. 16.

50. Saxenhouse, "The Philosopher and the Female," p. 211.

51. Susan Moller Okin, "Philosopher Queens and Private Wives: Plato on Women and the Family," *Philosophy and Public Affairs*, 6 (Summer 1977), p. 365. Okin first discussed the relation between female guardians and private wives in this article, and then in a slightly revised version in her *Women and Western Political Thought* (Princeton: Princeton University Press, 1979), in which the first three chapters are devoted to Plato.

52. See above, pp. 33ff.

53. Okin, "Philosopher Queens," pp. 346, 347.

54. Ibid., p. 361.

55. Okin, *Women and Western Thought*, p. 69.

56. Okin, "Philosopher Queens," p. 368.

57. Rousseau, *Emile*, 4: 699–700, quoted in ibid., p. 356.

58. Ibid.

59. In her earlier article she states only that Taylor does not give "any reasons" (ibid., p. 356), but in the later book she makes the accusation even stronger, referring to his dogmatism.

60. Taylor, *Plato: Man and Work*, p. 278.

61. Nohle, *Die Statslehre*, pp. 137–38.

62. Okin, "Philosopher Queens," p. 359.

63. William Jacobs, "Plato on Female Emancipation and the Traditional Family," *Apeiron*, XII, 1 (1978), p. 29.

64. Okin, *Women and Western Thought*, p. 38 and n.38. She nevertheless retains the expression "entails as a corollary," p. 41. See also p. 69.

65. Dover, *Greek Popular Morality*, p. 98.

66. Okin, *Women and Western Thought*.

67. Okin, "Philosopher Queens," p. 357.

68. See also Jacobs, *Plato on Female Emancipation*, p. 30 and p. 31, n. 3.

69. Okin, *Women and Western Thought*, p. 38.

70. Ibid., p. 29.

71. Although the usage is very common, I agree with A. E. Taylor's objection that the practices recommended have little to do with our modern understanding of the word. *Plato: Man and Work*, pp. 277–78.

72. Okin, *Women and Western Thought*, p. 29.

73. Ibid., p. 51.

74. Ibid., p. 52.

75. At one point she attempts a qualification of this nature-nurture bifurcation, but in general she argues for Plato's stress on nurture. Ibid., p. 57.

76. Ibid.

77. See *Phaedrus* and Okin, *Women and Western Thought*, p. 57.

78. For example, J. P. Sartre's existentialist ontology with its formulation "existence precedes essence" is designed to counter the Platonic stress on the fixity of human nature and the consequent devaluation of change and choice.

79. John Wild, *Plato's Modern Enemies and the Theory of Natural Law* (Chicago: University of Chicago Press, 1953), p. 150. Wild shows that for Plato the goal for any entity whatsoever is to realize its "essential tendencies and capacities," p. 73.

80. Cornford, *From Religion to Philosophy*, quoted in Okin, *Women and Western Thought*, p. 52.

81. Okin, *Women and Western Thought*, p. 53.

82. Cornford, *Republic*, 485.

83. Jowett, *Republic*, 485.

84. Okin, *Women and Western Thought*, p. 59.

85. Plato, *Laws*, 795.

86. Okin, *Women and Western Thought*, p. 64.

87. Ibid., pp. 64, 65.

88. Glen Morrow, *Plato's Cretan City*, p. 331, quoted in ibid., p. 316, n.48.

89. Taylor, *Laws*, 802e. In Hamilton and Cairns, *Collected Dialogues*, p. 1374.

90. Okin, *Women and Western Thought*, p. 71, and n.44.

91. Jowett, *Laws*, 781.

92. See discussion of F. A. Wright above, pp. 62-63.

93. Bloom translates "produce"; Rouse, "engender"; Shorey, "create"; and Jowett, "implant." Jowett assumes that Plato believed that good education has a cumulative force and "affects the breed." Jowett, *Greek Text*, III, p. 151.

94. *Laws*, 834d. The Greek text states that a woman may participate if her nature is not averse, *mē dyscherainē*; the reason a woman's nature might make her vexed or uncomfortable with horsemanship is not here specified.

95. Jowett, *Laws*, 834d, 781.

96. Okin, *Women and Western Thought*, p. 59.

97. Ibid., p. 68.

98. Plato, *Laws*, 805c–d.

99. The wording is *hoti malista*, which Jowett translates "to the greatest possible extent." Jowett, *Laws*, 805.

100. Okin, *Women and Western Thought*, pp. 40–41.

101. Jane R. Martin, "Equality and Education in Plato," in *Feminism and Philosophy*, ed. M. Vetterling-Braggin, F. A. Elliston, J. English, (Totoma, N.J.: Littlefield, 1977), pp. 280, 282.

102. Ibid., p. 1.

103. Ibid., pp. 286, 287.

104. Ibid. p. 289.

105. I have preferred to extend the terminology in English to "Philosopher-Kings" and "Philosopher-Queens" only because the former has become standard usage, and demands some equivalent. Of course "female philosopher-ruler" would be more accurate but also more awkward and less suggestive of the intended parallelism. Plato, of course, does not use

basileia. Jowett translates *archontas* as "governers" and *archousas* as "governesses." This choice may be well intentioned (since the Oxford English Dictionary defines "governess" first as a woman who governs, e.g. a kingdom, province, community, or religious institution), but it hardly conveys equality to the contemporary reader. Nussbaum points out that the frequently anthologized translation of Paul Shorey renders *archontas* as "rulers" and *archousas* as "women" rather than "female rulers." She connects this misleading usage to Shorey's endowment of a bequest for "single young men studying Plato" and sees both facts as instances of bias, bias of the sort I have detailed above in other earlier Plato scholars. She reports holding a different fellowship in the same classics department, an award which allowed her "(unjustly) to be the first female in that guardian class." This was possible because the term "men" in the conditions of her award was henceforth to be construed to mean "members of the human species." Twenty-five hundred years after Plato's formulation the powers in the university have finally come around to his conclusion! Nussbaum, "Plato and Affirmative Action."

106. Martin, "Equality in Plato," p. 288.
107. Ibid. See p. 298, n.29.
108. This was the observation of Mrs. Ferraro, made in a public broadcast after her daughter Geraldine Ferraro was nominated at the Democratic Party Convention in August 1984.
109. Martin, "Equality in Plato."
110. Ibid., p. 288.
111. I use this concept in the sense popularized by the British psychiatrist Winnicott who concluded that although perfect parents cannot exist, children's mental health can be adequately assured by "good enough" parenting.
112. E. O. Wilson points out that "the best women athletes are better than most male athletes," *On Human Nature* (Cambridge, Mass.: Harvard University Press, 1978) p. 127.
113. Martin, "Equality in Plato," p. 293.
114. Plato, Republic. 541a.
115. G. Mitchell agrees we should focus our research on power and leadership, on getting things done, rather than on gender-related variables. It is interesting, however, that she describes the masculine or "agentic" pattern in power situations as one that promotes the individual, glorifies individual achievement, and separates the individual from the group. Whereas the female or "communal pattern promotes the welfare of the group and stresses relations with others." By these criteria Plato's rulers follow the female pattern! See *Human Sex Differences: A Primatologist's Perspective* (New York: Van Nostrand, Reinhold, 1981), p. 18.
116. Jean B. Elshtain, *Public Man, Private Woman* (Princeton: Princeton University Press, 1981), pp. 20–41.
117. In her preface Elshtain writes "*Public Man, Private Woman* is a nasty book. It is intended to be" (p. xi). She justifies her tone by refer-

ring to a letter by Ludwig Wittgenstein. He wrote that thinking really honestly about our own and other people's lives is not really thrilling, but often downright nasty, and when nasty then it's most important. Quoted from Norman Malcolm, *Ludwig Wittgenstein, A Memoir*, p. 39. However, it should be noted that Wittgenstein was describing the process of thinking; and his own work, as published by his disciples, is *not* nasty. My disagreement with Elshtain here is pronounced. Nastiness generally provokes only more nastiness and does not in fact illuminate important questions. The temptation to respond in kind is strong and may result in the exaggeration of differences and the obscuring of crucial agreement. I am not sure I have succeeded in avoiding this trap.

118. She writes, "The key problem is not so much Plato's personal antipathy toward women but his conceptual adequacy to the task at hand. Here Plato's somewhat muddled treatment of the category "nature" becomes critical." *Public Man, Private Woman*, p. 37.

119. Jane R. Martin makes a similar point in her book *Reclaiming a Conversation: The Ideal of the Educated Woman* (New Haven: Yale University Press, 1985). According to Martha Nussbaum in her review essay, Martin makes the important point that contemporary theorists on women's education seldom consult the philosophical discussions that have taken place for centuries. The result is that public debate is impoverished and important public figures repeatedly make assumptions that have been successfully challenged. Nussbaum points out that the U.S. White House Chief of Staff Donald Regan made just such an erroneous assumption about women when he stated that they did not have the ability to comprehend arms negotiations. See Nussbaum, "Women's Lot," p. 7. Feminist thinkers who neglect previous scholarship may also make false assumptions.

120. Elshtain, *Public Man, Private Woman*, p. 21, n.4.

121. See Hans Kelson, "Platonic Love," *American Imago*, 3, 1–2 (April 1942). p. 3.

122. Elshtain, *Public Man, Private Woman*, p. xiii.

123. Russell wrote that Plato possessed the art to dress up illiberal suggestions in such a way that they deceived future ages who admired the *Republic* without ever becoming aware of what was actually involved in its proposals. "It has always been correct to praise Plato but not to understand him. . . . My object is the opposite. I wish to understand him, but to treat him with as little reverence as if he were a contemporary English or American advocate of totalitarianism." B. Russell, *History of Western Philosophy*, (New York: Simon and Schuster, 1945), p. 85. Elshtain's account, though more filled with that spirit of *ressentiment* that she elsewhere derides, would seem in intention at least to be similar.

124. E.g., Bertrand Russell complains that in spite of all the fine talk, skill in war and enough to eat is all that will be achieved by Plato's ideal society. The philosopher had lived through famine and defeat in Athens, and as Russell puts it, "perhaps *subconsciously* he thought the avoidance

of these evils the best that statesmanship could accomplish." (My emphasis.) *History of Western Philosophy*, p. 85.

125. Elshtain, *Public Man, Private Woman*, pp. 31–32.

126. Jean B. Elshtain, "Against Androgyny," *Telos*, 47, Spring 1981, p. 19.

127. Elshtain, *Public Man, Private Woman*, pp. 15, 16, 27. One cannot be sure of the extent to which Elshtain would be prepared to defend this idea. She writes in her introduction that "the question to be put, then, is not just what politics is for but what politics has served to defend against." Ibid., p. 16. But then in her chapter immediately following she describes her calling "normative ideals of collective life" a defense as "a playful and provocative note." Ibid., p. 19.

Hans Kelson, in his psychoanalytic analysis of Platonic love, takes a similar view of Plato's deficiencies. He, too, speculates on Plato's unconquered incest wish and accuses the philosopher of ignoring "the woman as such" and denying her any sexual peculiarity (*Platonic Love*, p. 17). Ultimately it is Plato's perverse sexual orientation that is responsible for his stance toward women in the *Republic*. Plato's mistaken view of the relations between the sexes stems from the fact that "nature has denied him all knowledge of motherhood." Ibid., p. 19.

128. Ibid., p. 335.

129. While Elshtain's attempt at a lively and personal style is admirable, her lack of precision places a burden on the reader. For example, in *Public Man, Private Woman*, she uses the word "imperative" repeatedly without clarifying its meaning. She speaks of "political and philosophic imperatives," p. 20; "psycho-social imperatives," p. 25; "feminist imperatives," p. 298; "public imperative," p. 299; "universal, bureaucratic, and socioeconomic imperatives," p. 305; "moral and theoretical imperative," p. 310; "inborn imperative," p. 318; "human imperative" and "familial imperative," p. 332; "humanizing imperative," p. 333; "Nazi imperative," p. 335; and "bedrock imperatives," p. 339, as well as numerous other vague uses of the term. Many of her metaphors are equally confusing, such as her assertion that those who undervalue the importance of the body "need to hold the body at arm's length."

130. She quotes with enthusiasm this view of what women's political urgency must be from Hélène Cîxous, "Poetry is/and (the) Political," in *The Second Sex—Thirty Years Later* (Mimeographed, New York Institute for the Humanities, 1979), p. 37. Quoted, *Public Man, Private Woman*, p. 335.

131. Elshtain, *Public Man, Private Woman*, p. 311.

132. Elshtain, "Against Androgyny," p. 14. Elshtain insists that such feminist theory automatically involves us in a belief in Lockean atomistic individuals as well as in the post-industrial capitalist use of people as interchangeable units. Ibid., p. 11.

133. Elshtain, *Public Man, Private Woman*, p. 318.

134. Ibid., p. 35. See also "Against Androgyny," pp. 7, 10, 16, 17,

where the assumption is that androgyny automatically means "blandness," p. 21.

135. See e.g., Elshtain, *Public Man, Private Woman*, p. 38. In "Against Androgyny" she speaks of the "iron cage of . . . liberal dualism," p. 11.

136. Elshtain, *Public Man, Private Woman*, pp. 326, 327.

137. Ibid., p. 39.

138. Ibid., p. 248.

139. Carol Gilligan, *In a Different Voice* (Cambridge, Mass.: Harvard University Press, 1982), pp. 335–36.

140. Elshtain, *Public Man, Private Woman*, pp. 335, 336.

141. Gilligan, *In a Different Voice*, pp. 2, 8ff.

142. Ibid., pp. 11–12, 19ff. She also argues very convincingly against the psychiatrist-researcher George Vaillant's minimizing of the value of attachment and using as models for mental health men distant in their relationships. I would claim that Gilligan's view of morality is not only different, but that her values, as the Greeks would say, are better. See p. 153.

143. Ibid., p. 37.

144. Elshtain, *Public Man, Private Woman*, p. 19.

145. She writes, "Whatever nightmares rocked his sleep and terrors filled his days, Plato's solution is an overreaction." Ibid., p. 35.

146. Ibid., p. 16 and n.12.

147. For Elshtain's objections to other interpretations of Freud see e.g., ibid., pp. 249, 273–74. Freud's view of the consequences of a lack of castration anxiety on women's mental life and the resulting different sense of justice appears in "Some Psychical Consequences of the Anatomical Distinctions Between the Sexes," *The Complete Psychological Works of Sigmund Freud*, ed. J. Strachey (London: Hogarth Press, 1961), vol. 19, p. 243.

148. Elshtain, *Public Man, Private Woman*, p. 310.

149. Ibid., p. 317.

150. Georges M. A. Grube, *Plato's Thought* (Boston: Beacon Press, 1935), p. 136.

151. Ibid. Adela N. Adam writes: "There is an element of passion and ardour in Plato's 'reason' which is very remote from our usual understanding of the term. Reason is afire with love of beauty and of goodness as well as love of truth, and so is capable of inspiring life and action. . . . " *Plato: Moral and Political Ideals*, p. 116.

152. Elshtain, *Public Man, Private Woman*, p. 27.

153. Ibid., p. 27.

154. Ibid.

155. Dover, *Greek Homosexuality*, p. 164.

156. Ibid.

157. Ibid., p. 157.

158. Erich Segal, "Platonic Love," review of Dover's *Greek Homosexuality* in the *New York Times Book Review*, April 8, 1979, p. 9.

159. Elshtain, *Public Man, Private Woman*, p. 27, n.22.
160. T. Gould maintains that the earlier speeches in the *Symposium* though representing false views most probably show Plato extracting the best from popular notions. *Platonic Love*, p. 21.
161. Anton-Hermann Chroust, *Socrates, Man and Myth* (South Bend: Notre Dame Press, 1957).
162. T. Gould, *Platonic Love*, pp. 54, 55.
163. Ibid., p. 54.
164. Ibid., p. 55.
165. Ludwig Wittgenstein, *Philosophical Investigations* (Oxford: Blackwell, 1972) I, 67, p. 32e.
166. Elshtain, *Public Man, Private Woman*.
167. Mary Midgley, *Beast and Man: The Roots of Human Nature* (Ithaca: Cornell University Press, 1978), p. 75.
168. Ibid., p. 353.
169. Ibid.
170. Ibid., pp. 75, 76.
171. Ibid., p. 331.
172. Ibid., p. 76, n.27.
173. Ibid.
174. Ibid., p. 327.
175. Elshtain, *Public Man, Private Woman*, p. 30.
176. Ibid.
177. *The Undergraduate Woman: Issues in Educational Equity*, ed. P. J. Perun (Lexington, Mass.: D.C. Heath, 1982), p. 406.
178. Lili S. Hornig makes this point about the reluctant support of women's sports, and offers this quote from Judge J. J. Fitzgerald of Connecticut. In ibid., p. 418.
179. Elshtain, *Public Man, Private Woman*, p. 37.
180. Opposition to androgyny has already "rallied" many in the United States. The leaders of the so-called Moral Majority have called vociferously for the elimination of text books in which women appear in nontraditional roles, and the question has become a political issue in the South and Midwest. See Elshtain, "Against Androgyny," p. 19.
181. For an excellent examination of the logical implications of Plato's argument, including a critique of Bloom's (and others') interpretation, see Brian Calvert, *Plato and Equality*, pp. 234ff. He points out that there is no inconsistency between saying that the class of men is superior to the class of women, and that "the best women are equal to the best men."
182. Katherine Ralls, "Mammals in which Females are Larger than Males," *Quarterly Review of Biology*, June 1976.
183. See above, pp. 45–47.
184. Dale Hall, "The Republic and the 'Limits of Politics,' " *Political Theory*, 5, 3 (August 1977), p. 296.
185. Ibid.

186. Bloom, *Republic, Interpretive Essay.*
187. Bloom, "Response to Hall," *Political Theory,* 5, 3 (August 1977), p. 315.
188. Ibid., p. 324.
189. Ibid.
190. It is interesting to note that even a scholar as open-minded as K. J. Dover seems to assume in his *Greek Homosexuality,* p. 156, that his readers will be either heterosexual or homosexual males. In quoting this passage from Kharmides to illustrate Plato's philosophical exploitation of homosexuality, Dover tries to make the fact that Socrates is "on fire" at the sight of Kharmides' torso or genitals more understandable to his readers. He writes: "If we translate this scene into heterosexual terms, so that Socrates' glimpse inside Kharmides' cloak becomes a glimpse of a young woman of extraordinary beauty, as she leans forward to ask an unaffected question, we come as close to seeing through ancient Greek eyes as we are likely to come." He also explains that those with a mainly or entirely homosexual orientation may see clearly enough through Greek eyes already. What he does not concern himself with at all is whether the appeal of Kharmides' anatomy would already sufficiently clarify the intended exploitation of erotic appeal for his female readers; or whether perhaps some other male type would be necessary. This oversight is particularly ironic since Dover cites the female classicist Wender in this very paragraph (though she is using the passage for other purposes). It may seem a trivial point, but after centuries of androcentric explications, it is surely time to address explanations to female as well as male audiences.
191. In the vaudeville review "Oh! Calcutta," where nightly nude dancing of men and women was a theatrical spectacle, just such control was exercised for hundreds of performances. I cannot vouch for the rehearsals, of course.
192. Bloom, "Response to Hall," p. 324.
193. See above, p. 43.
194. In an appendix to his edition of the *Republic,* James Adam reviews over 100 scholars who have discussed the subject, considering the nature of the connection far from self-evident, pp. 352–55. Adam himself argues that the idea of female guardians was part of a well-reasoned and deliberate attempt by the Socratic school to improve the position of women in Greece, p. 280, and asserts that Plato "touches with serious purpose on nearly all the proposals which Aristophanes had tried to make ridiculous" p. 355.
195. Aristophanes, *Ecclesiazusae,* ed. R. G. Ussher (London: Oxford University Press, 1973), p. xx.
196. A. Bloom, "Response to Hall," p. 324. It is simply not conceivable to Bloom that intelligent, imaginative thinkers living with a woman and priding themselves on speculation, exposed to females' intelligence despite their lack of education, might well have seriously considered

alternatives before Plato. The great classicist Schleiermacher, whose translation of the *Republic* Bloom admires, takes that view, though he states it without any of Bloom's dogmatism. About the subject of egalitarianism in Book V he writes: "It does not appear to me that the way in which it is introduced, Socrates' reluctance to enter upon it, and his wish to avoid the subject, refers to the circumstance that he was here about to introduce into the language of the people a thing contrary to all current opinion, and as yet unheard-of. I rather discover in this the clearest traces of the fact the *this doctrine was already known*, as it naturally might be from the oral lectures and the communications of his pupils, and had experienced some satirical treatment" (*my emphasis*). Bloom's arrogance contrasts sharply with the hesitance of Schleiermacher who adds: "But this is so completely a matter of critical feeling lying without the limits of argument, that I can do nothing but invite those readers who are interested in such questions . . . to an attentive consideration of the passage." F. Schleiermacher, *Introductions to the Dialogues of Plato* (New York: Arno Press, 1973), see pp. 377–81.

197. Bloom, "Response to Hall," p. 326.

198. Ibid., p. 318.

3: THE CONTINUING IMPORTANCE OF PLATO'S QUESTIONS

1. This frequently quoted dictum is from Whitehead's major work, *Process and Reality* (New York: Macmillan, 1929), p. 63. Okin (who evidently had difficulty locating it and speculated that he must have said it in some unpublished lecture) disagrees. This is because she believes Aristotle's functionalism and outright subordination of women have been ascendent in the history of philosophy. But of course Aristotle's discussion is in part an answer to his teacher Plato; and what Whitehead intends is precisely that Plato initiated the discussion of all the significant issues (not, of course, that all of his solutions have prevailed). See Okin, *Women in Western Thought*, p. 335 and chapter 10, n. 1.

2. Wilson, *On Human Nature.*

3. Ibid., p. 135.

4. Donald Symons, *Evolution of Human Sexuality* (New York: Oxford University Press, 1979).

5. Clifford Geertz, in "Sociosexology," his review of Symons' book in the *New York Review of Books*, Jan. 24, 1980, p. 4. Geertz refutes Symons' "sociosexology," saying, "to write a book that says men and women are radically mismatched in their basic sexual natures, that sex is a basic disruptive force in marriage and a primary obstacle to human happiness, that copulation is a female service provided to men for an appropriate return, that men want sexual novelty and women sexual constancy, that male sexuality is rigidly channeled and female highly

malleable, . . . and expect it all to be taken, at this time and in this place, as 'just the facts' is so wildly unrealistic as to suggest a highly uncertain grasp on the ways of the world."

6. David Barash, *The Whisperings Within* (New York: Harper and Row, 1979), p. 6.

7. Stephen Jay Gould, "Genes on the Brain," *New York Review of Books*, June 30, 1983, p. 6.

8. E. O. Wilson, *Sociobiology* (Cambridge, Mass.: Harvard University Press, 1975), p. 562. See also his *On Human Nature*, p. 5.

9. Wilson, *On Human Nature*, p. 132.

10. Hrdy, *Woman that Never Evolved*, pp. 200–201.

11. Wilson, *On Human Nature*, p. 135.

12. Ibid., pp. 133–34.

13. Ibid., p. 133.

14. Ibid.

15. Ibid., p. 134.

16. Melford Spiro, *Gender and Culture: Kibbutz Women Revisited* (Durham, N. C.: Duke University Press, 1979), p. 99.

17. Ibid., p. 86.

18. Ibid., p. 85.

19. See, e.g., the discussion of R. L. Blumberg, "The Erosion of Sexual Equality: A Structural Interpretation," in *Beyond Intellectual Sexism: A New Woman, a New Reality*, ed. J. I. Roberts (New York: David McKay, 1976). Blumberg rejects the "unilateral and deterministic view that, due to the intrinsic nature of human females, 'Laundry is Destiny,' " p. 331.

20. I am indebted to Barbara Tizard, Head of the Thomas Coram Research Unit of the University of London and an authority on early childhood development, for this suggestion.

21. Wilson, *Sociobiology*, p. 575.

22. Melvin Konner, *The Tangled Wing: Biological Constraints on the Human Spirit* (New York: Holt, Rinehart and Winston, 1982), p. 121, and n.

23. Ibid., pp. 106–07.

24. Ibid., p. 106.

25. R. Barnett, G. Baruch, and C. Rivers, *Life Prints: New Patterns of Love and Work for Today's Women* (New York: New American Library, 1983) pp. 38, 143–49.

26. Aristotle, on *The Generation of Animals*, 728a 18, quoted in Caroline Whitbeck, "Theories of Sex Difference," *The Philosophical Forum*, 5 (Fall 1973–74), p. 56.

27. Konner, *The Tangled Wing*, p. 126.

28. Ibid. The philosopher Mary Midgley, who would agree that considerations of our innate biological nature are crucial to planning a just society, also maintains that women are "rather less competitive by nature." But she sees that to arrive at the place where they could do something to bring about a saner climate, "they would have to compete

without catching the competitive spirit." She is less sanguine about this possibility than Konner, and admits that "this is a lot to expect." *Beast and Man*, p. 330. My own view is that there is no reason at all to believe that it would occur.

29. Hrdy, *Woman that Never Evolved*, pp. 42–43.

30. Symons, *Evolution of Human Sexuality*. More than 100 years before sociobiologists like Symons claimed that the existing sex roles were biologically prescribed, Herbert Spencer assumed before he even started investigating that there was an "unlikeness of mental facilities" which went along with the unlikeness of "parental activities" between the sexes. See J. Sayers, *Biological Politics*, pp. 34–35. Such "scientific" thought no doubt indirectly influenced nineteenth-century British Plato commentators.

31. Mitchell, *Human Sex Differences*, p. 205. Also see n.115 above.

32. Midgley, *Beast and Man*, p. 125, n.7.

33. David Barash, *Sociobiology and Behavior* (New York: Elsevier, 1977), p. 293.

34. See, for example, Barash, *The Whisperings Within*, p. 49.

35. Dover, *Greek Popular Morality*, p. 101. He writes that the Greeks tended to think that women desired and enjoyed sexual intercourse *more* than men. He quotes from Hesiod (fr.275), who "relates a myth in which Teiresias (since he had been both man and woman) was asked by Zeus and Hera to say which sex got more pleasure from intercourse, and his answer was that the woman got nine-tenths, the man one-tenth." See also Aristotle, "Females are naturally libidinous, incite the males to copulation, and cry out during the act of coition." *De Historia Animalium* 5.2.540 11–13.

36. Barash, *The Whisperings Within*, p. 87.

37. Barash, *Sociobiology and Behavior*, p. 301.

38. Barash, *The Whisperings Within*, pp. 233–34. His fellow sociobiologist, Daniel Freedman, also makes an attempt to allow for free will saying it is "universal" and "species-specific" but adding "therefore within the realm of biology." He reveals his prejudices when he writes that "[d]espite . . . shifting patterns, certain male-female differences can be expected to remain the same," in his section on "Male Bragging and the Double Standard." *Human Sociobiology* (New York: Macmillan, 1979), p. 18.

39. "His and Hers Brains," *Science*, 3, 7 (September 1982), p. 14.

40. David Gelman and John Carey, "Sex Research—On the Bias," *Newsweek*, May 18, 1981, p. 81.

41. Erik Erikson in *Childhood and Society*, and discussed in the excellent popular summary of recent scientific research, "Just How the Sexes Differ," *Newsweek*, May 18, 1981, p. 81.

42. Research of Paula Caplan, Toronto psychologist, reported in "Sex Research—On the Bias," p. 81.

43. It is well known that a drop in social status in monkeys can result in

224 Notes to Pages 188–193

a lower level of testosterone. See, e.g., Konner, *The Tangled Wing*, p. 119 and n. We have much to learn about the way women's destiny affects her anatomy.

44. University of Chicago psychologist Jerre Levy, a pioneer in studies of brain lateralization, withdrew from public discussion of her work after being harassed by hostile letters and phone calls. And S. B. Hrdy relates that when she participated in a panel discussing possible differences in male and female math ability, a feminist suggested to her that it was evil to do such studies. Reported in *Newsweek*, May 18, 1981.

45. Gould, *Platonic Love*, p. 84.

46. C. Lumsden and E. O. Wilson, *Genes, Mind and Culture* (Cambridge, Mass.: Harvard University Press, 1981), p. 172.

47. Lewontin, "A Simple Problem Science Can't Solve," p. 21.

48. The anthropologist Peter Wilson writes in *Man, the Promising Primate* (New Haven: Yale University, 1980), that "it is a distinguishing feature of the human species that although individuals are naturally impelled toward living in company and it is necessary for them to do so, there is no universal instinctive *form* that this company will take," pp. 160, 161.

49. See, e.g., C. Benbow and J. Stanley, "Sex Differences in Mathematical Ability: Fact or Artifact?" *Science*, December 12, 1980.

50. W. D. Wandersee points out in *Women's Work and Family Values 1920–1940* (Cambridge, Mass.: Harvard University Press, 1981), that the family was as often a source of power as a tool of oppression. She says if family life is to be revolutionized to allow for women's full equality, because of women's historical commitment to the family, "the revolution will have to be gentle" if it is to have a broad base of support, pp. 121–22. But, of course, a gentle revolution is a contradiction in terms. Wandersee herself finds this a feminist dilemma, and "one that is not much closer to being resolved today than it was half a century ago." In the light of *Republic* V and Aristotle's pro-family rejoinder to it, one might say the dilemma is as unsolved as it was twenty-three centuries ago! The important point as Plato saw was that changes of some kind are essential.

References

Adam, Adela M. *Plato: Moral and Political Ideals.* Cambridge: Cambridge University Press; New York: G. P. Putnam's, 1913.

Adam, James. *The Republic, ed. with Critical Notes, Commentary, and Appendix.* Cambridge, 1905.

Allen, Christine G. "Plato on Women." *Feminist Studies,* 2, 2–3 (1975), p. 132.

Annas, Julia. "Plato's *Republic* and Feminism." *Philosophy,* 51 (1976), p. 309.

Aristophanes. *Ecclesiazusae.* Ed. R. G. Ussher. London: Oxford University Press, 1973.

———. *Ecclesiazusae.* Trans. B. B. Rogers. Vol. III. Cambridge, Mass.: Harvard University Press, 1924.

Aristotle. *Politics.* Trans. Benjamin Jowett, in *The Basic Works of Aristotle.* New York: Random House, 1941.

Arnheim, Rudolf. "Plato of Two Minds." In *Visual Thinking.* Berkeley: University of California Press, 1971.

Arthur, Marylin B. " 'Liberated' Women: The Classical Era." In *Becoming Visible: Women in European History.* Ed. R. Bridenthal and C. Koonz. Boston: Houghton Mifflin, 1977.

Asmus, V. F., ed. Platon: *Sochinenia v Trekh Tomakh Tom 3.* Moscow, 1971.

Bakewell, Charles M. *Plato: The Republic with Introduction.* New York: Charles Scribner's, 1928.

Bannes, Joachim. *Hitlers Kampf und Platons Staat.* Berlin: W. de Gruyter, 1933.

Barash, David. *The Whisperings Within.* New York: Harper and Row, 1979.

———. *Sociobiology and Behavior.* New York: Elsevier, 1977.

Barker, Ernest. *Greek Political Theory: Plato and His Predecessors.* London: Methuen, 1947.

———. *The Political Thought of Plato and Aristotle.* New York: Dover, 1959.

Barnett, R., G. Baruch, and C. Rivers. *Life Prints: New Patterns of Love and Work for Today's Women.* New York: New American Library, 1983.

Beard, Mary. *Women as a Force in History.* New York: Colliers, 1971.

de Beauvoir, Simone, *The Second Sex*. New York: Bantam Books, 1968.
Bell, Susan G., ed. *Women from the Greeks to the French Revolution*. Stanford: Stanford University Press, 1980.
Benbow, C., and J. Stanley. "Sex Differences in Mathematical Ability: Fact or Artifact?" *Science*, December 12, 1980.
Benn, A. W. *Greek Philosophers*. New York: Dutton, 1974.
Bloom, Allan. "Response to Hall." *Political Theory*, 5, 3 (August 1977).
————, trans. *The Republic of Plato, with Interpretive Essay*. New York: Basic Books, 1968.
Blumberg, R. L. "The Erosion of Sexual Equality: A Structural Interpretation." In *Beyond Intellectual Sexism: A New Woman, a New Reality*, ed. J. I. Roberts. New York: David McKay, 1976.
Blunt, Anthony. *Artistic Theory in Italy, 1450–1600*. New York: Oxford University Press, 1956.
Boas, George. "A Sermon for Humanists." *The Johns Hopkins Magazine*, October 1984, 16.
Borsook, Eva. *The Companion Guide to Florence*. London: Collins, 1973.
Bosanquet, Bernard. *A Companion to Plato's Republic*. London: Rivingtons, 1925.
————. *The Education of the Young in The Republic of Plato*. Cambridge: Cambridge Press, 1900.
Calvert, Brian. "Plato and the Equality of Women." *Phoenix*, 29, 3 (1975).
Campese, Silvia, and Silvia Gastaldi. *La donna e i filosofi: archeologia di un' immagine culturale*. Bologna: Zanichelli, 1977.
Chroust, Anton-Hermann. *Socrates, Man and Myth*. South Bend: Notre Dame Press, 1957.
Cohart, Mary, ed. *Unsung Champions of Women*. Alburquerque: University of New Mexico Press, 1915.
Cornford, F. M., trans. *The Republic of Plato*. London: Oxford University Press, 1941.
Croiset, Maurice, *La République de Platon: étude et analyse*. Paris: Edition Mellottée, 1946.
Crombie, I. M. *An Examination of Plato's Doctrine*. Vol. I. London: Routledge & Kegan Paul, 1962.
Crossman, Richard C. *Plato Today*. New York: Oxford University Press, 1939.
Currie, H. M. *The Individual and the State*. London: Dent, 1973.
Davis, Elizabeth G. *The First Sex*. New York: Putnam, 1971.
Dickason, Anne. "Anatomy and Destiny: The Role of Biology in Plato's Views of Women." *The Philosophical Forum*, V (Fall-Winter 1973–1974).
Diesendruck, Z. *The Republic: Translated into Hebrew with Introduction and Notes*. Tel Aviv: Newman, 1953.
Diogenes Laertius. *Lives of Eminent Philosophers*, with English translation by R. D. Hicks. Cambridge, Mass.: Harvard University Press, 1966.

Dover, K. J. *Greek Homosexuality*. New York: Random House, 1978.
―――. *Greek Popular Morality in the Time of Plato and Aristotle*. Berkeley: University of California Press, 1974.
Edelstein, Ludwig. "The Function of the Myth in Plato's Philosophy." *Journal of the History of Ideas*, 10 (October 1949).
Elshtain, Jean B. *Public Man, Private Woman*. Princeton: Princeton University Press, 1981.
―――. "Against Androgyny." *Telos*, 47 (Spring 1981).
Erikson, Erik. *Childhood and Society*. New York: Norton, 1950.
al-Fārābī. *De Platonis philosophia*, ed. F. Rosenthal and R. Walzer. London: Warburg Institute, 1943.
Fau, Guy. *L'Émancipation féminin dans la Rome antique*. Paris, 1978.
Fehl, N. E. *A Guide to the Study of Plato's Republic*. Hong Kong: Chung Chi College, 1961.
Field, G. C. *Plato and His Contemporaries A Study in Fourth-Century Life and Thought*. London, 1930.
Finley, M. I. *The World of Odysseus*. Revised Edition. New York: Viking Press, 1978.
Fite, W. *The Platonic Legend*. New York: Charles Scribner's Sons, 1934.
Fortenbaugh, W. W. "On Plato's Feminism in *Republic V.*" *Apeiron*, IX, 2, (1975).
Freedman, D. *Human Sociobiology*. New York: Macmillan, 1979.
Freud, Sigmund. *Analysis Terminable and Interminable*. Standard Edition. London: Hogarth Press, 1964.
Friedlander, Paul. *Plato: The Dialogues*. 2nd and 3rd Periods. Princeton: Princeton Unversity Press, 1969.
Gauss, H. *Philosophischer Handkommentar zu den Dialogen Platos*. Bern, 1958.
Geertz, Clifford. "Sociosexology" *New York Review of Books*, January 24, 1980.
Gelman, David, and John Carey. "Sex Research—On the Bias." *Newsweek*, May 18, 1981, p. 81
Ghougassian, Joseph. *Toward Women*. San Diego: Lukas, 1977.
Gilligan, Carol. *In a Different Voice*. Cambridge, Mass.: Harvard University Press, 1982.
Gomperz, Theodor. *Greek Thinkers*. Vols. I–V. London, 1905.
Gould, Stephen Jay. "Genes on the Brain." *New York Review of Books*, June 30, 1983.
Gould, Thomas. *Platonic Love*. New York: Free Press, 1963.
Grant, W. V., and Thomas D. Snyder. *Digest of Education Statistics: 1985–1986*. Washington, D.C.: U.S. Government Printing Office, 1986.
Grote, George. *Plato and the Other Companions of Socrates*. Vol. IV. London: John Murray, 1888.
Grube, Georges M. A. *Plato's Thought*. Boston: Beacon Press, 1935

228

Hall, Dale. "The *Republic* and the 'Limits of Politics.' " *Political Theory*, 5(3) (August 1977).
Hamilton, Edith, and Huntington Cairns, eds. *The Collected Dialogues of Plato*. Princeton: Princeton University Press, 1963.
Heim, A. M. "Harvard Study Reveals Gender Inequality in the Classroom." *Second Century: Radcliffe News*, April 1986.
"His and Hers Brains." *Science*, 3, 7 (September 1982).
Holmes, G. *The Florentine Enlightenment: 1400–1450*. New York: Pegasus, 1969.
Hoole, C. H. *An Analytical Paraphrase of the Republic of Plato*. Oxford: J. Vincent, 1875.
Hrdy, Sarah B. *The Woman That Never Evolved*. Cambridge, Mass.: Harvard University Press, 1981.
Ithurriague, Jean. *Les idées de Platon sur la condition de la femme*. Paris: Librarie Universitaire, 1931.
Jacobs, William. "Plato on Female Emancipation and the Traditional Family." *Apeiron*, XII, 1 (1978).
Jaeger, Werner. *Paideia*. Vol. II. London: Oxford University Press, 1943.
Jaggar, Alison. "Political Philosophies of Women's Liberation." In *Feminism and Philosophy*. Ed. M. Vetterling-Braggin, F. A. Elliston, J. English. Totowa, N.J.: Littlefield, 1977.
James, William. *Some Problems of Philosophy*. New York: Longmans, Green, 1948.
Janeway, Elizabeth. *Powers of the Weak*. New York: Knopf, 1980.
Jenkyns, Richard. *The Victorians and Ancient Greece*. Cambridge, Mass.: Harvard University Press, 1980.
Jowett, Benjamin, trans. *The Dialogues of Plato*. 3rd Edition. Oxford: Clarendon Press, 1892.
Jowett, B., and L. Campbell, eds. *Plato's Republic: The Greek Text, Edited, with Notes and Essays*. Oxford: Clarendon Press, 1894.
"Just How the Sexes Differ." *Newsweek*, May 18, 1981.
Kelson, Hans. "Platonic Love." *American Imago*, 3, 1–2 (April 1942).
Konner, Melvin. *The Tangled Wing: Biological Constraints on the Human Spirit*. New York: Holt, Rinehart and Winston, 1982.
Koyre, A. *Discovering Plato*. Trans. L. C. Rosenfield. New York: Columbia University Press, 1945.
Lacey, W. K. *The Family in Classical Greece*. Ithaca: Cornell University Press, 1968.
Lange, Lynda. "The Function of Equal Education." In *The Sexism of Social and Political Theory*, ed. Lorenne M. G. Clark and L. Lange. Toronto, 1979.
Langer, W. C. *The Mind of Adolf Hitler*. London: Secker & Warburg, 1973.
Lee, Desmond. *The Republic*, translated, with Introduction. London: Penguin, 1974.

Lefkowitz, M. R., and M. B. Fant. *Women in Greece and Rome*. Toronto: Samuel Stephens, 1977.

Lerner, Gerda. *The Female Experience*. Indianapolis: Bobbs-Merrill, 1977.

Lewontin, Richard C. "Plato's Women." Letters to the Editors. *New York Review of Books*, Oct. 25, 1984.

———. "A Simple Problem Science Can't Solve." *New York Review of Books*, April 12, 1984.

Lodge, R. C. *Plato's Theory of Education*. With an appendix on the education of women according to Plato, by Rabbi Solomon Frank. London: K. Paul, Trench, Trubner, 1947.

Lumsden, C., and E. O. Wilson. *Genes, Mind and Culture*. Cambridge, Mass.: Harvard University Press, 1981.

Martin, Jane R. "Equality and Education in Plato." In *Feminism and Philosophy*, ed. M. Vetterling-Braggin, F. A. Elliston, and J. English. Totowa, N. J.: Littlefield, 1977.

———. *Reclaiming a Conversation: The Ideal of the Educated Woman*. New Haven: Yale University Press, 1985.

Midgley, Mary. *Beast and Man: The Roots of Human Nature*. Ithaca: Cornell University Press, 1978.

Mill, John Stuart. "The Subjection of Women." In *The Feminist Papers*, ed. Alice S. Rossi. New York: Bantam, 1974.

Mitchell, G. *Human Sex Differences: A Primatologist's Perspective*. New York: Van Nostrand, Reinhold, 1981.

Neal, Marie Augusta. "Women in Religious Symbolism and Organization." In *Religious Change and Continuity*, ed. H. M. Johnson. San Francisco: Jossey-Bass, 1979.

Nettleship, Richard. *Lectures on The Republic of Plato*. New York: Macmillan, 1967.

Nohle, Karl. *Die Statslehre Platos*. Leipzig, 1880.

Nussbaum, Martha, "Plato and Affirmative Action: Nussbaum-Lewontin Exchange." *New York Review of Books*, January 31, 1985.

———. "Women's Lot." *New York Review of Books*, January 30, 1986.

Okin, Susan Moller. "Philosopher Queens and Private Wives: Plato on Women and the Family." *Philosophy and Public Affairs*, 6 (Summer 1977).

———. *Women and Western Political Thought*. Princeton: Princeton University Press, 1979.

Osborne, Martha Lee. "Plato's Unchanging View of Woman: A Denial That Anatomy Spells Destiny." *The Philosophical Forum*, Summer 1975.

Ostwald, Martin, ed. *Aristotle, Nichomachean Ethics*. New York: Bobbs-Merrill, 1962.

Parker, Douglass, trans. *Aristophanes, The Congresswomen*. Ann Arbor: University of Michigan Press, 1967.

Pater, Walter. *Plato and Platonism*. London: Macmillan, 1910.

Peirce, C. S. "The Fixation of Belief." In *Collected Papers of Charles S.*

Peirce, vols. V & VI, ed. C. Hartshorne and P. Weiss. (Cambridge, Mass.: Harvard University Press, 1965).

Pierce, Christine. "Equality: *Republic* V." *The Monist,* 57, 1 (Jan. 1973).

Perun, P. J., ed. *The Undergraduate Woman: Issues in Educational Equity.* Lexington, Mass.: D.C. Heath, 1982.

Pomeroy, Sarah. *Goddesses, Whores, Wives, and Slaves: Women in Classical Antiquity.* New York: Schocken, 1975.

———. "Feminism in Book V of Plato's *Republic.*" *Apeiron,* VIII, 1 (1974).

Plato. *Republic.*

———. *Timaeus.*

———. *Laws.*

———. *Symposium.*

Popper, Karl. *The Open Society and Its Enemies.* (London: Routledge & Kegan Paul, 1945).

Ralls, Katherine. "Mammals in which Females are Larger than Males." *Quarterly Review of Biology,* June 1976.

Rankin, H. D. *Plato and the Individual.* London: Methuen, 1964.

Ritter, Constantin. *The Essence of Plato's Philosophy.* New York: Russell & Russell, 1933.

Rosenthal, Abigail. "Feminism Without Contradictions." *The Monist,* 57, 1 (January 1973).

Rosenthal, E. I. J. "The Place of Politics in the Philosophy of Ibn Rushd." *Bulletin of the London School of African Studies,* XV:2.

———, ed. *Averroës Commentary on Plato's Republic.* Cambridge: Cambridge University Press, 1966.

Russell, Bertrand. *History of Western Philosophy.* New York: Simon and Schuster, 1945.

Ryle, Gilbert. *The Concept of Mind.* New York: Barnes and Noble, 1971.

———. "Plato: Moral and Political Theory." In *Encyclopedia of Philosophy,* ed. Paul Edwards. New York: Macmillan, 1967, Vol. VI.

Saxenhouse, Arlene. "The Philosopher and the Female in the Political Thought of Plato." *Political Theory,* 4(May 1976).

Sayers, J. *Biological Politics: Feminist and Anti-Feminist Perspectives.* London: Tavistock, 1982.

Schleiermacher, F. *Introductions to the Dialogues of Plato.* New York: Arno Press, 1973.

Segal, Erich. "Platonic Love." *New York Times Book Review,* April 8, 1979.

Simon, Bennett. *Mind and Madness in Ancient Greece.* Ithaca: Cornell University Press, 1978.

Spens, H., trans. *Republic of Plato.* London: Dent, 1906.

Spiro, Melford. *Gender and Culture: Kibbutz Women Revisited.* Durham, N. C.: Duke University Press, 1979.

Sprague, Rosamond. *Plato's Philosopher-King: A Study of the Theoretical Background.* Columbia, S.C., 1976.

Strauss, Leo. *The City and the Man*. Chicago: Rand McNally, 1964.

Symons, Donald. *Evolution of Human Sexuality*. New York: Oxford University Press, 1979.

Taylor, A. E. *Plato: The Man and His Work*. New York: Meridian, 1956.

Tennyson, A. *The Poetical Works of Alfred Lord Tennyson*. Boston: Houghton-Mifflin, n.d.

Wandersee, W. D. *Women's Work and Family Values 1920–1940*. Cambridge, Mass.: Harvard University Press, 1981.

Warren, T. H., trans. *The Republic*. London: Macmillan & Co., 1888.

Weiss, Paul. *Sport: A Philosophical Inquiry*. Carbondale: Southern Illinois University Press, 1969.

Wender, Dorothea. "Plato: Misogynist, Paeodophile and Feminist." *Arethusa*, VI, 1 (Spring 1973).

Whitbeck, Caroline. "Theories of Sex Difference." *The Philosophical Forum*, 5 (Fall 1973–74).

White, James E. *Contemporary Moral Problems*. St. Paul: West, 1985.

White, Nicholas. *A Companion to Plato's Republic*. Oxford: Blackwell, 1979.

Whitehead, A. N. *Process and Reality*. New York: Macmillan, 1929.

Wilamowitz-Moellendorff, U. V. *Die Griechische und der Platonische Staatsgedanke*. Berlin: Weidmannsche Buchhandlung, 1919.

———. *Platon: Beilagen und Textkritik*. Vol. II. Berlin: Weidmannsche Buchhandlung, 1919.

Wild, John. *Plato's Modern Enemies and the Theory of Natural Law*. Chicago: University of Chicago Press, 1953.

Wilson, E. O. *On Human Nature*. Cambridge, Mass.: Harvard University Press, 1978.

———. *Sociobiology*. Cambridge, Mass.: Harvard University Press, 1975.

Wilson, Peter. *Man, the Promising Primate*. New Haven: Yale University Press, 1980.

Winspear, Alban Dewes and Tom Silverberg. *Who Was Socrates?* New York: Russell & Russell, 1960.

Wittgenstein, Ludwig. *Philosophical Investigations*. Oxford: Blackwell, 1972.

Wright, F. A. *Feminism in Greek Literature: From Homer to Aristotle*. Port Washington: Kennikat Press, 1969.

Xenophon. *Memorabilia*. With English translation by E. C. Marchant, Cambridge, Mass.: Harvard University Press, 1965.

Index

*Only those references to the Republic that are not clearly indicated in the Contents have been included.